S0-CCM-648

THE NO B.S. GUIDE TO RED HAT LINUX

BOB RANKIN

THE NO B.S. GUIDE TO RED HAT® LINUX

no starch press

San Francisco

THE NO B.S. GUIDE TO RED HAT® LINUX. Copyright © 2000 by Bob Rankin

All rights reserved. No part of this work may be reproduced or transmitted in any form or by any means, electronic or mechanical, including photocopying, recording, or by any information storage or retrieval system, without the prior written permission of the copyright owner and the publisher.

Printed in the United States of America

1 2 3 4 5 6 7 8 9 10—00

Printed on acid-free recycled paper ✪

Trademarked names are used throughout this book. Rather than use a trademark symbol with every occurrence of a trademarked name, we are using the names only in an editorial fashion and to the benefit of the trademark owner, with no intention of infringement of the trademark.

Publisher: William Pollock
Project Editor: Karol Jurado
Cover and Text Design: Derek Yee Design
Compositor: Black Hole Publishing Services
Technical Editor: Stephen Smoogen
Copyeditor: Judy Ziajka
Proofreader: John Carroll
Indexer: Nancy Humphreys

Distributed to the book trade in the United States and Canada by Publishers Group West, 1700 Fourth St., Berkeley, CA 94710, phone: 800-788-3123 or 510-548-4393, fax: 510-658-1834.

For information on translations or book distributors outside the United States, please contact No Starch Press directly:

No Starch Press
555 De Haro Street, Suite 250, San Francisco, CA 94107
phone: 415-863-9900; fax: 415-863-9950; info@nostarch.com; http://www.nostarch.com

The information in this book is distributed on an "As Is" basis, without warranty. While every precaution has been taken in the preparation of this work, neither the author nor No Starch Press shall have any liability to any person or entity with respect to any loss or damage caused or alleged to be caused directly or indirectly by the information contained in it.

Library of Congress Cataloging-in-Publication Data

```
Rankin, Bob.
        The no b.s. guide to Red Hat Linux / Bob Rankin.
            p.      cm.
        ISBN 1-886411-30-1 (pbk.)
        1. Linux.  2. Operating systems (Computers)   I. Title.
    QA76.76.063R366     1999
    005.4'469--dc21                               99-18467
```

BRIEF CONTENTS

CONTENTS

1

2

3

4

5

THE LINUX FILE SYSTEM

6

IMPORTANT LINUX COMMANDS

7

TEXT EDITORS

8

SLICING AND DICING 184

9

ROLLING YOUR OWN: LINUX PROGRAMMING 202

10

MANAGING YOUR EMAIL 226

11

COMPRESSION, ENCODING, AND ENCRYPTION 244

12

13

14

15

INTRODUCTION

About this Book

This book is about Linux, a version of Unix that runs on ordinary personal computers. It's for people who want to learn the basics of installing and using Linux (and thereby Unix) without getting bogged down in too much detail or technobabble.

To be sure, there are other Linux books on the shelf—but you'll find this one unique because it's short and to the point. Oddly enough, most computer books seem to be written for people who already understand the topic. This book has been carefully crafted and edited so that both the novice and the more experienced computer user will get what they want—Linux on their PCs with a minimum of fuss, and the know-how to use Linux effectively.

Because Unix is the foundation for much of the Internet, many people are using or encountering it nowadays. As the Internet grows, Unix will become more popular, creating an array of new opportunities. If you're simply curious, looking to gain new job skills, or thinking about Linux as a low-cost platform for operating your own Internet server, this book is for you.

What's Inside

You'll find plain-English information here about installing Linux on a personal computer and using it productively. After a brief history and overview of Linux, the book provides a concise and occasionally light-hearted treatment of these topics:

- File systems
- Useful commands
- Text editors
- Email tools

- Data manipulation
- Shell programming
- Internet access and tools
- Running your own Linux Web server

The CD-ROM accompanying this book contains **Red Hat™ Linux version 6.** The Red Hat distribution was selected because it's the most popular Linux product on the market, is very easy to install, and requires minimal configuration.

What's So Great about Linux?

Until recently, running Unix meant investing in a powerful workstation that cost megabucks. Linux changes all that, because it's a complete version of the Unix operating system (software that controls the basic functions of the personal computer) that runs on ordinary 386, 486, and Pentium systems. The added fact that it's freely available and "open source" makes it all the more attractive.

Linux is perfect for people who want to operate their own low-cost Internet servers, and it's robust enough to satisfy the needs of many Internet service providers. Linux is a multiuser and multitasking environment, and it can access huge amounts of memory (gigabytes) and huge amounts of disk storage space (terabytes). Linux offers virtually everything that Windows NT has been promising for years and may not deliver in a truly stable form for some time to come.

Don't make the mistake of assuming that Linux is some kind of watered-down or underpowered Unix for the masses. Linux is Unix. POSIX certification (compliance with the industry standards for Unix) makes it official that Linux can do everything that a Unix system is supposed to do. The only difference is that Linux works on a personal computer, whereas other versions of Unix run on larger workstations or mainframes.

Linux is also being taken very seriously by the computer industry, with new Linux-compatible versions of popular software packages being announced every month. The Apache Web server software running on Linux platforms powers about half of all Web sites today. Even more telling, Microsoft considers Linux a major threat to its Windows NT operating system.

What Is Linux?

In the early 90s, a geek named Linus Torvalds at the University of Helsinki in Finland thought it would be fun to write a Unix kernel from scratch. He called it Linux, and it was cool but pretty much useless without all the utility programs needed to make it a complete operating system. At the same time, Richard Stallman and his pals at the Free Software Foundation were writing a bunch of freeware Unix utilities collectively known as the GNU Project. It was cool but pretty much useless without a kernel to make it a complete operating system. Fortunately, the two parties decided to collaborate.

News of Linux spread quickly over the Internet, and many other Unix programmers joined the effort to enhance it. What we now know as Linux is a combination of Torvald's Linux kernel, the GNU Project software, and some other nifty software bit and pieces developed by programmers from all around the world.

Today Linux is a complete and reliable implementation of the Unix operating system, with the following notable features:

- 32-bit operation (it uses all the speed and power of your CPU, unlike 16-bit DOS systems)

- Virtual memory (it can use all of your system's RAM; there's no 640K memory limit)

- Full support for X Windows (Unix's standard graphical user interface)

- TCP/IP networking support (allowing connection to the Internet)

- GNU software support (including a huge amount of free Unix software from the GNU Project)

■ **NOTE:** *GNU is one of those recursive acronyms that computer scientists love; it stands for GNU's Not Unix. The GNU Project is an effort sponsored by the Free Software Foundation to provide freely available Unix software. See Appendix C for related information.*

Most flavors of Unix require an expensive, high-powered workstation, but Linux is unique in that it runs on personal computers (Intel-based 386, 486, and Pentium machines) and was written totally from scratch without using any of the original AT&T UNIX code. (Throughout this book, *UNIX* refers to the original trademarked UNIX project invented by AT&T. The term *Unix* is used here as a generic term for other variants of the operating system.)

Because of that (and because the author is a nice guy), Linux is free. Appendix C has more information on the GNU General Public License—the terms under which Linux can be distributed—but the gist of it is this: You can modify and sell or give away the software so long as you provide full source code and don't impose any restrictions on what others do with it.

What You Need to Use This Book

Although it's not essential, a working knowledge of DOS will help you grasp the concepts in this book. You don't need to be a hacker to use Linux, but it is an operating system, and operating systems can be technically challenging. Still, the book aims to provide enough background for most people to tackle just about any Linux problem they may encounter.

A Really Brief History of Unix

Sometime in the mid 1960s, a bunch of geeks at AT&T's Bell Labs decided it would be fun to create a new operating system called Multics. (This was no small task, because computers at the time were about the size of a football field and two stories high.) Multics fizzled in 1969 when Bell cut the cord, but some of the geeks continued work on what became known as UNIX; and it became wildly popular inside AT&T.

Since AT&T was not allowed to sell computer software at the time, it gave away UNIX (complete with source code) to any educational institution. AT&T produced new versions of UNIX called System III and System V in the early 1980s, but all the while, geeks at the University of California at Berkeley and other places were busy hacking away on their own versions of Unix based on the AT&T code. Some cross-pollination did occur, but there are still significant differences between the Berkeley (commonly called BSD Unix) and AT&T flavors. In the early 1990s, AT&T sold UNIX to Novell, which was bought by Digital Equipment Corporation, which sold it to SCO (Santa Cruz Operation), which markets it as UNIXWare.

Today, there are now lots of Unix variants sold or given away by many different companies and universities. While these various flavors can make it difficult to write portable software, efforts to standardize Unix (two of the more notable ones being POSIX and COSE) offer hope for greater compatibility in the future.

Like any operating system, Unix has some cryptic commands and less-than-intuitive aspects. (Three of the most important Unix commands have the peculiar names *cat, grep,* and *awk*.) Either serious hallucinogens or a warped sense of humor came into play at some point in the creation of Unix. I don't let this bother me, though, taking comfort in my favorite platitude: "Unix was written by geeks on drugs." Seriously, though, Unix is really no more difficult to learn than DOS or Windows—it's just different.

Uh, What's an Operating System?

For a computer to do anything useful, it needs both application software (programs you use) and an operating system (programs the computer uses). The operating system sits between the physical hardware that makes up a computer (the monitor, keyboard, CPU, hard drive, and so forth) and the end-user software that people use to process documents, play games, and all that good stuff.

My brother Tom and I are both into computers. We're computer programmers by trade, but I'm quick to point out that we produce very different kinds of software. The difference, as I like to explain it, is this: I write software for people; Tom writes software for computers.

We commonly think of the CPU as the brain of a computer, but in reality, it can't do much besides crunch numbers and move data around in the computer's memory. The job of the operating system (OS) is twofold:

1. To work with computer hardware to process user requests by

    •interpreting keystrokes from the keyboard,

    •displaying images on the screen,

    •storing files on the hard disk,

    •sending documents to a printer,

    •communicating over a modem.

2. To manage the application software's use of memory (RAM) and processor time.

If you've used a multitasking environment like Windows or a multiuser mainframe system, you've seen the concept of "time-slicing" in action. While your computer has only one CPU, which can do only one thing at a time, the OS can make it seem like several people or programs are using the CPU simultaneously. Similarly, even though the real memory (RAM) is shared by all running applications, the OS can make it seem like you have it all at your disposal, all the time, by sharing it between applications—using a technique called paging.

The OS time-slices by giving one user or application exclusive use of the hardware for a brief instant, and then doing the same for the next user or application. On systems with adequate horsepower, this approach works so that you never even know about that little game of round-robin going on behind the scenes. On a wimpy computer or a mainframe with too many users, it's toe-tappin' time for everybody.

MY LAWYER MADE ME DO IT

Red Hat is a registered trademark and the Red Hat Shadow Man logo, RPM, the RPM logo, and Glint are trademarks of Red Hat Software, Inc. *Linux* is a registered trademark of Linus Torvalds. *Motif* and *UNIX* are registered trademarks of The Open Group. *Netscape* is a registered trademark of Netscape Communications Corporation in the United States and other countries. *TrueType* is a registered trademark of Apple Computer, Inc. *Windows* is a registered trademark of Microsoft Corporation.

All other trademarks and copyrights referred to are the property of their respective owners. Your mileage may vary. No warranty expressed or implied. Objects in mirror are closer than they appear. Consult your physician before using this product.

UPDATES TO THIS BOOK

Changes happen fast in the Linux world, but we'll do our best to keep you posted about anything that affects the content of this book after press time. Visit http://www.nostarch.com/rhl_updates.htm for more information.

WHERE AM I?

In this introduction to Linux, you've learned the basic tasks of an operating system and how it differs from application software. You're now an expert on Unix history, you understand that Linux is a version of Unix for ordinary PCs, and you can even pronounce the name correctly. You don't have a clue about hardware requirements or installation, but that's coming next.

INSTALLING LINUX ON YOUR PC

N ow that you've had a bit of history, it's time for the real fun—installing the Linux operating system on your own personal computer. This chapter assumes that you have a PC currently running some version of DOS, but installing Linux is going to be very different from installing a new DOS or Windows software package. There will be no pointing, clicking, or hand-holding installation programs to guide you through the process. And most important, when you're done, you'll be booting up something entirely different from the DOS-based system you've grown to know and, uh, tolerate.

ABOUT THE CD

The version of Red Hat Linux provided on the CD accompanying this book is Red Hat Linux version 6.0. There are many distributions of Linux available, but I chose Red Hat because it's very stable and extremely popular with Linux aficionados. Red Hat is also known for its add-ons that make installing, configuring, and running Linux much easier.

If your DOS system is properly configured, Red Hat Linux installs directly from the CD-ROM with one simple command—and when you're done, you have a fully functioning Internet-ready Linux system with a graphical user interface. All the arcane file system and graphical user interface (GUI) setup and network configuration is done automatically—not the case with other Linux versions.

SAYONARA, DOS?

You'll be running Linux (Unix for your PC), but you can take comfort in the knowledge that your DOS system is still available in case you ever want to return from the Land of Grep and Awk. (These are two Linux commands that sound weird, but are quite useful. You'll learn about them in Chapter 6, "Important Linux Commands".)

In fact, you can even access your DOS files directly from Linux, and in some cases you can run DOS or Windows programs under Linux. In Chapter 12, "Linux Does DOS and Windows," I'll show you how to keep in touch with DOS and even boot up Windows 95/98 while running Linux.

What Hardware Will I Need?

You don't need an expensive state-of-the-art monster machine to run Linux. Almost any PC with a 386, 486, or Pentium processor will do nicely. That's because Linux, unlike Microsoft Windows and other Unix flavors, is not a disk-chomping, memory-swilling CPU hog. It runs quite happily on a 386SX with 16MB of memory and a 150MB hard drive. Of course, it will run faster on a 500-MHz Pentium with 128MB of RAM and a 10GB hard drive, but that's your choice—you can get to work in a Yugo or a Cadillac.

It's a pretty safe bet that your PC will run Linux if you already have Windows 95 installed and working, but not every piece of hardware is supported by Linux. Here are the major system components, in terms of compatibility and requirements:

- **CPU** Intel 80386, 80486, Pentium, or the AMD/Cyrix variants (that is, almost any 386 or better); Linux will emulate a math coprocessor if one is not present.

- **Video** Almost any VGA/SVGA card that works with DOS is acceptable.

- **Floppy drive** A 3.5-inch floppy drive is required.

- **Hard disk** Most MFM, RLL, IDE, and SCSI drives/controllers are supported; a minimum of 300MB of free space is required for the installation detailed here, but 550-600MB is more reasonable for serious use.

- **Memory** Minimum 16MB of RAM is recommended, but more memory dramatically improves performance; 48MB is recommended if the user wishes to use the GNOME GUI; mixing RAM of various speeds (that is, 60 ns, 70 ns) can cause problems.

- **CD-ROM** Almost any IDE- or SCSI-based CD-ROM drive will work.

- **Modem** Required if you want to connect to or host Internet services; the faster the better, but 33.6 Kbps or better is recommended.

■ *NOTE: The most recent list of hardware supported by Red Hat Linux can be found at at http://support.redhat.com/hardware. It's a good idea to check your hardware against this list before proceeding.*

TAKING INVENTORY

Not sure what hardware lurks in the heart of your computer? If you are running Windows 95/98, hold down the **ALT** key and click on the "My Computer" icon. A pop-up menu (Figure 1-1) should appear, showing the type of processor and the amount of installed RAM.

Next, click on the "Device Manager" tab (Figure 1-2). The System Properties window will show a list of your computer's hardware components. (Make sure the "View devices by type" button is selected.)

At this point, you can double-click on any of the icons to learn more about the component and how it's configured. You can also print a summary by clicking on the "Print" button. When prompted, choose the "All Devices and System Summary" report.

You should also check your computer's BIOS (use the SETUP feature at boot time) to determine if your hard drive uses LBA (large block access). You'll need to know this to answer one of the questions during the installation process.

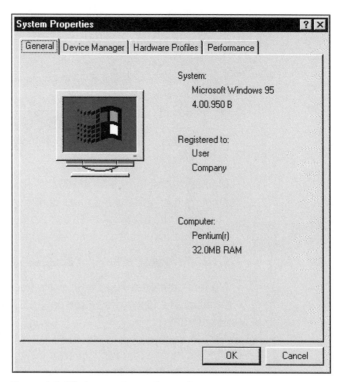

FIGURE 1-1: *Windows 95 System Properties*

Don't forget you can also learn a lot about your hardware components by reading the documentation that came with them! If you don't have a spare PC lying dormant in the closet that fits the bill for your Linux machine, the type of machine you should get depends on whether you want to run Linux for business or pleasure. If you're just experimenting with Linux for fun, you can probably find an old 486 system in the classifieds for a few hundred dollars. If you're planning on running a busy Web site, a high-end Pentium will set you back about $2000.

The important thing to remember when choosing your Unix machine is that the more RAM you have, the better your system's performance will be. And since memory and hard disk prices have fallen so much recently, don't skimp. My personal Linux machine has an Intel Celeron 300A processor, 64MB of RAM, 2.5GB hard disk, S3/Virge video card, no-name 24X CD-ROM, and US Robotics 56K modem. That's by no means a hot rod, but it runs Linux very nicely.

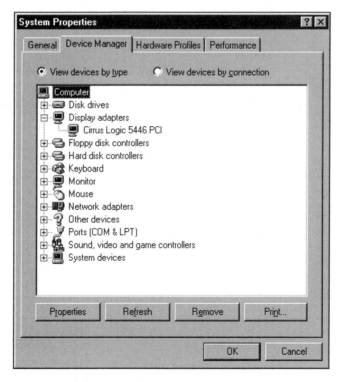

FIGURE 1-2: *Windows 95 Device Manager*

THE INSTALLATION AT A GLANCE

That's it for the preliminaries. Here's an overview of the installation process you will follow to get up and running with Linux on your PC. It's a good idea to understand what's coming and to know about the possible gotchas before you start anything so drastic as installing a new operating system, so please read through to the end of this chapter before you begin the process. Trust me—you'll be glad you did!

Here are the steps in brief:

1. Repartition your hard disk with FDISK or FIPS.

2. Create a Linux boot floppy (optional).

3. Start the installation program.

4. Answer a few simple questions.

5. Use Disk Druid to create Linux partitions.

6. Select the Linux components to install.

7. Copy the Linux files from the CD-ROM to the hard drive.

8. Configure your hardware for Linux.

9. Install LILO.

10. Shut down and reboot.

■ *NOTE: You may run into a number of pitfalls during your installation due to quirky hardware, careless keystrokes, or failure to follow these instructions closely. But you can' t really hurt anything if the installation isn' t successful. If you have trouble with your installation, you can always start over and try it again. If you get really stuck, see Chapter 15, "Learning More about Linux," which lists people and places on the Internet that you can turn to for help.*

REPARTITION YOUR HARD DISK

Since you're running DOS, it's a given that your hard disk has at least one partition. (A partition is simply a division of your hard disk.) And unless you're very adventurous, it's almost a sure bet that your hard disk has a single DOS partition that occupies the entire disk. Since you need partitions to install multiple operating systems on a single hard disk, you'll have to change the current partitioning of your disk so that there is room for a new partition (or two) for Linux.

Note that in this step you will *not* be creating any Linux partitions, though you will use a DOS utility to reduce the size of an existing partition. (You'll use a Linux utility later to create the Linux partitions.)

You have a choice of two tools to reduce the size of your DOS partition. Which one you choose depends on how much you value the existing data on your DOS disk, and whether or not you're a gambler at heart.

The **FDISK** command, which comes with DOS, is the official disk partitioning tool. But since it can't change the size of a partition, it makes you delete your existing partition before it will re-create it as a smaller one. Unfortunately, this means you lose all the data on the disk, so you'll need to perform a full backup and restore operation (along with reinstalling DOS) if you use **FDISK**. **FDISK** is a nuisance, but it works.

The alternative utility, **FIPS** (which you'll find in the **DOSUTILS** directory on the CD), can resize an existing partition without deleting it, but it's a "use at your own risk" program. Have a look at the FIPS documentation and give it a try if you feel comfortable with it. FIPS has been around for several years and is said to be very reliable, but don't call me if you choose to use FIPS and something screws up.

Regardless of the utility you choose, the amount of space you leave for your Linux partitions will depend on the size of your hard disk, how much space is currently occupied, and how you intend to use Linux. I recommend that you devote 500MB or more to Linux, but you can slide by with only 120MB if space is tight.

■ *NOTE: The installation outlined in this chapter requires about 300MB of hard disk space and is the basis of future chapters, so I recommend you follow it pretty closely. If you don' t have that much space available, you can omit the X Windows components (about 75MB), but you' ll have a very boring Linux system with no GUI. You could also skip the Emacs and Games components (about 20MB) if you wish, but what' s an operating system without a little fun?*

In the example that follows, we'll start with a 1.2GB hard disk, reduce the DOS partition to 600MB, and use the remaining 600MB for Linux.

If you choose to use **FDISK,** do this:

- *NOTE: This process assumes that you are starting with only one partition. If you have multiple partitions, keep in mind that you don't necessarily have to delete and re-create all of them. If you have two partitions, you can probably whack a piece off the second one and leave the primary partition untouched. You should leave the unallocated space at the end of your disk for use by Linux.*

    1. Back up your hard drive. (A tape drive is preferable to dozens of floppies.)

    2. Create a bootable DOS floppy with the **FORMAT A: /S** command and copy **FDISK.EXE** and **FORMAT.COM** to it. Follow the instructions for your backup program to ensure that you have the restore software available on floppy disk, too.

    3. Insert the floppy disk and restart your system. The computer should boot from the floppy instead of the hard disk. If it doesn't, you may have to fiddle with your machine's CMOS parameters so that it will boot from the floppy first. Typically, you can change these settings by pressing the **DEL** key just after turning on your machine. (See your system manual for help.)

    4. Use the **FDISK** utility to delete the existing partition and create a smaller one. (FDISK is pretty straightforward, but you should refer to your DOS manual if you've never used it before.)

    5. Use the **FORMAT C: /S** command to format the new partition.

    6. Finally, restore your hard drive using the backup from step 1. (You did make a backup, right?)

THE LINUX INSTALLATION PROCESS

Now that you've partitioned your hard disk, you're ready to begin the Red Hat Linux installation process. As I mentioned earlier in this chapter, it's possible to run the install program directly from the CD—but only if your system supports it. If not, don't worry—just follow the simple instructions provided later to create a Linux boot floppy.

If you have a newer system that supports bootable CDs, you can pop in the Red Hat Linux CD and reboot your computer, and the installation program will start automatically. Give it a try! If your computer ignores the CD and boots DOS or Windows as usual, you still might be able to avoid creating the boot floppy.

To try this alternative method, get yourself to a "real" DOS prompt. (An MS-DOS prompt running under Windows is *not* going to work!) If your CD-ROM drive is accessible from outside the Windows environment, you can use the LOADLIN program to start the Linux install process from the CD-ROM. You'll need to do one of these things to get to a real DOS prompt:

- Shut down Windows 95/98 and choose the "Restart in MS-DOS Mode" option.

- Exit from Windows 3.1 to the DOS command prompt.

- Reboot your computer with a DOS boot floppy.

At the DOS prompt, enter the following command (assuming your CD-ROM drive is drive D):

```
D:
```

If you don't get an error such as "Invalid drive specification," continue with the following commands to start the installation program:

```
cd \dosutils
loadlin autoboot\vmlinuz initrd=autoboot\initrd.img
```

If your CD-ROM drive is available, the installation program will start, and you can skip the next section dealing with the boot floppy.

CREATE A LINUX BOOT FLOPPY

If it turns out you can't boot directly from the CD or access the CD-ROM drive from the DOS prompt, you must create a Linux boot floppy. To do so, return to Windows and start a DOS prompt. Insert a formatted diskette into drive A and enter these commands:

```
D:
cd \dosutils
rawrite -f \images\boot.img -d A:
```

When the rawrite program finishes, leave the floppy in the A drive and reboot your computer. The installation program will start, and the CD-ROM whirs into action.

Do You Need a Supplemental Diskette?

If you will be using a PCMCIA device *during the installation* (for example, you have a PCMCIA SCSI card and will be installing from a SCSI CD), you'll need to create a supplemental diskette and supply it when prompted during the installation process. Note that you don't need install-time PCMCIA support if you're installing using a laptop's built-in CD-ROM drive—only if the drive is connected via the PCMCIA card. To create the supplemental diskette, enter the following:

```
D:
cd \dosutils
rawrite -f \images\pcmcia.img -d A:
```

Start the Linux Install Program

When Linux starts, a whole bunch of stuff will flash across the screen. Unless you did really well in that Evelyn Wood speed reading program, you won't be able to read much of it, but that's okay. After a few moments, you'll be greeted by a series of screens that will guide you through the installation process.

On each screen, you'll make a choice and then select **OK** to continue. Since the mouse is not active at this point, you must use the **TAB** and arrow keys to navigate and make selections. The install program will ask you some questions about your hardware in this start-up phase—here's how to respond.

Selecting a Language

When asked to choose a language (see Figure 1-3), "English" is probably your best bet, unless you happen to be more comfortable with German or Turkish. Select the appropriate language, tab to the **OK** button, and press **ENTER** or **F12** to continue.

Selecting a Keyboard Type

Next, you'll need to tell Linux about your keyboard (see Figure 1-4). Selecting the default, **us**, is the best choice, unless you know you have one of the other keyboards listed. Select **OK** to continue.

SELECTING PCMCIA SUPPORT

Next, the installation program will probe your system to determine whether you require PCMCIA support during the installation. If you will be using a PCMCIA device during the installation (for example, you have a PCMCIA SCSI card and will be installing from a SCSI CD), you should select "Yes."

If you do answer "Yes," you must then insert the PCMCIA support diskette that you created earlier. Select **OK** to continue, and the installation program will display a progress bar as the support diskette is loaded. Note that support for post-installation use of PCMCIA devices will be included, no matter how you reply here. The supplemental PCMCIA diskette is needed only if you require PCMCIA support *during* the installation process.

SELECTING THE INSTALLATION METHOD

When the Installation Method screen (Figure 1-5) appears, choose "Local CDROM" and select **OK** to continue. This is a good time to verify that your Red Hat Linux CD is in the CD-ROM drive, instead of inside the plastic sleeve in the back of the book. :-)

CHOOSING INSTALL OR UPGRADE

If you have an existing version of Red Hat Linux (version 2.0 or higher), the install program will ask if you wish to upgrade it to version 6. If you select "Upgrade," your existing system will be preserved, and only

FIGURE 1-3: *Choosing a language*

FIGURE 1-4: *Selecting a keyboard type*

the items needed to bring you up to date will be installed. If you select "Install," the install program will wipe out all files on the Linux partition and fully install Red Hat version 6.

SELECTING AN INSTALLATION CLASS

When you're asked to select an installation class (see Figure 1-6), choose "Custom" and select **OK** to continue.

GOT ANY SCUZZY DEVICES?

After you choose an installation class, the installation program will poke around your hardware for SCSI adapters. In some cases, the installation program will ask if you have any SCSI adapters. Most systems do not use SCSI adapters, so unless you're sure that your hard drive, CD-ROM, or some other peripheral is attached to a SCSI adapter card, choose "No."

If you choose "Yes," you'll have to select from a list the software driver that corresponds to your SCSI adapter. You'll also have an opportunity to specify options for the selected SCSI driver, but most SCSI drivers should detect your hardware automatically. Unless told otherwise, leave the options field blank and select **OK** to continue.

CREATE LINUX PARTITIONS

You're now ready to create those Linux partitions on your hard disk that we discussed earlier. To run Linux, you need a *root partition* and a *swap partition*. The root partition is where all your operating system

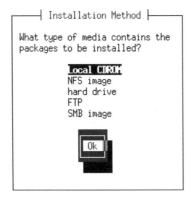

FIGURE 1-5: *Selecting the installation method*

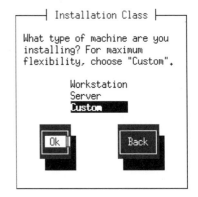

FIGURE 1-6: *Selecting an installation class*

and user data files reside. Linux uses the swap partition to simulate physical memory (installed RAM), in much the same way that Windows or a Macintosh uses a chunk of hard-drive space to create virtual memory.

You need a minimum of 16MB of RAM to run Linux, so if you have less than 16MB of physical memory installed, you have to make up the difference with a swap partition. For example, if you have only 8MB of RAM, you can create a 16MB swap partition, and Linux will think it has 24MB of RAM to use. The more memory you can muster, the faster Linux will fly.

■ **NOTE:** *For non-PCMCIA (normal) installations, 16 MB of RAM is suffi-cient, but 24MB is required for an upgrade or PCMCIA install, and 32MB is required if it is an upgrade with PCMCIA.*

USING THE DISK DRUID UTILITY

When the Disk Setup screen (Figure 1-7) appears, choose "Disk Druid" and then select **OK** to continue. When the Disk Druid screen (Figure 1-8) appears, it should show a single partition called hda1, with a size of 600MB, labeled "DOS 16-bit." (If you have a SCSI hard drive, look for scd1 instead of hda1.) This assumes you started with a 1.2GB hard disk and used **FDISK** or **FIPS** to reduce the size of your DOS partition to 600MB.

Your goal is to do four things with the Disk Druid program:

• Create a Linux root partition.

• Create a Linux swap partition.

• Assign a mount point for the root partition.

• Assign a mount point for the DOS partition.

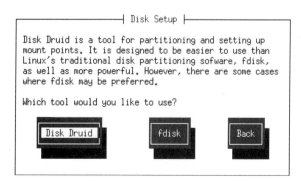

FIGURE 1-7: *Starting Disk Druid*

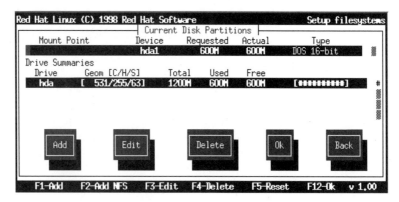

FIGURE 1-8: *Partitioning with Disk Druid*

CREATING THE ROOT PARTITION

Use the "Add" button to create the root partition. Enter **/** for the mount point and **580** for the size, and select "Linux Native" for the type (see Figure 1-9). Select **OK** to return to the main Disk Druid screen.

CREATING THE SWAP PARTITION

Use the "Add" button to create the swap partition. Leave the mount point blank, enter **20** for the size, and select "Linux Swap" for the type (see Figure 1-10). Select **OK** to return to the main Disk Druid screen.

■ *NOTE: If you have enough disk space available, Red Hat recommends a minimum 32MB of swap space for systems with less than 128MB of RAM. For low memory systems (<32MB), a good rule of thumb is to have swap space equal to four times your system memory to avoid problems with large applications like Netscape and GNOME.*

SETTING THE PARTITION MOUNT POINTS

Select the "DOS" (**hda1**) partition and use the "Edit" button (see Figure 1-11). Change the mount point to **/dos** (indicating the DOS C drive partition). Do not change any other settings for this partition. Select **OK** to return to the main Disk Druid screen.

Your screen may show hda1, hda5, and hda6 partitions as shown in the illustration, or you may have hda1, hda2, and hda3. If you started with two hard drives and opted to put Linux on the second drive, you may have hda1, hdb1, and hdb2.

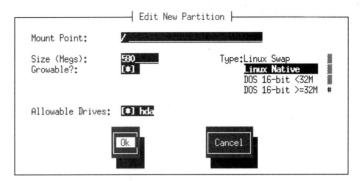

FIGURE 1-9: *Creating the root partition*

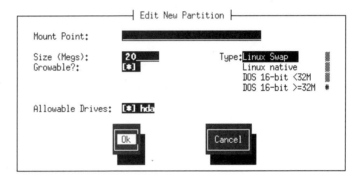

FIGURE 1-10: *Creating the swap partition*

The important thing is to have one DOS partition, one Linux native (root) partition, and one Linux swap partition. If your hard drive is not the same size as the one in this example, it's fine to adjust the partition sizes accordingly or to suit your own preferences.

PREPARE THE PARTITIONS

Continuing with the installation process, the installation program will ask you to confirm the activation of your swap partition (see Figure 1-12). Select the box next to **/dev/hda6** to confirm, and Linux will format and prepare the swap space for use.

You've just increased the amount of your system's available RAM by creating a pool of virtual memory in the swap space—and you didn't have to spend a penny or install new SIMMs!

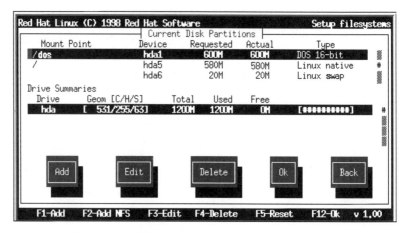

FIGURE 1-11: *Setting the partition mount points*

Next you must confirm the formatting of your root partition (see Figure 1-13). Select the box next to **/dev/hda5** to confirm, and Linux will format and prepare the root partition.

SELECT THE COMPONENTS TO INSTALL

At this point you've created a root partition to store all of your Linux files, but it's empty. You still need a file system (the physical structure and organization of files on the disk) and a bunch of files to get Linux rolling.

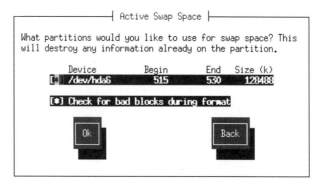

FIGURE 1-12: *Activating the swap space*

The installation program will show you a long list of packages you can select, each of which is an optional part of the Linux system (see Figure 1-14). Some will be preselected, but I recommend that you also select the following packages:

- Printer Support

- DOS/Windows Connectivity

- X Games

- Web Server

- Emacs

- Extra Documentation

This installation will require about 300MB of hard disk space. As mentioned earlier, you can skip the "X" packages but you won't get the X Windows GUI or some nifty system configuration tools. If you're a programmer and some of the other packages look interesting, go ahead and select them if you know you have enough disk space. You can always install additional packages later with the **rpm** (text-based) or **gnorpm** (X Windows–based) utilities. Select **OK** when you've finished making your selections, and the install program will start copying the selected files to your hard disk. This will take several minutes.

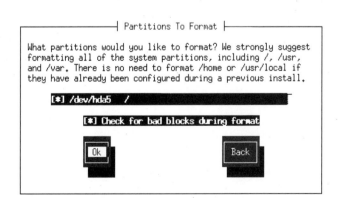

FIGURE 1-13: *Formatting the root partition*

FIGURE 1-14: *Selecting the components to install*

Configure Your Hardware for Linux

The installation program will now ask you a series of questions about your hardware in order to configure each device for use with Linux.

Configuring the Mouse

When you are presented with a list of mouse options (shown in Figure 1-15), choose the one that matches your system. If you're unsure, look at the plug on the end of the cable. If it's rectangular, you have a serial mouse. If it's round, you have a PS/2-style mouse. Choose the corresponding Generic Mouse entry, depending on the number of buttons your mouse has. If you have a two-button mouse, select the "Emulate 3 Buttons?" box and you'll be able to simulate the middle button by pressing the left and right buttons together.

Select **OK**, and if you have a serial mouse you'll be asked which port your mouse is connected to (see Figure 1-16). The correct answer will probably be highlighted already, but you should check to see if it matches the port that DOS or Windows uses for the mouse. If the mouse doesn't work after installation, you can run the **mouseconfig** command again and try different settings.

If you're left-handed and you want to configure your mouse as a left-handed mouse, you can reset the order of the mouse buttons with

Figure 1-15: *Configuring the mouse*

the **gpm** utility. After the installation is complete, start your system and enter the following command at the prompt. It would also be a good idea to log in as **root** and put the same command in your **/etc/profile** file so you don't have to enter it each time you boot up Linux.

`gpm -B 321`

CONFIGURING A NETWORK

The install program will next ask if you want to configure the system for a LAN network. Answer "No" unless you have a network card and your PC is part of a network. If you do want to configure a network, respond to the prompts with the information supplied by your network administrator.

CONFIGURING THE SYSTEM CLOCK

Choose your time zone from the list and then select **OK** (see Figure 1-17). Generally, you do *not* want to select the Hardware clock set to GMT box, unless you are on a network.

SELECTING STARTUP SERVICES

The install program will present you with a long list of strange-looking system services (shown in Figure 1-18) that are to be started when you boot up Linux. The best thing to do is select **OK** to continue without making any changes to the list. But if you're curious, you can highlight an item and press **F1** to see what it's supposed to do.

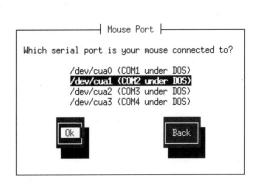

FIGURE 1-16: *Selecting a mouse port*

FIGURE 1-17: *Configuring the time zone*

CONFIGURING A PRINTER

The install program will ask if you want to configure a printer (see Figure 1-19). If you have one, by all means select "Yes." When asked how the printer is connected to your computer, the most likely response is "Local," which means it's plugged directly into the back of your computer. If your printer is on a network, ask the administrator for the information needed to configure it for Linux.

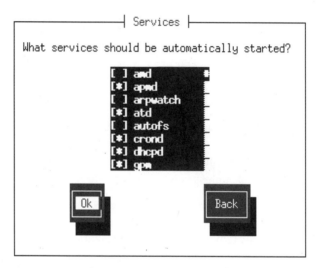

FIGURE 1-18: *Selecting startup services*

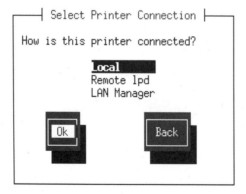

FIGURE 1-19: *Selecting a printer connection*

When the Standard Printer Options and Local Printer Device screens appear (Figures 1-20 and 1-21), select **OK** to accept the defaults that are presented.

On the Configure Printer screen (Figure 1-22), select the printer that most closely matches yours; then choose the appropriate paper size and resolution (Figure 1-23).

Select **OK** when you're ready to proceed, and then select **OK** again when you see the Verify Printer Configuration screen.

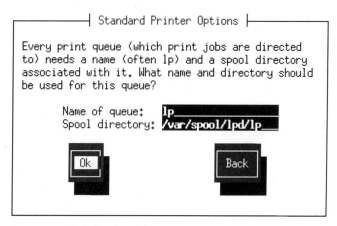

FIGURE 1-20: *Defining the printer queue*

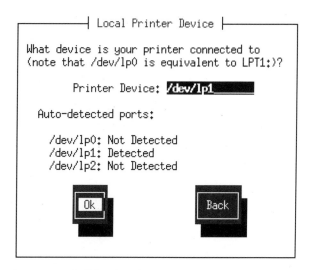

FIGURE 1-21: *Defining the printer port*

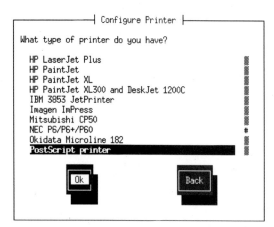

FIGURE 1-22: *Configuring the printer*

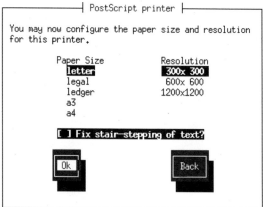

FIGURE 1-23: *Selecting the paper size and resolution*

CHOOSE A ROOT PASSWORD

When you start Linux after installation, you'll log in with the username **root** and a password you choose. If you plan to allow others to use your Linux system, it's important to choose a root password that cannot be easily guessed. Pick a winner, enter it twice, and select **OK** (see Figure 1-24).

Because the root user (also called the superuser) has complete access to everything on a Linux system, root should be used only for system administration tasks such as installing new software and configuring system services. You'll learn how to create new users for everyday use in Chapter 4, "Living in a Shell."

CREATE AN EMERGENCY BOOT DISK

Just in case you ever have trouble booting up your Linux system, you should have an emergency Linux boot disk on hand (see Figure 1-25). This will allow you to boot the system using a floppy disk and access the files on your Linux partition.

You can accidentally wipe out the LILO code (see the next section) on your boot partition if you install a DOS or Windows upgrade, leaving you unable to boot into Linux—another good reason to have an emergency disk on hand.

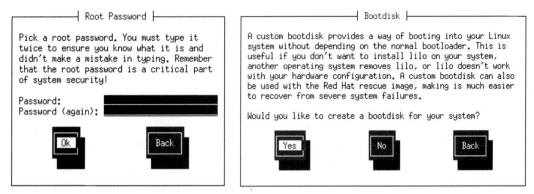

FIGURE 1-24: *Choosing a root password*　　　**FIGURE 1-25:** *Creating an emergency disk*

Oh; don't forget to put a nice new floppy in drive A first, and remove it afterward. You should also label the disk "Red Hat Linux Boot Disk."

INSTALL LILO: THE LINUX LOADER

Next, the install program will ask if you want to install LILO (Figure 1-26). You do. LILO (the Linux Loader) lets you boot Linux directly from the hard disk when you turn on your PC. Without LILO, you have to create a special floppy disk and boot Linux from it, which is slow and inconvenient.

Specify that LILO is to be installed on the Master Boot Record (**/dev/hda** or **/dev/sda**, as shown in Figure 1-26), and do not specify any kernel options (as shown in Figure 1-27). Before installing, you should review your computer's BIOS settings to see if your computer accesses a hard drive in LBA mode. If it does, select the "Use linear mode" box.

When the Bootable Partitions screen appears, you'll see a list of all the bootable partitions on your system. In our case, there should be just two—the DOS 16-bit and the Linux Native partitions. Note the column labeled "Default." The partition that contains an asterisk under that column is the partition LILO will boot by default, unless you respond to the **LILO:** prompt at startup.

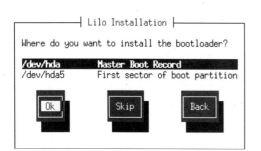

FIGURE 1-26: *Installing LILO*

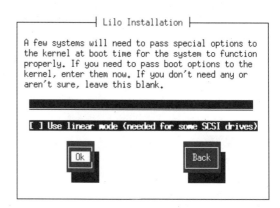

FIGURE 1-27: *Specifying kernel options*

Your Red Hat Linux root partition will be selected as the default. If you'd like to boot DOS by default (with the option of booting Linux), use the arrow keys to highlight the DOS partition and press **F2**.

LILO will display a **LILO:** prompt at startup that lets you select which operating system to start. If you want to start the default operating system, just press **ENTER**. If your default is to boot Linux, you can boot DOS by entering **dos** at the prompt. Similarly, if your default is to boot DOS, you can boot Linux by entering **linux** at the prompt.

CONFIGURE X WINDOWS

At this point, the installation program starts the Xconfigurator (the X Windows configuration program), which will probe your system to figure out what type of video card and monitor you have and install the proper XFree86 server. XFree86 is an implementation of the X Windows system for PC-compatible processors and is part of the GNU project.

DEFINING YOUR VIDEO CARD

If Xconfigurator can tell which video card you have, it will display a screen showing the name of your card. Just press **ENTER** to continue, as shown in Figure 1-28. If Xconfigurator cannot automatically determine your video card, it will display a list of video cards from which you must make a selection. If your video card does not appear on the list, it may be unsupported. However, if you have the technical documentation for your card, you can choose "Unlisted Card" and try to configure it by closely matching your card's video chipset with the options presented by Xconfigurator.

DEFINING YOUR MONITOR

After a video card is selected, Xconfigurator presents a list of monitors (see Figure 1-29). If your monitor is on the list, select it. If it's not on the list and you have the manufacturer's technical specifications, select "Custom," and Xconfigurator will prompt you to select the characteristics of your monitor. Be careful, though—if you select a monitor "similar" to yours, and your monitor can't handle a certain display mode, it's possible to damage the monitor. A safer choice would be "Generic Monitor" or "Generic Multisync."

If Xconfigurator asks to probe for your monitor's characteristics, allow it to do so, and accept the default results it presents (see Figure 1-30). Unless you built your own video card from molten silicon, you probably won't know the difference.

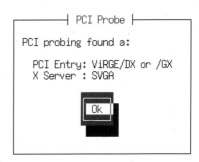

FIGURE 1-28: *Video probing results*

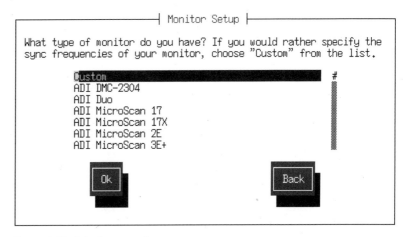

FIGURE 1-29: *Selecting a monitor*

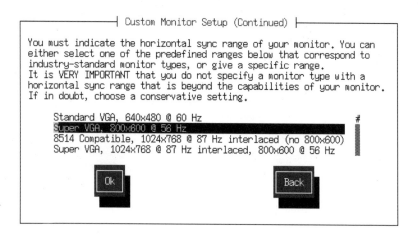

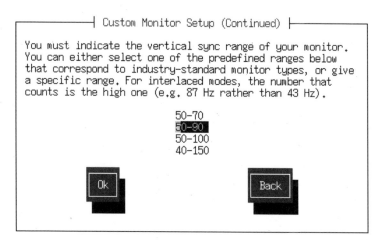

FIGURE 1-30: *Defining monitor characteristics*

MORE VIDEO SETUP QUESTIONS

Xconfigurator may prompt you for the amount of video memory installed on your video card (see Figure 1-31). If you don't know, check the documentation for your video card. You can't damage your card by choosing the wrong amount, but X Windows may not work if you guess wrong.

Xconfigurator may also present a list of clock chips (Figure 1-32). Unless you're sure you know better, choose "No Clockchip Setting," since XFree86 can automatically detect the proper clock chip in most cases.

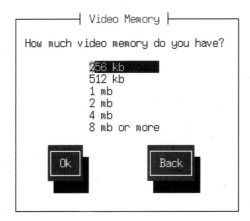

FIGURE 1-31: *Defining video memory*

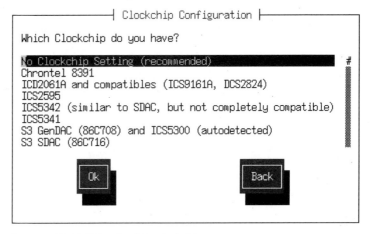

FIGURE 1-32: *Defining the video clock chip*

Xconfigurator will then probe for your video card to set the video mode (see Figure 1-33). If you don't want to accept the default settings, choose "Let Me Choose" and you'll be prompted to select the video modes you wish to use (see Figures 1-34). For most people, running at 800 x 600 with 16-bit color will do nicely. If your monitor and video card support higher resolutions, go for it. If you select more than one, you can cycle through the modes by pressing **CTRL-ALT-+** while running X Windows.

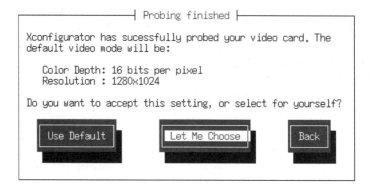

FIGURES 1-33: *Probing your video card*

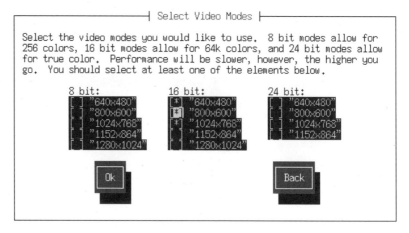

FIGURE 1-34: *Selecting a video mode*

When you are finished, Xconfigurator records all of your configuration choices in the **/etc/X11/XF86Config** file. You may find it interesting to browse this file, but unless you really know what you're doing, don't make any changes to it.

If you can't get X Windows running, or if the display looks poor (too big, too small, wrong colors, and so on), you can run **Xconfigurator** again and try different settings. You can even run the **Xconfigurator** command again after installation, if you want to finish the installation and try different setup options later.

```
┤ Done ├
─────────────────────────────────────────

Congratulations, installation is complete.

Remove the floppy from the drive and press return to
reboot. For information on fixes which are available
for this release of Red Hat Linux, consult the Errata
available from http://www.redhat.com.

Information on configuring your system is available in
the post install chapter of the Official Red Hat Linux
User's Guide.

                      ┌──────┐
                      │  Ok  │
                      └──────┘
```

FIGURE 1-35: *Installation complete*

START X WINDOWS AT BOOT TIME?

Finally, you will see a screen that gives you the option of starting your
system in X Windows mode when you boot. I recommend against this,
because it's tricky to get back to the text-mode shell prompt if you do.
My suggestion is to use the **startx** command after booting up in text
mode to fire up X Windows, but if you prefer the GUI interface at boot
time, go for it!

SHUT DOWN AND REBOOT

You're almost at the finish line. When you see the Done screen (Figure
1-35), remove any floppies from the disk drive and select **OK**. A bunch
of messages will show various systems shutting down, and then you'll
boot up into your grand and glorious new Linux system.

AFTER INSTALLATION: MOUNTING YOUR CD-ROM DRIVE

After you reboot your system, you'll most likely want to access files on
the installation CD or some other CD-ROM disk, either to view some of
the helpful documentation found there or to install additional software
packages. But before you can access the CD-ROM drive, you have to
mount it. Mounting means you assign a physical device (the CD-ROM) to
a directory on your hard disk.

Normally, the CD-ROM is mounted automatically, and you can view the files on a CD by looking in the **/mnt/cdrom** directory. If the CD is not mounted automatically, you can mount the drive with a command like this:

```
mount -t iso9660 XXXXX /mnt/cdrom
```

Before you issue that command, you must substitute the device name of your CD-ROM for *XXXXX*. The following information will help you select the correct device name.

CD-ROM TYPE	DEVICE NAME
IDE on Controller 0	/dev/hdb
IDE on Controller 1	/dev/hdc or /dev/hdd
SCSI Interface	/dev/scd0 or /dev/scd1
SoundBlaster or compatible	/dev/sbpcd

Check your manual to determine what type of CD-ROM drive you have. If you have an IDE drive, either your CD manual or your IDE controller manual will tell you what controller is in use for the CD-ROM drive. (The most common ones are **/dev/hdb** and **/dev/hdc**.)

Be especially careful to check the manual if you have a SoundBlaster CD. Some are actually IDEs, and some IDE drives are configured to use controller 3. If this is the case, refer to the manual for instructions on how to change the controller, since Linux will not find a CD unless it is on controller 0 or 1. (It's a matter of fooling with the jumpers on the controller card to which your CD is connected.)

ACCESSING FILES ON THE CD-ROM
After you issue the mount command, list the files on the CD-ROM to see if the mount worked, using these commands:

cd /mnt/cdrom	Switch to the CD directory.
ls	List the files on the CD.

If you try a device name in the mount command and get an error, or if your **ls** command doesn't display any files, just pick another device name and try again—you won't hurt anything.

For now, just be happy if you can list the files on the CD-ROM. In Chapter 5, "The Linux File System," you'll learn more about navigating directories, as well as about listing and viewing files.

I Need Help!

If the installation does not work, or if you have trouble with your system after installation, refer to Chapter 15, "Learning More about Linux." You should also look at the Red Hat Installation manual on the CD for help with the most common installation problems if following the instructions in this chapter doesn't get you up and running. To view the manual, start your Web browser under Windows and open the file:

```
D:\DOC\RHMANUAL\MANUAL\DOC000.HTM
```

You will also find lots of helpful information, including the Linux FAQ (Frequently Asked Questions) files and the Linux HOWTO files, in these directories on the CD:

```
D:\DOC\FAQ
D:\DOC\HOWTO
```

Shut Down and Reboot

You're almost at the finish line. When you see the "Done" screen, remove any floppies from the disk drive and select **OK**. A bunch of messages will show various sysytems shutting down, and tnen you'll boot uo into your grand and glorious new Linux system. If you chose the text-mode shell prompt for your bootup option, you'll be greeted by a prompt like this:

```
[root@localhost/root] #
```

If you're familiar with Linux commands, you can enter them at the pound sign (#) prompt. Otherwise, use the **startx** command to start the GNOME graphical interface, and proceed to Chapter 2, "GNOME: The Linux GUI."

GNOME: THE LINUX GUI

T he graphical user interface (GUI) for Linux systems is XFree86, a PC-based implementation of X Windows. Red Hat Linux version 6 adds GNOME (GNU Network Object Model Environment), a friendly desktop manager that makes it easy to use and configure X Windows and Enlightenment, a window manager that allows you to control the look and feel of the desktop with themes, wallpaper, sound, screensavers, and special effects.

Using GNOME is a lot like using other graphical user interfaces— you can have several applications open in different windows on the screen, and you can move from one to another using your mouse. If you're familiar with Windows 95/98 or the Macintosh, you'll have no trouble adapting to GNOME. Later, you may want to check out "The GNOME Control Center" and "Customizing Enlightenment" in Chapter 13, "Tweaking Linux," to learn how to make your desktop more fun and personal. See the sample GNOME desktop in Figure 2-1.

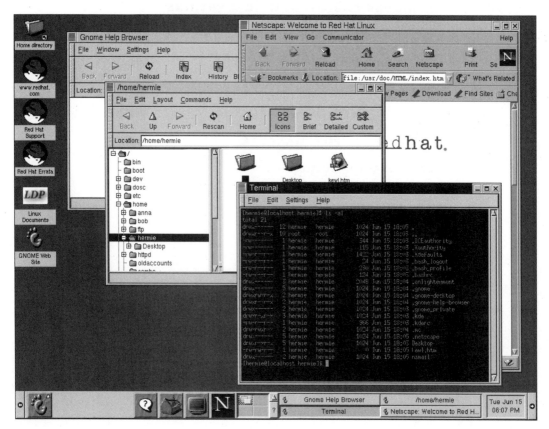

Figure 2-1: *The GNOME desktop*

DESKTOP AND WINDOW MANAGERS

One of the fundamental principles of X Windows architecture is the cooperation of separate components. X Windows' client-server model of operation and the capability it provides that allows users to replace major pieces of functionality with alternative plug-in modules make it very flexible and popular in the Unix world. The most prominent examples of this flexible architecture are the X Server, Desktop Manager, and Window Manager.

Many people are confused by these terms, and frankly, understanding the difference between the server, the desktop manager, and the window manager is not all that important to the average Linux user. If you want to think of them simply as components of the X Windows environment, that's fine—you can safely ignore the rest of this section. If, however, you're prone to endless tinkering with your system, you should read on to get a better understanding of these terms.

The X server is the low-level program that handles the details of writing text and graphics widgets to the screen with the specified size, colors, and location. When you ran the Xconfigurator utility, it selected an X server appropriate for your video hardware. The server listens for the various client programs to ask for these widgets to be drawn. One of those client programs is the Window Manager, which works as a layer between the client programs and the X server. It puts borders around windows, resizes windows, and allows for controls to move things.

The Desktop Manager works at an even higher level than that, giving a unified look and feel to programs running on the desktop and acting as an intermediary so that programs can interact and exchange data. The Desktop Manager also gives you a set of desktop applications such as a file manager, text editor, and other productivity tools. Your Red Hat Linux system is shipped with both GNOME and KDE (K Desktop Environment), the two most popular Desktop Managers. The default X Windows configuration for Red Hat version 6 is GNOME with the Enlightenment Window Manager. GNOME was selected because it's very popular and is the only fully open source desktop environment. At the time Red Hat version 6 was released, Enlightenment was the only Window Manager that was 100 percent compliant with GNOME. For more information on customizing the look and feel of your GNOME desktop, see "The GNOME Control Center" and "Customizing Enlightenment" in Chapter 13, "Tweaking Linux."

Here are some other Window Managers that work with GNOME, but which may not be fully compliant:

Window Maker   http://www.windowmaker.org

FVWM   http://www.fvwm.org

Icewm   http://www.kiss.uni-lj.si/~k4fro235/icewm

See Chapter 13 for information on downloading other Window Managers and trying them out using the Window Manager applet in the GNOME Control Center. If you want to try out KDE, use the **switchdesk** command and select the "KDE" option. To return to GNOME, use the **switchdesk** command again and select "GNOME."

MOUSE AND WINDOW CONVENTIONS

Have a close look at the windows on your GNOME desktop, and you'll see some common features, namely the title bar; "System Menu" button; "Minimize," "Maximize," and "Close" buttons; and grab handles.

Refer to Figure 2-1 as we explore some of the ways you can interact with a window. (I've used LMB and RMB as abbreviations for left mouse button and right mouse button in the following table.)

FEATURE	LOCATION	FUNCTION
System menu	Upper left	Click with LMB to reveal System menu or double-click to close.
Title bar	Top middle	Click with LMB to bring window to front, or click with RMB to send window to rear. You can also move a window by dragging while holding down LMB on the title bar.
Maximize button	Top right (square inside button)	Click with LMB to make the window occupy the full screen (or its maximum size). Click again to resume former size.
Minimize button	Top right (underscore inside button)	Click with LMB to send the window to the Pager on the bottom of the screen. Double-click an item in the Pager to restore it to a window.
Grab handles	Corners, left, right, and bottom borders	Hold down LMB and drag to resize the window.

The left mouse button is used to mark, select, and drag items. To copy text, click and drag with the left mouse button across the text you want to copy, move the pointer to the place you want the text placed, and press the middle mouse button. (If you have a two-button mouse, press the left and right buttons simultaneously to simulate the middle button.) Clicking the right mouse button will display a menu for the selected object, if one applies.

MAJOR FEATURES OF GNOME

Major features of GNOME include the following:

- The GNOME Panel. This is similar to the Windows 95/98 taskbar, but of course more fun and powerful. The GNOME Panel is used to launch applications, manage virtual desktops, and display the system status. The panel is the long bar located at the bottom of the screen.

- The desktop. This is the place for data, applications, and active windows.

- A set of tools and productivity applications, such as the File Manager, text editor, spreadsheet, calendar, and calculator.

- A set of conventions that make it easy for applications to cooperate and be consistent with each other. This makes life easier for both programmers and end users.

GNOME is part of the GNU project, so it's free software and is open source. This means that the source code is available for anyone to inspect and modify. You can learn more about the GNOME project or get involved in the development yourself by visiting the GNOME Web site at http://www.gnome.org/.

THE GNOME PANEL

The GNOME Panel, located at the bottom of the screen (see Figure 2-2) is the heart of the GNOME interface and is the place for your application launchers, applets, the Pager, and the main menu. The panel is also designed to be highly configurable, and you'll learn how to set up the menus and applications just the way you want them to be.

Figure 2-2: *The GNOME Panel*

Using the GNOME Panel is very simple and will come easily to anyone who has used a GUI-based operating system. You can launch programs, add application launchers to the panel, add various applets (little programs that run inside the panel), or even create multiple panels. All of these functions and more will be described in this section.

USING THE MAIN MENU

The button on the bottom left of the panel that looks like a footprint (shown at the left) is the "Main menu" button, sometimes called The Foot. Just click on the "Main menu" button and you'll see a menu of preloaded applications and actions (as in Figure 2-3), including a logout command.

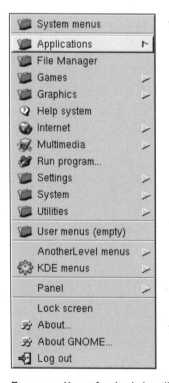

The "Main menu" button is a convenient means of starting any of the applications installed on your system, and it works a lot like the "Start" button on Windows 95/98 systems. Some of the menu items on the Main menu have cascading submenus that appear when you click on them. If you click and hold down the left mouse button, you can navigate the menus just by moving the mouse. When you find the application you want to start, release the button.

Figure 2-3: *Menu of preloaded applications*

If you find that the cascading menus are a little too sensitive, click and release the left button to reveal a submenu; then carefully move the mouse into the submenu. The right mouse button has a special function in the main menu area, which we'll learn about later in this section.

CHANGING THE MAIN MENU PROPERTIES

The Main menu is divided into two areas: the System menus and the User menus. To change the properties of the Main menu, right-click on the "Main menu" button and select "Properties" to launch the Menu Properties dialog box (see Figure 2-4).

The only thing you can customize here is whether the various submenus appear within the Main menu, in a submenu, or not at all. For example, if you change the selection for User menu from "On the main menu" to "In a submenu," you will no longer see the items from the User menu when you first display the Main menu. You'll have to click on "User menu" to make them appear.

CUSTOMIZING THE MAIN MENU

If you want to add or delete items in the Main menu, use the Menu Editor. To start the Menu Editor, click on the "Main menu" button and select "Settings" and then "Menu Editor" (see Figure 2-5).

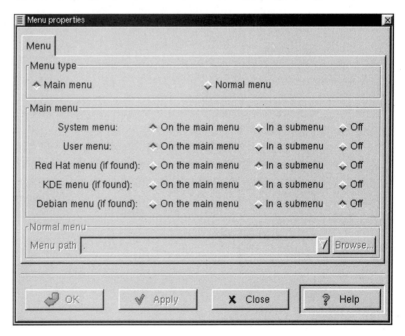

Figure 2-4: *Menu Properties dialog box*

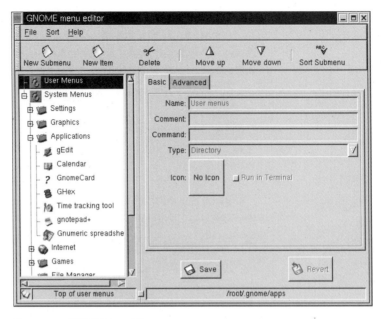

Figure 2-5: *GNOME Menu Editor*

The Menu Editor is divided into two main panels. On the left panel, you will see a tree-like view of your current menus. Clicking on a plus sign will expand the tree to reveal the items in a menu, and clicking on a minus sign will reverse the process. The right panel is a dialog box where you can specify the particulars for new applications you want to add to the menu.

You can use the buttons at the top of the screen to add or delete items or to add a new submenu. The position of a menu item can be changed by pressing the "Move up" and "Move down" buttons on the toolbar or by dragging the item with the left mouse button. The Menu Editor supports drag-and-drop, which allows you to drag applications from other windows (such as the File Manager or the GNOME Panel) to the menus you want them in.

■ *NOTE:* *Any user can modify the User menus, but only the root user can modify the System menus.*

THE GNOME PAGER

The Pager (Figure 2-6) is a tool on the GNOME Panel to help you manage the applications currently active on your desktops. You can use it

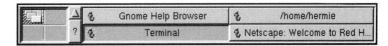

Figure 2-6: *The GNOME Pager*

to restore minimized applications to your desktop or to switch from one desktop area to another.

The area on the left side of the Pager is the desktops view, which shows all of your desktops and the applications within them. Each desktop is represented by a small rectangle, and the applications on the desktops are outlined in miniature form. By default, all applications are started in the upper-left desktop, but if your screen gets too cluttered, switch to another desktop by clicking on one of the rectangles.

The task list on the right side of the Pager displays the active applications on the current desktop. If you minimize an application, you can return it to your desktop by clicking on its entry in the task list. The arrow button in the middle of the Pager displays a list of all the applications active on any desktop. You can also restore minimized windows by clicking on this list.

CUSTOMIZING THE PAGER

The Pager is very customizable. To open the Pager Properties dialog box (see Figure 2-7) right click on "Pager" and select "Properties" from the pop-up menu. You can tweak the maximum width of the task list, the number of rows and columns in the task list, and the number

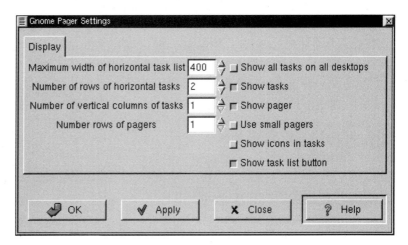

Figure 2-7: *Pager Properties dialog box*

of rows in the pager. You can also try out various options such as viewing all applications on all desktops (instead of just the current desktop), turn the task list off, turn the Pager off, or use small pagers. Try the various options to configure the Pager just the way you like it.

HIDING THE PANEL

If the GNOME Panel is getting in your way, you have several options. You can hide the panel by pressing either of its "Hide" buttons. There are hide buttons on both sides of the Panel, so you can slide it away in either direction. Even more useful is the auto-hide feature, which makes the panel slide off the bottom of the screen. The panel springs back up when you bring the mouse into the panel area. To enable auto-hide, select **Panel • This Panel Properties** from the "Main Menu" button (see Figure 2-8).

If you use auto-hide all the time, it might be wise to disable the "Hide" buttons, to regain a little extra space on the panel.

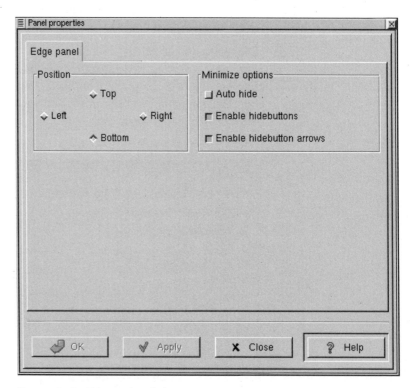

Figure 2-8: *Panel Properties window*

Moving the Panel

You can also use the Panel Configuration dialog box to change the position of the panel on your screen. Select "Top," "Right," "Left," or "Bottom"; then click the "Apply" button to move the panel.

Adding Application Launchers

If you want to add an Application Launcher (an icon that starts a particular application) to the panel, right-click the panel and select "Add New Launcher" from the pop-up menu. After selecting the Add New Launcher menu item, you will see a dialog box that enables you to set the properties for the application launcher you want to add.

In the Create Launcher Applet dialog box (see Figure 2-9), you can add a name for your launcher, a comment, and the command line to launch the application, and you can define the application type. You can also click the icon button and choose an icon to represent the application from the icon picker. If no icon is chosen, a default icon will be used.

Another, quicker method of adding an application launcher to the GNOME Panel is to go to the Main menu and right-click on an application menu item. You will be given another menu that contains the

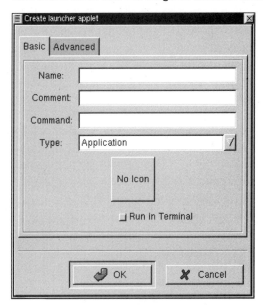

Figure 2-9: *Create Launcher Applet dialog box*

selection "Add this launcher to panel." If you select this menu item, it will automatically add a launcher for that application to the panel in which you invoked the Main menu. At this point, you can right-click on the launcher and select the "Properties" menu item to change any options for that launcher.

ADDING DRAWERS AND MENUS TO THE PANEL

If you want to group a subset of applications together, you can use a *drawer*. A drawer is simply a small menu-like button that sits on your panel that groups application launchers together is one place. Once you have placed a drawer on the panel, you can click on it to raise the menu of applications and click again to lower it.

There are a couple of ways to place a drawer on your panel. First, you can right-click on the panel and select "Add drawer" from the pop-up menu. Second, if you want a whole subset of menus from the Main menu to become a drawer, you can right-click on the title bar of that menu and select "Add this as drawer to panel" from the pop-up menu.

You can add *menus* to your panel in the same way as you add drawers. Menus are very similar to drawers except that they do not use large icons to represent application launchers. Instead, they use a style similar to the Main menu: small icons and the application name. You can add a menu by right-clicking on the title bar of a menu and selecting "Add this as menu to panel" from the pop-up menu. You can also add system directories to the panel as menus by dragging a directory out of the GNOME File Manager and dropping it on the panel. The image at the left shows the Menu and Drawer icons as they appear on the GNOME Panel.

Clicking on a drawer or menu will open it. Figure 2-10 shows samples of an open drawer and menu. Note that drawers stay open after you click on one of the icons inside and have to be closed by clicking the down arrow. Menus automatically close after you make a selection.

Figure 2-10: *Open drawer (left) and menu (right)*

CREATING MULTIPLE PANELS

If you think having one GNOME Panel is fun, why not throw a few more on the screen? To add a new panel to your desktop, press the "Main Menu" button and then select **Panel • Add New Panel**. You can add either an Edge panel or a Corner panel. Edge panels stretch the full length of the screen edge where they are placed, and Corner panels stretch only far enough to hold the applets they contain. Having a second panel can be useful if you want to try out some panel applets, but you have limited space on the main panel.

PANEL APPLETS

Applets are tiny programs that run inside the panel. The clock on the right side of the panel is one example, but there are lots of optional applets you can add to your panel. To access these applets, right-click on the panel and select "Add new applet" from the pop-up menu. Here are some of the applets you can run:

AMUSEMENT APPLETS

Fifteen Lets you play that little rearrange-the-scrambled-squares game.

Game of Life Simulates the *Life* game in a tiny window.

SlashApp Displays a ticker with Linux news from SlashDot.Org.

MONITORING APPLETS

Battery Monitor Shows how much time you have left on your laptop battery.

Battery Charge Monitor Shows how much your battery has been charged and how much time is needed to complete the task.

CPU/MEM Usage Monitor Shows current use of the CPU, memory, and swap space.

CPULoad Displays a graph that shows your current CPU use.

MEMLoad Displays a graph that shows your current memory use.

SWAPLoad Displays a simple graph that shows your current swap space use.

MULTIMEDIA APPLETS

CD Player Plays music CDs.

Mixer Sets the sound level.

NETWORK APPLETS

Mail Check Lets you know when your email has arrived.

Modem Lights Simulates the flashing lights on an external modem.

PPP Dialer Turns your PPP connection on or off.

Web Control Provides a command line for entering URLs and launching the browser.

UTILITY APPLETS

AfterClock Provides a clock much cooler than the Clock applet that's included by default on the GNOME Panel. To access the

AfterClock properties, right-click on the clock and select the "Properties" menu item from the pop-up menu. A dialog box will appear, where you can change the look of the clock. Several options are shown at left.

Printer Applet Provides a small printer icon that lives on your GNOME Panel. If you drag a file to the Printer applet, the applet will print the file for you. To set up the Printer applet, right-click on it and select the "Properties" menu item from the pop-up menu.

Drive Mount Applet Allows you to mount or unmount a floppy drive, hard disk, or CD-ROM drive on your system by clicking the icon.

Quicklaunch Gives you a place to put tiny launchers. Drag and drop existing launchers onto the Quicklaunch applet to create small (and barely readable) launcher buttons.

Mini Commander Puts a command line on your taskbar. This applet is handy if you want to run a command quickly without first opening a terminal window. The Mini Commander also features a command history so you can select a command to run again without reentering it.

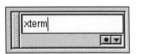

The GNOME Help Browser

The GNOME Help Browser (Figure 2-11) is a convenient path to all the available help files on your system. Click on the taskbar button with the big question mark and you'll launch the GNOME Help Browser. From there, you can browse a catalog of help information in man, info, and html format, along with special help files for the GNOME interface.

The GNOME Desktop

Outside of the panel, the rest of the screen space is called the desktop. If you have programs or data files that you use often, you can place them on your desktop and then double-click to use them. If the item is a program, the program will start. If it's data, the appropriate program will start with that data loaded. If it's a WWW link, the Netscape browser will start and display the Web page. If it's a directory, the File Manager will start and show the contents of that directory.

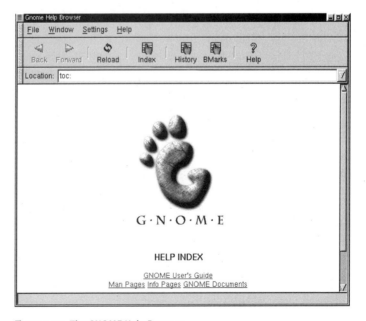

Figure 2-11: *The GNOME Help Browser*

The desktop supports drag-and-drop operation, so you can easily move items between the desktop and other windows. You can drag data files from the File Manager to a program icon on the desktop to launch the program with that data loaded, or you can drag a link from Netscape and drop it on the desktop to create a shortcut.

DESKTOP AREAS

Earlier in this chapter we touched on the subject of desktop areas while discussing the GNOME Pager. If your screen gets too cluttered with active windows, you can click on the desktop switcher in the Pager to move to another desktop area and open more windows. If you're a keyboard addict, you can use the **ALT-F1** through **ALT-F4** keys to switch among the desktop areas.

If you're wondering why they're called desktop areas and not just desktops, there is a good reason: The four desktop areas actually make up one big desktop. You can see how this makes sense by dragging a window to the right side of the screen so that half of it disappears. Now move to the second desktop area and you'll see that the other half of the window is there. This doesn't make much practical sense, but it does illustrate the point.

MOVING WINDOWS BETWEEN DESKTOPS

If you want to move a window from one desktop area to another, click on the "System Menu" button in the upper-left corner of the window and then select "Desktop" and choose the target desktop area.

If you want a certain window to appear on all four desktop areas, click on the "System Menu" and select the "Stick/Unstick" option. This doesn't mean that you'll have four copies of that program running. When you move from one desktop area to another, this window will follow as you go.

| Close |
| Annihilate |
| Iconify |
| Raise |
| Lower |
| Shade/Unshade |
| Stick/Unstick |
| Desktop ▶ |
| Window Size ▶ |
| Remember State ▶ |
| Set Stacking ▶ |
| Set Border Style ▶ |

FILE MANAGER

The File Manager application (see Figure 2-12) lets you manipulate your files. The left side of its window shows directories, and the right side shows the selected directory's contents. If you have used the File Manager application for Windows, you'll be right at home. Here are some quick tips:

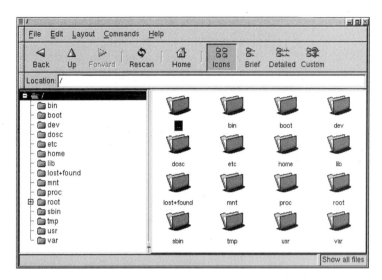

Figure 2-12: *The File Manager*

- Click on a plus sign in the left panel to expand a branch of the file tree (to reveal subdirectories) or click on a minus sign to hide a branch of the file tree.

- Use the "Icon," "Brief," "Detailed," and "Custom" buttons to change the style of the file listing in the right panel.

- To run a program or edit a data file, double-click it.

- To move a file or directory, just drag and drop it to another folder, window or the desktop.

- To copy a file, hold down the **CTRL** key while dragging.

- Start two File Manager windows with different directories to easily move or copy files between directories.

- To rename a file, right-click on it and select "Properties."

- To delete a file, select with a single-click and then press the **DELETE** key.

SELECTING FILES

To select more than one item, hold down the **SHIFT** key and click on the items. You can also use a *rubber-band selection*, by holding down the left mouse button and dragging the mouse over a group of files.

A small dotted line will show the selected files. For more flexibility in selecting files, use the "Select Files" option in the "Edit" menu. This will display a pop-up menu where you to enter criteria for your selection. For example, you could select all HTML files in the directory by entering ***.html** as the criterion.

FILE ACTIONS

If you right-click on any file in the right panel, you can choose several actions from a pop-up menu:

Open Opens the file with the associated application. (Refer to the section on editing your GNOME Mime Types in Chapter 13, "Tweaking Linux".)

Open With Opens a file with an application you select, if you don't want to use the default associated application.

View Lets you view the file with a simple text browser.

Edit Opens the file in an editor associated with that file type. (Refer to the section on editing your GNOME Mime Types in Chapter 13, "Tweaking Linux.")

Copy Copies the file to the clipboard so that it can be pasted elsewhere.

Delete Deletes the selected files.

Move Moves the selected files to another folder.

Properties Allows you to change the properties for the selected file. You can change the name of the file; the default open, view, and edit actions; and the read, write, and ownership permissions.

GAMES AND PRODUCTIVITY APPLICATIONS

Your Red Hat Linux system comes with a set of nifty applications to boost your productivity or help waste time—whatever your needs may be! You can launch any of these applications by selecting them from the Main menu on the GNOME Panel.

Terminal Your command-line interface to Linux.

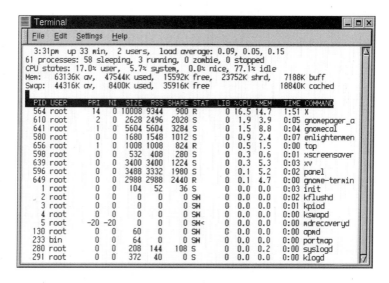

Text editor Gnotepad+ editor: a handy little editor with HTML support.

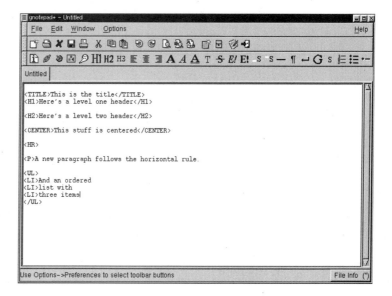

Calendar A calendar and appointment scheduler.

Calculator A calculator with memory and scientific functions.

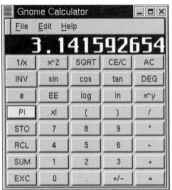

Spreadsheet A nifty spreadsheet program. Not as powerful as Microsoft Excel, but it's being actively enhanced by the developers.

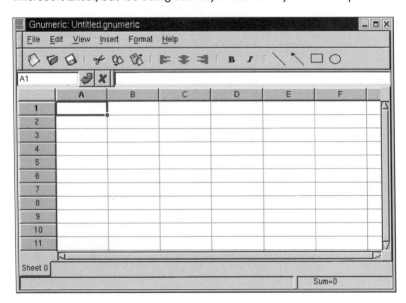

GAMES

These are just a few of the games shipped with Red Hat Linux. You can find other games by poking around in the Main menu.

Freecell A solitaire variant.

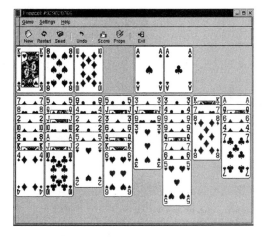

GNOME Mines A minesweeper clone.

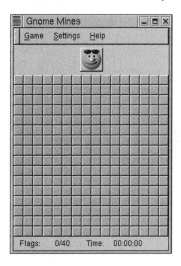

GNOME Tetravex One of those maddening rearrange-the-squares thingies.

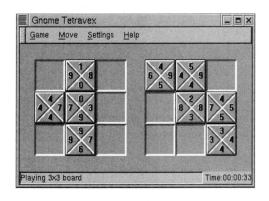

GNOME Mahjongg A very nicely done mahjongg game, with impressive attention to detail on the tiles.

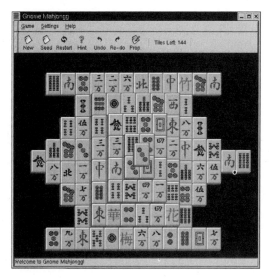

Same GNOME A fun click-the-spinning-balls-until-they're-gone game.

Xgammon A backgammon game.

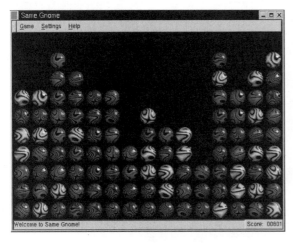

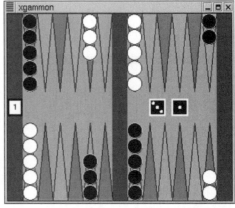

GRAPHICS

Here are some of the most useful graphics utilities shipped with Red Hat Linux. You can find other these and a few others other by poking around in the Main menu.

GIMP Graphical Image Manipulation Program, aka the freeware "PhotoShop for Unix."

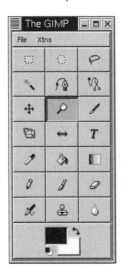

Electric Eyes   An image viewer that supports many graphical formats.

Xpaint   A paintbrush-type program.

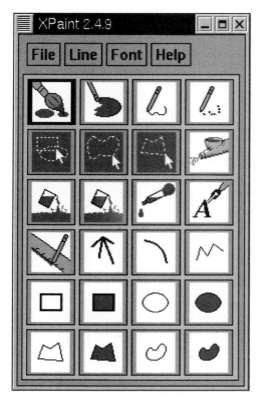

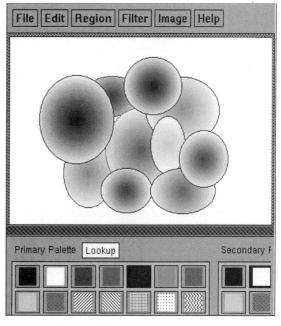

OTHER APPLICATIONS

If you don't find the software you need already installed on your Linux system, there's a good chance you can download it for free or buy a commercial package that suites your needs. One good place to start is the GNOME Software Map at http://www.gnome.org, which lists freely available software in the categories listed here. The numbers in parentheses indicate the number of packages in each category, as this book goes to press.

Core (9)

Development Tools (26)

Entertainment (35)

Internet Tools (30)

Mail Clients (6)

Math and Science Tools (13)

Miscellaneous (34)

Network Talk Clients (IRC, ICQ, and so on) (9)

Productivity (32)

Sound Tools (16)

System Utilities (26)

Window, Session, and Desktop Managers (7)

You can also follow the links listed here for some commercial software packages.

StarOffice

StarOffice is a fully-integrated and Microsoft Office–compatible suite of productivity applications. It provides powerful Web-enabled word processing, spreadsheet, presentation graphics, email, news, charting, and graphics applications. The download file is over 70MB, and a minimal install requires about 100MB. For more information, see http://www.stardivision.com/office.

ApplixWare

Applix Office is a fully-integrated, cross-platform suite of desktop productivity tools. Included in the suite are graphical tools for word processing and document publishing, spreadsheets, business graphics, graphics editing, data access, and email. For more information, see http://www.applix.com.

Corel WordPerfect

Corel WordPerfect Version 8 for Linux: Personal Edition is an office solution that offers the same word processing capabilities as the Windows version, plus many features available only for Linux. It contains support for over 1,000 printers and is a free (24MB) download. For more information, see http://linux.corel.com.

AbiWord

AbiWord is a small, fast, and full-featured word processor. It works on most Unix systems (including Linux) and also on Windows 95/98/NT. AbiWord can import Word97 and RTF documents, is available for free, and is open source. The download file is a slim 770KB, and the installed version needs only 1.2MB of disk space.

If you've ever wanted to see the source code behind a word processor, here's your chance. Download the AbiWord source, make your own improvements, and you can build your own personal version of AbiWord. For more information, see http://www.abisource.com.

Development Tools

Code Warrior by Metrowerks is a popular cross-platform development environment for Linux, Macintosh, and Windows 95/98/NT. For more information, see http://www.metrowerks.com.

Code Fusion by Cygnus Solutions combines the latest open-source GNU tools (compilers, debuggers, libraries, and utilities) with a graphical interactive development environment that includes a code editor, class browsing, build, and debugging tools. For more information, see http://www.cygnus.com.

KAI C++ is a cross-platform development environment designed to make C++ programmers more efficient. Also available is the KAI C++ debugger. For more information, see http://www.kai.com.

Logging Out of GNOME

To log out from GNOME, select the "Logout" menu item found in the Main menu. For convenience, you can also add a Logout button to the GNOME Panel by right-clicking on the Panel and then selecting "Add logout button" from the pop-up menu.

After you select the Logout menu item or clicking the Logout button, a dialog box will prompt you to confirm the log-out (see the image below). Click "Yes," and your GNOME session will end. Depending on your system configuration, you'll return to a text-mode shell prompt or the graphical log-in screen. If you decide not to log out, click the "No" button.

There are a few selections you can make in the GNOME Logout dialog box. If you check the "Save current setup" box, your next GNOME session will start with the same settings and active applications. In other words, if you exit GNOME with the File Manager and Netscape windows on your screen, they'll start again when you come back to GNOME.

Also, in the Action panel, you can select "Logout," "Halt," or "Reboot." Logout will end your GNOME session, Halt will shut down your computer (in preparation for a power-off), and Reboot will restart the machine.

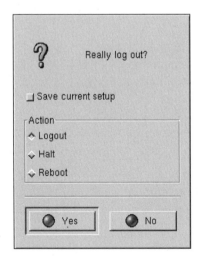

CONNECTING TO THE INTERNET

Linux is an excellent platform for exploring the online world and for providing Internet services of your own. As a personal "surfboard," Red Hat Linux comes with everything you need to connect to an Internet service provider (ISP), including TCP/IP software; client programs such as FTP, Telnet, Finger, Mail, Ping, Lynx, and Netscape.

Linux also makes it easy to set up your own servers so you can operate FTP or Web sites and even provide Telnet or dial-up access to your system. If you have dreams of becoming an ISP, the Red Hat Linux product is an excellent platform to build on. The really nice thing is that TCP/IP and all the popular network services are installed automatically and preconfigured for you. If you've ever tried to configure a Unix network, set up email delivery, or get a Web server running, you will really appreciate this feature. (In technical terms, it means that local loopback, sendmail, inetd, httpd, and several other network daemons are configured and running when you boot up Red Hat Linux.)

In this chapter, you'll learn the following:

- How to connect your Linux system to the Internet with a dial-up PPP connection

- What tools are available for Internet access (text and graphical)

- How to operate your own Internet site

- Where to get more information on Linux networking

SETTING UP YOUR SERIAL PORT TO WORK WITH YOUR MODEM

By default, Red Hat Linux is configured to run your serial (modem) port at a speed of 9600 bps. But faster modems, with speeds of 33.6 and 56 Kbps, for instance, are quite common now. It would be a shame to spend money on a fast modem and not use it to the fullest, so to get the best performance, you'll have to tweak your serial port settings.

Unless you have a very slow modem (9600 bps or less), you should use the **setserial** command to enable Linux to make a high-speed connection. Depending on your modem speed, at the command prompt enter one of the commands shown here. It would also be a good idea to log in as root and put the same command in your **/etc/bashrc** file so you don't have to enter it each time you boot up Linux.

setserial /dev/modem spd_hi	For a 14.4 Kbps modem
setserial /dev/modem spd_vhi	For a 28.8 Kbps or faster modem

Since modems have built-in compression capabilities, you can transfer data at speeds up to 57.6 Kbps with a 14.4 Kbps modem, or 115.2 Kbps with a 28.8 Kbps modem. (Compression enables a theoretical data rate of four times the speed of your modem). But if you don't issue the **setserial** command, your maximum data rate will be four times 9600 bps, or 38.4 Kbps.

MODEM SETUP UNDER LINUX

In a DOS environment, a modem is assigned to a COM (communications) port, an IRQ (interrupt request) number, and an I/O (input/output) address. Here are the most common configurations:

PORT	IRQ	ADDRESS	LINUX DEVICE NAME
COM1	4	3F8	/dev/ttyS0
COM2	3	2F8	/dev/ttyS1
COM3	4	3E8	/dev/ttyS2
COM4	3	2E8	/dev/ttyS3

You can find out your settings under DOS by using the **MSD** command. Under Windows 95/98, hold down the **ALT** key, double-click on the "My Computer" icon, and then click on the "Device Manager" tab to find the settings. If your modem is configured like one of the entries in the preceding table, Linux should automatically detect and configure your modem just fine.

After booting up Linux, make sure that your modem was detected properly. Since Linux knows the modem by the generic name **/dev/modem**, you can use the **ls** command to verify that it exists and is assigned to the correct COM port. Try this command:

```
ls -al /dev/modem
```

The response should look something like the output shown here. For now, ignore everything except the rightmost columns of output.

```
lrwxrwxrwx  1 root    root  5  Feb 19 22:19 /dev/modem -> /dev/ttyS1
```

In this case, the modem device **/dev/modem** is assigned to **/dev/ttyS1,** which corresponds to COM2. If the assignment is wrong, or if you get a "No such file" error message, you can fix it with one of these commands:

ln -s /dev/ttyS0 /dev/modem	For a modem on COM1
ln -s /dev/ttyS1 /dev/modem	For a modem on COM2
ln -s /dev/ttyS2 /dev/modem	For a modem on COM3
ln -s /dev/ttyS3 /dev/modem	For a modem on COM4

VERIFYING THE MODEM SETUP

Okay—you think your modem is ready to roll? Let's test it using Minicom, the basic communications software that comes with Linux. Enter the command

```
minicom
```

to start the program and wait for the OK response to appear on the screen. Then enter the command **ATDT *NNN-NNNN*** (where *NNN-NNNN* is your Internet service provider's dial-up number, the access number of a BBS, or some other local number). If you get a dial tone and the modem begins to make dialing noises, you're in business (see Figure 3-1).

We really don't need to do anything online just yet, so press **CTRL-A,** then **Z,** and then **X** to hang up the modem and exit Minicom. If you didn't get an OK response, or if the modem wouldn't dial out, read the next section. Otherwise, skip to "Making a Dial-Up Connection to the Internet."

IF YOU HAVE TROUBLE CONNECTING

Under certain uncommon circumstances (for instance, if you have nonstandard IRQs or multiple I/O cards in your computer), you may

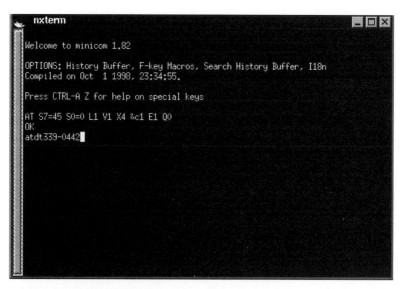

Figure 3-1: *The minicom opening screen*

need to set some special options of the **setserial** command to use your modem with Linux. Something else that might cause trouble is a plug-and-play modem. Linux has very limited support for plug-and-play devices, so if you have one, it probably won't work without some fiddling.

If you have trouble dialing out with your modem, there are two things you can try to solve the problem. The first is to issue the **man setserial** command for information on how to set your serial port for nonstandard IRQ or COM port configurations. If you have a plug-and-play modem, the **isapnptools** utility in conjunction with **setserial** may help to configure the modem for use by Linux. The second option is to rearrange your computer's hardware settings so that the modem can operate on one of the standard configurations.

In my case, I had a US Robotics plug-and-play modem on COM3 and IRQ5 that Linux could not detect. Using the manufacturer's instructions, I disabled the plug-and-play feature on the modem, changed the computer's BIOS settings to disable the built-in COM2 port, and then set the modem to operate on COM2 and IRQ3. After rebooting and verifying that Windows was able to successfully run the modem with these settings, I had no trouble getting it to work under Linux.

Making a Dial-Up Connection to the Internet

To connect your Linux system to the Internet with a modem, the first thing you will need is a PPP account with a local ISP. If you're lucky, you might be able to get a free account through a local university or library. PPP is a protocol that allow you to use TCP/IP networking over a serial (dial-up) line.

You will need the following pieces of information from your ISP to connect using Linux:

- Your ISP's name-server address(es)
- Your ISP's dial-up phone number
- Your log-in ID
- Your password

What's in a Name Server?

When you want to access a site on the Internet, your TCP/IP software must first translate the site name (for example, www.yahoo.com) into an IP address (205.216.146.102). A name server performs this translation, and since your connection to the Internet is through your ISP, you must use your ISP's name servers.

To tell your computer's TCP/IP software to use your ISP's name servers, enter the command

```
linuxconf
```

Then choose **Config • Networking • Client Tasks • Name server specification (DNS)** (see Figure 3-2).

Your ISP will supply you with one or more name-server addresses, which must be plugged in on this screen. Be sure to use *your* ISP's domain and name-server addresses, not the ones in this example! After filling in the fields as shown in Figure 3-3, exit back to the first linuxconf menu.

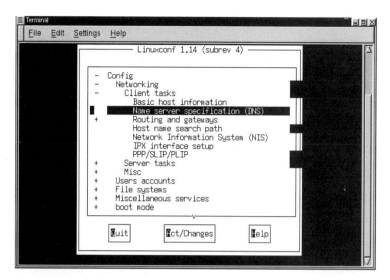

Figure 3-2: *The Linuxconf main menu*

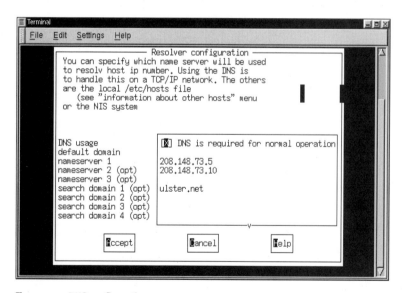

Figure 3-3: *DNS configuration*

Defining a PPP Connection

After setting up the name server, you can start the PPP configuration to connect to your ISP from Linux.

From the linuxconf main menu, choose **Config • Networking • Client Tasks • PPP/SLIP/PLIP**. Then click the "Add" button (see Figure 3-4).

Select the "PPP" option and then click "Accept" to continue (see Figure 3-5).

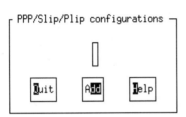

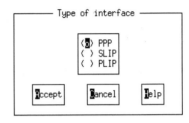

Figure 3-4: *Adding a new connection*   **Figure 3-5:** *Adding a PPP interface*

Enter your ISP's dial-up access number, your PPP log-in name, and your password (see Figure 3-6). In most cases, this completes the PPP connection setup.

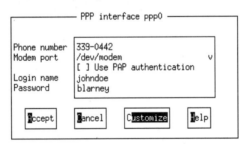

Figure 3-6: *Defining a PPP interface*

Your ISP's terminal server may present a dialog box with prompts like this (many do):

```
            Welcome to Ed's Garage Internet Services




    Please enter your login: <your login here>

    Please enter your password: <your password here>

    Starting PPP ...
```

The PPP setup just defined will work without any changes. The default behavior of the PPP connection process is to wait for the **login:** prompt, enter the log-in name you provide, wait for the **password:** prompt, and enter the password you provide. If your screen looks like this, click "Accept" to complete the PPP setup and exit all the way out of linuxconf to the command prompt.

CUSTOMIZING PPP CONNECTION PROMPTS

It's quite common for ISP terminal servers to operate in the manner just described, but let's assume the dialog box looks like the one shown below instead, where you have to supply a command to enter PPP mode first and then supply a log-in name and password. And just for fun, let's assume the ISP sends a **username:** prompt instead of a **login:** prompt.

```
                 Welcome to the CyberSurf Domain, Dude!
                               Options Menu
     1 - Display Help

     2 - Account Information and Rates

     3 - Online signup form

     PPP - Start a PPP connection


     Enter command: PPP


     Please enter your username: <your login here>

     Please enter your password: <your password here>


     Starting PPP ...
```

In such case, you will need to change your PPP setup so that the order of the "Expect" and "Send" prompts matches the order and spelling of the terminal server's prompts. In this case, click the "Customize" button (shown in Figure 3-6) and scroll down to the "Chat" section of the page shown in Figure 3-7. This example will work for the terminal dialog box that expects you to respond to the "command:," "username:," and "password:" prompts, in that order. Your goal is to match the command prompts presented by your ISP's terminal server by filling in the "Expect" and "Send" prompts on this screen accordingly. Click "Accept" to complete the PPP setup and exit all the way out of linuxconf to the command prompt.

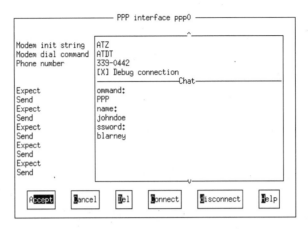

```
                      ── PPP interface ppp0 ──
                                   ^
  Modem init string   ATZ
  Modem dial command  ATDT
  Phone number        339-0442
                      [X] Debug connection
                      ────────────────────Chat──
  Expect              ommand:
  Send                PPP
  Expect              name:
  Send                johndoe
  Expect              ssword:
  Send                blarney
  Expect
  Send
  Expect
  Send

     Accept    Cancel    Del    Connect    Disconnect   Help
```

Figure 3-7: *Customizing a PPP log-in screen*

STARTING PPP

Once your setup is complete, you can make a PPP connection by entering this at a Linux command prompt:

```
ifup ppp0
```

Unfortunately, nothing appears on the screen as you connect, so if something goes wrong, it may not be obvious at first. To find out if your Internet connection was successful, examine the output of the **ifconfig** command (issue it with your connection up and running), which might look like this:

```
lo0    Link encap: Local Loopback
       inet addr:127.0.0.1  Bcast:127.255.255.255
       UP BROADCAST LOOPBACK RUNNING  MTU:2000  Metric:1

ppp0   Link encap: Point-Point Protocol
       inet addr:205.161.119.112  P-t-P:205.161.119.3
       UP POINTOPOINT RUNNING  MTU:1500  Metric:1
```

The first few lines show the status of **lo0**, your local loopback interface. The local loopback is like your *intranet*—a local network that allows you to exchange email with other users on your system, access files on the local Web server, and so on. The **lo0** device will always have an IP address of 127.0.0.1, and the status line should say UP and RUNNING.

If you see a **ppp0** device listed in the **ifconfig** output, you have an active PPP connection to the Internet. Your computer is now a peer to all the other computers on the Internet, with its very own IP address (205.161.119.112 in this example). In fact, anyone on the Internet could connect to this address via Telnet, FTP, or a Web browser! But be aware that this IP address is dynamically assigned from a pool of addresses that your ISP makes available for dial-up users. Next time you connect, you will likely get a different IP address.

Your ISP can probably assign you a permanent IP address (for a fee) if you like, but that would require some changes to your PPP connection setup. Refer to the **PPP-HOWTO** file for information on how to specify a permanent IP address for use with pppd. (Visit the Linux Documentation Project home page on the Web at http://sunsite. unc.edu/mdw/linux.html to find all the HOWTO files.)

STOPPING PPP

To hang up the modem and terminate a PPP connection, enter this at a Linux command prompt:

```
ifdown ppp0
```

HELP—IT DIDN'T WORK!

If you hear the modem hang up unexpectedly while trying to dial in to the Internet, or if you never get a PPP connection, look in the **/var/log/messages** file for any message that might help you identify the problem. You should be able to modify your setup to correct the problem by following the interplay of prompts and commands and making corrections to fix any glitches. It may also be helpful to use Minicom to dial up your ISP and write down exactly the prompts and the correct responses to get connected. Minicom can't actually make a PPP connection, but it may help you clearly see what needs to be done in terms of prompts and responses.

TEXT-BASED INTERNET TOOLS

Believe it or not, the Internet existed prior to the advent of the graphical Web browser. Before the invention of Mosaic in 1990, netizens were emailing, transferring files, logging into remote machines, and even surfing the Web using text-based tools from a Unix command line.

Many users actually prefer to use text-based clients (tools that enable end users to connect to various types of Internet servers) because the graphical environment adds a lot of overhead, slowing things down. And some people just prefer the keyboard to a mouse.

- **NOTE:** *It's important to know the basics of using the Net from a command line, since you might not want (or have the hardware) to run X Windows on your system. These same techniques will come in handy if you have a Unix shell account through your ISP.*

USING FTP

FTP (which stands for *file transfer program* or *file transfer protocol*, depending on how many pencils you wear in your pocket protector) is the Internet file mover. You use it to transfer files from one computer to another. Most often, you'll be using it to download software to your computer, so try that now. To start a text-based FTP client from your Linux command line, enter the **ftp** command followed by a site name, like this:

```
ftp ftp.devolution.com
```

When prompted, specify anonymous as the log-in name and your email address as the password. You'll be connected to devolution.com's FTP site, where you can download Maelstrom—a cool Asteroids-like game for X Windows. After getting logged in to the server, you can enter these commands to download the compressed binary file for Maelstrom:

```
bin
cd /pub/maelstrom/Maelstrom-binaries/linux-x86/
get Maelstrom.tar.gz
quit
```

Use the **help** command if you're not familiar with FTP. After the **get** command is finished, **quit** will return you to the Linux command prompt, and you'll have a file named **Maelstrom.tar.gz** in the current directory. To uncompress the file and create the executable on your system, enter this:

```
tar xvfz Maelstrom.tar.gz
```

Refer to Chapter 11, "Compression, Encoding, and Encryption," for more information on handling compressed files.

USING TELNET

Telnet is a tool that lets you log in to other computers on the Internet. Why would you want to do that? Simple: to access the interesting stuff on those other computers, such as databases, games, card catalogs, and information services. If you have a shell account with your ISP, you might want to telnet there from your Linux system and check your email with Pine.

Telnet is strictly text-based—you can't point or click on anything. Whether you telnet from a command line or from a GUI, your Telnet session will look pretty much the same, and all your navigation in a Telnet session is via the keyboard. To start a text-based Telnet client from your Linux command line, enter the **telnet** command followed by a site name (and, sometimes, a port number), like this:

```
telnet cybersurf.com
```

This is a fictitious example that shows how you might log in to a shell account on your ISP's system. Here's a real example that will connect you to the Ham Radio Call Book database at the University of Buffalo (commands you enter are shown in boldface):

```
telnet electra.cs.buffalo.edu 2000

Connected to electra.cs.buffalo.edu.
Callbook v1.3 -- Type 'help' for help
>> help
Available commands:
     call [filters] callsign   - lookup callsign
     city [filters] city       - lookup city
     name [filters] surname     - lookup last name
     quit                      - exit the server
     zip [filters] zipcode     - lookup zip code
> city Tillson
Call-Sign: WA2TNV               Class: GENERAL
Real Name: DONALD G WOOD         Birthday: OCT 31, 1919
Mailing Address: BOX 873 ROSE AVE, TILLSON, NY  12486
Valid From: DEC 29, 1987        To: DEC 29, 1997
>> quit
```

Using Finger

Finger is a nifty little tool that can tell you who owns a particular email address, or sometimes display other interesting data. As the name implies, when you use Finger you are "pointing" at someone. When you finger an address, you send a request to another system asking it to tell you everything it knows (or is willing to tell) about that address. The results of fingering vary widely from system to system, and some systems will not even honor Finger requests at all, for privacy reasons. Still, most Finger requests will return some limited information about the user, such as the user's real name or the last time the user logged in to the system. To use the Finger client from your Linux command line, enter the **finger** command followed by an email address, like this:

```
finger jsmith@hotdog.edu
```

```
Home: /user/jsmith     In real life: Janet Smith
Shell: /bin/csh
New mail received Thu May 16 13:33:18 1996;
    unread since Tue May 14 07:50:31 1996
Janet Smith (jsmith) is not presently logged in.
```

And as you'll see in this next example, sometimes people connect strange things to the Net and allow you to query them via Finger. . .

```
finger coke@cs.cmu.edu
```

```
  M & M                 Coke Buttons
 /-----\        C: CCCCCCCCCCCCCCCCCCCCCCCC
 |?????|        C: ...........   D: ...........
 |?????|        C: ...........   D: ...........
 |?????|        C: ...........   D: ...........
 |?????|                         C: CCCCCCCCCCC
 \-----/                         S: CCCCCCCCCCC
     |     Key:
     |      0 = warm;  9 = 90% cold;  C = cold;   . = empty
     |      Beverages: C = Coke, D = Diet Coke, S = Sprite
     |      Leftmost soda/pop will be dispensed next
  ---^---   M&M status guessed.
```

This example shows how to get the status of a Coke machine, which has been connected to a minicomputer and wired into the Internet at Carnegie-Mellon University!

EMAIL HANDLING

In Chapter 10, "Managing Your Email," you will learn about the mail and Pine programs, which are text-based email handlers on your Linux system. With a SLIP or PPP connection, you can send email to Internet addresses, but you can't receive Internet mail directly on your system without a permanent connection and a registered domain name.

The **fetchmail** utility is the next best thing, though, if you don't have a permanent Internet connection. Once you have established a dial-up connection to your ISP, the **fetchmail** program will transfer any new mail waiting on your ISP's mail server to a local mail folder on your Linux system. You can then read and respond to emails using your favorite Linux email client. You may find this more convenient than using **telnet** to log in to your ISP and checking your email with Pine. Use the **man fetchmail** command for usage details.

If you want to be able to receive mail directly on your Linux system, you'll have to work with your ISP to register a domain name and get either a permanent or UUCP connection to the Internet. You can create a permanent connection (up to 56 Kbps) with a modem and a dedicated phone line, or you can install some expensive equipment and special phone connections to forge a high-speed link.

A UUCP connection is one where you occasionally dial up your ISP to send outgoing and receive incoming email messages. Any mail destined for your domain will queue up at your ISP until you dial in to receive it. UUCP is much less expensive than a dedicated phone connection to your ISP and is quite common on BBS systems in rural areas of the United States, and in other countries, where long-distance telephone costs are much higher.

Refer to the **UUCP-HOWTO** file and the "Help with Linux Networking" section later in this chapter for more details on UUCP connections. (Visit the Linux Documentation Project home page on the Web at http://metalab.unc.edu/LDP to find all the HOWTO files.)

Using Ping

Ping is a simple utility that can tell you the status of another computer on the Internet and the quality of the connection between your computer and the remote host. Ping works by throwing electronic pebbles at other computers. Every computer on the Internet has a little daemon just waiting for other computers to "ping" it, and when this happens, it tries to catch the pebbles and throw them back. If the network connection is sluggish, some of the pebbles might never hit their target, and if the other computer is slow or busy, the little daemon might miss or drop some pebbles.

To use the Ping client from your Linux command line, enter the **ping** command followed by a domain name or IP address, like this (press **CTRL-C** to stop after a few lines of output):

```
ping cqu.edu.au
PING cqu.edu.au: 56 data bytes
64 bytes from cqu.EDU.AU (138.77.1.23): icmp_seq=1 time=8100 ms
64 bytes from cqu.EDU.AU (138.77.1.23): icmp_seq=2 time=7354 ms
64 bytes from cqu.EDU.AU (138.77.1.23): icmp_seq=3 time=6281 ms
^C
----cqu.edu.au PING Statistics----
13 packets transmitted, 3 packets received, 77% packet loss
round-trip (ms)  min/avg/max = 6281/7245/8100
```

This output tells you three things:

- The other computer (located at a university in Australia, represented by the "au" in its address) is running and connected to the Internet. We know this because we didn't get a "no such host" or "host is not responding" message.

- It has an IP address of 138.77.1.23. This is the value in parentheses on the second line of the output.

- The connection is lousy. We can tell this because of the Statistics section at the end of the output. We sent out thirteen pebbles, er, packets, and only three were acknowledged. The "77% packet loss" and the average response time of 7245 milliseconds (7.245 seconds) is terrible. A more reasonable Ping response time would be under 750 milliseconds.

You can use Ping to test the speed of a connection before trying to connect via Telnet or FTP. Especially with FTP, you often have a choice of servers that all mirror the same set of files, so pick the quickest one.

USING TIN FOR USENET

Tin is a text-based program you can use to read and post to Usenet newsgroups. From the initial menu, you can select a newsgroup to read, and Tin will display the current postings in that group, as shown here:

```
                  Group Selection (news.myserver.com 5)

  1    884   alt.internet.services
  2    167   news.announce.newusers
  3    343   news.newusers.questions
  4     49   news.answers
  5    183   comp.internet.net-happenings




<n>=set current to n, TAB=next unread, /=search pattern, c)atchup,
g)oto, j=line down, k=line up, h)elp, m)ove, q)uit, r=toggle unread,
s)ubscribe, S)ub pattern, u)nsubscribe, U)nsub pattern, y)ank in/out
```

You do all your navigating with the cursor keys.

To start Tin, you must first set the NNTPSERVER (Network News Transport Protocol Server) environment variable to the name of your ISP's news server (usually **news** will work fine). Issue the command shown here from the prompt, and also add it to the **/etc/bashrc** file (you must log in as **root**) so it will be set automatically the next time you boot up.

NNTPSERVER=news

After setting the environment variable, enter one of the Tin startup commands shown here:

rtin -rq   Use the first time only

rtin -rqn   Use after the first time

The first time you use Tin, it will download a huge list of all available newsgroups from your ISP's server, so don't be surprised if it takes several minutes for the first screen to appear.

For more information on using Tin, use the **man tin** command to read the excellent online help for this program.

USING LYNX

Lynx is a text-based Web browser. You don't get to see the graphics on a Web page, but for some people, that's a plus. Many Web pages are loaded with gratuitous images that take forever to load and add little or no real value. So Lynx can usually get you to the information you're after a lot faster than a graphical browser. Here's what a Lynx screen might look like:

```
                              Yahoo!


          [ Reuters News Headlines | What's New | Cool Sites ]
             [ Write Us | Add URL | Random Link | Info ]




          _____ Search Options


    * Arts -- Humanities, Photography, Architecture ...

    * Business and Economy [Xtra!] -- Directory, Investments ...

    * Computers and Internet [Xtra!] -- Internet, WWW, Software

    * Education -- Universities, K-12, Courses ...

    * Entertainment [Xtra!] -- TV, Movies, Music, Magazines ...

    * Government -- Politics [Xtra!], Agencies, Law, Military ...

    * Health [Xtra!] -- Medicine, Drugs, Diseases, Fitness ...

    * News [Xtra!] -- World [Xtra!], Daily, Current Events ...

    * Recreation and Sports [Xtra!] -- Sports, Games, Travel ...


Arrow keys: Up/Down to move. Right to follow link; Left to go back.
          H)elp  O)ptions  P)rint  G)o  M)ain screen  Q)uit  /=search
```

In addition to displaying Web pages, Lynx can navigate FTP sites and download files for you. It can also send email, read or post Usenet newsgroups, and display information stored on gopher servers. To start the Lynx client from your Linux command line, enter the **lynx** command, optionally followed by a Web address (URL), like this:

lynx	Show the default Web page.
lynx http://www.yahoo.com	Show a specified Web page.
lynx ftp://ftp.netscape.com	Show files at an FTP site.
lynx gopher://cwis.usc.edu	Show files at a gopher site.
lynx mailto:user@site.com	Prepare to send email.
lynx news:rec.humor.funny	Show postings in a newsgroup.

Use the **help** command in Lynx to learn more about navigating the Web without a mouse.

USING WHOIS

The **whois** command will search the central domain registry at InterNIC and give you information about a domain, such as who owns it, where it is located, and how to contact the owners. Here's an example of **whois** output:

```
whois aol.com
    America Online (AOL-DOM)
    12100 Sunrise Valley Drive
    Reston, Virginia 22091 USA


    Administrative Contact:
        O'Donnell, David B  (DBO3)  PMDAtropos@AOL.COM
        703/453-4255 (FAX) 703/453-4102
    Technical Contact, Zone Contact:
        America Online  (AOL-NOC)  trouble@aol.net
        703-453-5862
```

USING NSLOOKUP

The **nslookup** command will tell you the IP address associated with an Internet domain name, or vice versa:

```
nslookup well.com
```

Server: ns.myserver.com	Your ISP's name server.
Address: 239.0.0.2	Your ISP's IP address.
Name: well.com	
Address: 206.15.64.10	The IP address of well.com.

USING TRACEROUTE

The **traceroute** command will show you the path your network connection would take to reach a remote host. You might find it interesting to learn the actual geographic location of the routers that sit between you and a remote destination on the Internet. Here's an example:

```
traceroute cqu.edu.au
traceroute to cqu.edu.au (138.77.1.23), 30 hops max, 40 byte packets

 1  router.mhv.net (199.0.0.1)  8 ms   103 ms   3 ms

 2  sl-pen-10-S3/4-T1.sprintlink.net (144.228.160.41) 560 ms 34 ms   33 ms

 3  sl-pen-1-F0/0.sprintlink.net (144.228.60.1)  136 ms   200 ms   217 ms

 4  core4-hssi5-0.WestOrange.mci.net (206.157.77.105)  23 ms   22 ms   22 ms

 5  core2-hssi-3.LosAngeles.mci.net (204.70.1.237)  141 ms   159 ms   140 ms

 6  border7-fddi-0.LosAngeles.mci.net (204.70.170.51)  111 ms   146 ms   92 ms

 7  qld-new.gw.au (139.130.247.227)  315 ms   311 ms   368 ms

 8  qldrno.gw.au (139.130.5.2)  322 ms   319 ms   321 ms

 9  hub.questnet.net.au (203.22.86.241)  328 ms   386 ms   331 ms

10  cqu-gw.questnet.net.au (203.22.86.146)  349 ms   331 ms   338 ms

11  centaurus.cqu.EDU.AU (138.77.5.1)  410 ms   360 ms   336 ms

12  janus.cqu.EDU.AU (138.77.1.23)  327 ms   346 ms   331 ms
```

If you look at the router names carefully, you can see that the route from my ISP in southeastern New York to Columbia Queens University in Australia passes through a local SprintLink router to MCI routers in West Orange (New Jersey) and Los Angeles before hopping Down Under.

Using Minicom

Minicom is a communications program, similar to Telix or Procomm. It's not really an Internet tool, but you can use it to dial in to your shell account or access a bulletin board system. Use the **minicom** command to start this program.

Graphical Internet Tools for X Windows

For those who prefer point and click to hunt and peck, Red Hat Linux provides you with graphical tools to handle your email and explore the Web. This section introduces you to some graphical tools for email, Web browsing, FTP, and IRC. All of these are free and already installed on your system.

Using exmh

The exmh program is a full-featured email client for the X Windows environment, similar to the popular Eudora mail program (see Figure 3-8). It sends, receives, and stores mail in folders. Just as with

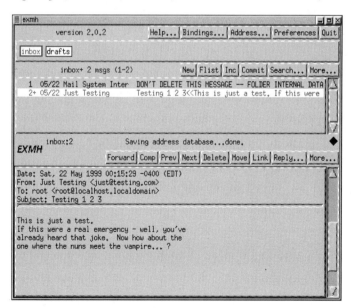

Figure 3-8: *The exmh email client*

the text-based mail clients, you can't receive Internet mail directly on your system without a permanent (or UUCP) connection and a registered domain name.

For more information on using exmh, use its help facility, available via the "Help" button.

USING NETSCAPE

Red Hat Linux comes with Netscape Navigator version 4 (see figure 3-9). It's an excellent browser, works well with FTP sites, and comes with a built-in email client and Usenet newsgroup reader, making it the Swiss army knife of Internet tools.

If you're already using Netscape Communicator's email client on Windows, I recommend that you use it on Linux also, instead of exmh, so you won't have to learn another program (see Figure 3-10).

Figure 3-9: *The Netscape Navigator browser*

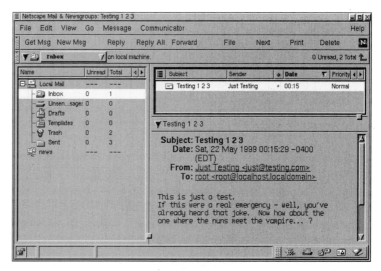

Figure 3-10: *The Netscape Communicator email client*

FILE TRANSFER WITH gFTP

If you download often from FTP sites, you can use the gFTP program under X Windows to make things a little nicer (see Figure 3-11). This client allows you to store the addresses of frequently used FTP sites so you can connect quickly and features point-and-click file transfer from remote sites to your hard drive, or vice versa.

IRC CHAT WITH X-CHAT

You can interact live with other Internet users around the world using IRC—Internet Relay Chat (see Figure 3-12). Using IRC is similar to being in a chat room on commercial services such as America Online and CompuServe. IRC can be compared to a CB radio—you tune in to a specific chat channel, give yourself a *handle* (nickname), and partici-pate in a live conversation with one or more people by typing mes-sages back and forth. Anyone connected to the same channel can read your messages.

A detailed discussion of IRC is beyond the scope of this book, but you can find a good IRC tutorial online at http://www.irchelp.org/.

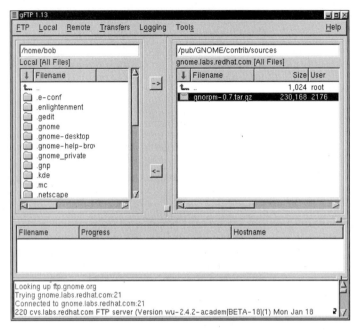

Figure 3-11: *The gFTP file transfer client*

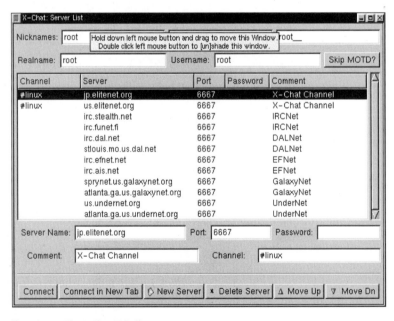

Figure 3-12: *The X-Chat IRC client*

Operating an Internet Site

If you plan to run a public Web site from a Linux system, you will have to register a domain name and make arrangements to connect your computer permanently (24 hours a day) to the Internet.

Registering Your Domain Name

To register a domain name, contact InterNIC (keepers of the central name registry for the Internet) at http://rs.internic.net. Complete details and online registration forms are available at this site. After you register your domain name, you will have to update the **/etc/hosts** and **/etc/HOSTNAME** files to reflect the new domain name.

You'll have to work with your ISP to get the domain registered and operational. The InterNIC fee for domain-name registration is currently $70 for the first two years, and $35 per year thereafter. Your ISP will probably charge an additional $50 to $100 to set things up locally.

- **NOTE:** *As an alternative to registering your own domain name with InterNIC, there are some programs for people with dynamic IP addresses (as with a typical dial-up connection) to have static domain names. Ask your ISP if they provide this service, or visit Domain Host Services at http://www.dhs.org for more information on their free services.*

Getting Yourself Connected

You have a number of options for full-time connectivity, depending on the expected traffic at your site and the amount of money in your budget. You'll have to pay the telephone company for installation and monthly use, and your ISP will charge a monthly connection fee, too.

Depending on the type of connection you choose and the local telephone company rates, your monthly connectivity bill could range from several hundred to several thousand dollars. The following sections summarize the types of connections possible. In addition, the book *How to Build an Internet Service Company* by Charles Burke (see http://www.index.mis.net/kanti) offers a wealth of information on this subject. You should also get a copy of *Boardwatch* magazine's *Directory of Internet Service Providers* (see http://www.boardwatch.com) to help you find a quality Internet service provider in your area. The Unix BBS FAQ at http://www.dsnet.com/unixbbsfaq may also provide some helpful information.

DIAL-UP MODEM LINE

A dial-up modem line is the least expensive option because it uses a regular phone line and a standard modem. But your visitors are limited to a maximum connection speed of 33.6 Kbps (even if you have a 56K modem), which would service only three or four visitors at once. This approach is recommended for hobby use only.

56K LEASED LINE

As the name implies, a 56K leased line is a line you lease from the phone company with a maximum speed of 56 Kbps. It will handle seven or eight concurrent users. It requires the installation of a router (about $1000), and it's upgradable to T1 speeds.

ISDN

A digital phone service available in many areas, with a top speed of 128 Kbps, ISDN will handle about 15 concurrent users. It requires an ISDN adapter, which costs about $500. ISDN is a good choice for many startups but it cannot be upgraded to higher speeds.

ADSL AND CABLE

In some areas, high-speed ADSL or cable modem connections are available and rates tend to be less than ISDN services. An ADSL connection allows you to serve data at about 1000Kbps, and cable modem throughput can be even higher. Check with your phone company or cable provider to see if they offer these services.

T1 CONNECTION

A T1 connection is a high-speed (1544 Kbps) and expensive digital connection that can handle 300 or more concurrent users—sufficient for all but the busiest sites. You can also get fractional T1 service, which provides either 256 or 512 Kbps for less than the cost of a full T1 connection. T1 connections typically require the installation of a router (a piece of hardware that the T1 line plugs into).

One alternative to a router is the RISCom/N2 adapter card from SDL Communications (http://www.sdlcomm.com), which allows you to plug a full or fractional T1 line directly into a Linux box. This card is much cheaper than other alternatives and has great performance.

Onsite ISP Connection

An onsite ISP connection requires no phone line, because your computer resides at your ISP's place of business. In this case, your Linux system is cabled directly into the ISP's ethernet network, and you have T1 access. The downside is that you don't have physical access to your computer, so you have to log in via Telnet.

Setting Up Your Web Site

Red Hat Linux comes with the very popular Apache Web (httpd) server. Best of all, it's preconfigured and already running when you boot up! To test it, start the Lynx browser and display the default Web page, which is stored as **index.html** in the **/home/httpd/html** directory. Of course, you'll want to create your own home page, so edit the **index.html** file to suit your needs, and you're in business.

If you want other Internet users to connect to your Web server, you'll have to provide them with your IP address and tell them to connect with a URL like this:

```
http://205.161.119.112
```

The IP address comes from the **ifconfig** command, but remember that it changes each time you connect to your ISP, unless you've arranged for a static IP address or obtained your own domain name, as discussed earlier.

The default Apache configuration files in the **/etc/httpd/conf** directory will work fine for most people, but if you're curious about ways to change the behavior of the server, have a look at the other files in this directory. Refer to the Apache home page at http://www.apache.org for help.

Help with Linux Networking

If you run into trouble establishing your dial-up connection, or if you have questions about Linux networking, visit the Linux Documentation Project home page on the Web at http://sunsite.unc.edu/mdw/ linux.html to find the **Net-2-HOWTO, PPP-HOWTO,** and **Serial-HOWTO** files.

This site is also home to a very comprehensive document called the Linux Network Administrator's Guide, which goes into great detail on SLIP and PPP connections, setting up your system to allow others to dial in, and security-related procedures you should follow.

You may also find some helpful tips in the "PPP Setup Tips" document from Red Hat, at http://support.redhat.com/docs/PPP-Client-Tips/PPP-Client-Tips.html.

These documents will be useful in answering any questions you may have about Linux networking, and I highly recommend them if you have trouble making a PPP connection, or if you plan to allow others to make PPP connections to your Linux machine.

LIVING IN A SHELL

To use Linux—or any Unix-like system, for that matter—you need to know a few things about shells. A shell is a program that acts as an intermediary between you and the guts of the operating system. In a DOS environment, **command.com** acts as your shell. Linux shells have more interesting names (like bash, pdksh, and tcsh), but they do pretty much the same thing. In addition to translating your commands into something the kernel can understand and act upon, the shell adds some important functions that the base operating system doesn't supply.

Using a Linux shell means working with a command line, which is much like working from a DOS prompt. You've already been introduced to the X Windows environment and the GNOME graphical interface in the previous chapter, but some Linux tasks can only be done from the command line. The knowledge of how Linux works that you'll gain in this chapter will provide the foundation you need to use Linux successfully and efficiently. Here's a description of the basic features of all Linux shells, a preview of the functions they perform, and a rundown of what you'll learn in this chapter.

Prompts   A prompt is a character or string of characters (such as $ or #) that the shell displays when it is ready to receive a new command. You'll learn about the different types of prompts and how to customize them to suit you and the way you work.

Command resolution   When you enter a command, the shell must determine which program to run in order to perform that command. You'll learn how shells do this and how to change the command resolution process to suit your needs.

Job control   Linux lets you multitask (run more than one command at a time). You'll learn how to start, list, and stop tasks; you'll also learn the difference between foreground and background task execution.

Command history and completion   When you're entering lots of commands, sometimes you want to repeat the previous command or issue a similar one. You'll learn how to recall and modify previously entered commands, as well as find out about some keyboard shortcuts that can automatically complete your commands for you.

Wildcards and aliases Wildcards let you process a whole bunch of files at once, instead of having to repeat the same command for each file. You'll learn how to use two types of wildcards and how to create aliases for commonly used commands.

Piping and I/O redirection Sending the output of one program directly to another program or to a file can save you time and keystrokes. You'll learn how to pipe program output (connect programs together) and how to make a program get its input from a file instead of the keyboard.

This chapter will look at each of these functions in detail and teach you how to use them to your advantage. But first—a few shell preliminaries.

LOGGING IN

Unlike DOS, Linux is a multiuser operating system. This means you have to log in before you can use it. After you log in, by default Linux places you in the bash shell (see Figure 4-1). At this point, you can type a command and press ENTER, and the system will respond. It's just you and the keyboard; the mouse has little to do in this environment.

If you've modified your system to start the X Windows GNOME interface automatically at bootup, you can start a windowed bash shell (Figure 4-2) by clicking on the taskbar button that looks like a computer terminal (as shown in Figure 4-3), at the bottom of the screen. (This is analogous to running a Windows 3.x system, where

```
Red Hat Linux release 6.0 (Hedwig)
Kernel 2.2.5-15 on an i686

localhost login: root
Password:

[root@localhost /root]# █
```

Figure 4-1: *The bash shell prompt just after login*

Figure 4-2: *The GNOME taskbar with the terminal button*

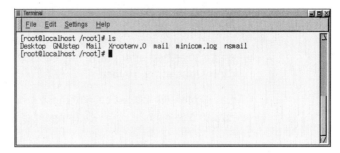

Figure 4-3: *A windowed shell prompt in X Windows*

you start in the **command.com** shell, or launching an MS-DOS prompt after booting Windows 95/98.) In either case, the shell is a text-based environment, with no point-and-click amenities.

THE ROOT USER

When you installed Linux, you logged in as **root**. The root user is called a *superuser* because it has powers far beyond those of mortal users (and it's not even affected by kryptonite). As **root,** you can access files and change the system in ways other users cannot. But you can also wipe out your entire hard drive in just ten keystrokes. You can tell when you have root privileges because your prompt ends in # instead of $—more on this later in the chapter.

Unless you plan to install new software or tweak your system, you should log in to Linux as a user other than **root**. The problem is, assuming you've followed the steps I've outlined so far, at this juncture there *are* no other accounts. We'll use this superuser account to change that.

EX NIHILO: ADDING NEW USERS

In the Linux universe, new users do not evolve—they are created by a benevolent superuser. To add a new user account, log in to the root account and enter a command like the one shown here. There's no limit to the number of new users you can add.

```
adduser hermie
```

After using the **adduser** command, you must assign a password to the new account before it can be used. Use this command to set the password:

```
passwd hermie
```

. . . and enter the initial password for hermie when prompted.

WHAT VIRTUAL CONSOLES ARE GOOD FOR

Remember that bit about multiple log-ins? Even though you may not have more than one physical console (a monitor plus a keyboard) connected to your PC, you can use *virtual consoles* to log in simultaneously to more than one account on your system.

You can use virtual consoles to perform two activities in parallel. For example, I used one virtual console to write this chapter and another to test the commands as they were introduced. You can even use your mouse to cut and paste text from one virtual console to another. When you start your Linux system and get the log-in prompt, you're looking at console number 1. Go ahead and log in as **root** here; then press **ALT-F2**. You should then see another log-in prompt. You can log in as user **hermie** on this console and then press **ALT-F3** to access a third console or press **ALT-F1** to return to the first console.

Virtual consoles come in particularly handy if you have a long-running task to perform, like installing a big software package from a CD-ROM —you can pop over to another console and log in again to stay productive while your CD-ROM churns away.

■ *NOTE: You don' t have to use a different user account for each console. Linux lets you log in to an account multiple times simultaneously.*

By default, your Linux system already has a bunch of virtual consoles waiting in the wings when you start your system, and pressing **ALT-F***n* at any time will bring the *n*th one up on your screen. You can also cycle through the consoles with **ALT–left arrow** or **ALT–right arrow**.

If you're running in the X Windows environment, there's not much need for virtual consoles because you can accomplish the same thing with multiple shell-prompt windows. But if you really want to use virtual consoles under X Windows, you must use **CTRL-ALT-F*n*** to switch to another (full-screen) virtual console. X Windows runs as virtual console 7, so you can switch back with **CTRL-ALT-F7**.

Multitasking under Linux isn't really much different from having multiple windows active on a Windows 95/98 or Macintosh system. The major difference is that if you've started multiple consoles, you can see only one at a time on the screen, though the others are still working away behind the scenes.

STOP THE SYSTEM, I WANT TO GET OFF!

If you're ready to cash in your console and call it a day, use the **logout** command. Entering

---

`logout`

---

at the command prompt exits your current user account and returns you to the log-in prompt. (The **exit** command does the same thing as **logout**.) To log out from multiple consoles, use **ALT-F*n*** to switch between consoles and then log out from each one. But note that even if you log out from all of your active consoles, Linux is still running.

If you were to power off your machine at this point, a voice from your computer would drone, "You have chosen *unwisely*!" The floor would shake, and your PC would glow white hot while your hard disk melted into a pool of molten silicon. Just kidding . . . sometimes the floor doesn't shake, but powering off a running Linux system without using the **shutdown** command will most certainly cause Bad Things to happen to your hard disk. So if you really want to exit Linux, be sure that you're logged in as the root user and enter the command

---

`shutdown -h now`

You'll see some messages indicating that various subsystems are being shut down, and then the computer will be reset. When you see a message indicating that shutdown is complete, it's safe to turn off your PC.

■ *TIP: Pressing **CTRL-ALT-DELETE** will also safely shut down your Red Hat Linux system. Just remember to power off as soon as you see your PC's normal bootup screen. Note that some other Linux distributions will do a hard reset (which may cause filesystem damage) instead of* *gracefully shutting down, so don' t use **CTRL-ALT-DELETE** on non-Red Hat systems unless you know it' s safe.*

BASH (AND OTHER SHELLS)

Bash, the default Linux shell, is popular and offers lots of advanced features. It combines many of the niceties found in the Bourne shell (the original Unix shell) and other modern shells.

But there are alternatives. The Korn shell is popular among many Unix users because it offers a rich scripting (programming) facility. Korn is commercial software, but there is a public-domain (free) version for Linux called pdksh. Another shell that's popular with C language programmers is the C shell, which exists for Linux as tcsh.

The CD that comes with this book provides both pdksh and tcsh, and you can try them out by entering their names at your shell prompt. If you decide to make a permanent switch to something other than the default bash shell, you must log in as **root** and edit the entry for your user ID in the **/etc/passwd** file.

Entries in the **/etc/passwd** file look like the following example. Just change "bash" at the end of the line to "pdksh" or "tcsh," and you're done. (If you're not familiar with Linux-based text editors, see Chapter 7, "Text Editors.")

```
hermie:x:501:1::/home/hermie:/bin/bash
```

Though there are alternatives, I suggest you familiarize yourself with bash's features first, because bash is the most commonly used Linux shell. In the rest of this chapter, we'll go over the basics of working in the bash shell, so go ahead and log in as user **hermie** now and follow right along. It'll help a lot to enter the commands as you go, experiment with them on your own, and see the actual output.

LINUX COMMANDS

When you enter a command in Linux, you type a command at a prompt and then press **ENTER**. Commands can be more than one word—some require switches (which modify the command's behavior) and/or file names (which tell the command what data to act on). Let's dissect the command shown here:

```
ls -l sample.doc
```

LINUX COMMANDS ARE CASE SENSITIVE

One of the most important things to remember about entering commands in any Unix environment is that case matters. In DOS, you can type **DIR** or **dir** or even **DiR** and get the same result, but not in Linux. Linux will be quite put out if you type **LS** instead of **ls** to list your files. With file names, you have to be even more careful, since nearly identical files (save for capitalization) can exist in the same directory, though they may have completely different contents—**Cookie_Recipe** and **cookie_recipe** would appear as distinctly different files to Linux, though they may look pretty much the same to you except for the capital letters.

The best rule to follow is this: Almost everything in Linux is lowercase, so avoid capital letters when naming your files.

COMMAND PROMPTS CAN VARY

When the Linux shell is ready for a command, you see a command prompt. As in DOS, Linux's command prompts vary. For example, when you log in as **root,** your default command prompt is the pound (#) sign, but if you log-in as a regular user (like **hermie**), the prompt changes to a dollar sign ($).

Bash uses the different prompts to clue you in to your user privileges. Pay attention to the prompts so you don't inadvertently wipe out important files while logged in to the root account with superuser privileges, for example.

It's especially important to mind the prompts if you use the **su** (switch user) command, which allows you to act temporarily as the root user while you're logged in as a regular user. Watch how the prompt changes in the following example. (User input is in boldface.)

```
$ who am i
hermie

$ su - root
Enter password for root: xxxxxxx

# who am i
root
# exit

$ who am i
hermie
```

In this example, entering the command **who am i** tells you who the system thinks you are—**hermie**. Then the **su - root** command switches you to the root user (note the prompt change to the pound sign). The **exit** command exits the root user account and brings you back to **hermie**; the prompt changes back to a dollar sign. (See Chapter 6, "Important Linux Commands," for more information on the **su** command.)

This example used the prompt and the **who am i** command to show the logged-in user, but customizing your prompt is a better way to keep track of where you are.

For example, the command

PS1="\u \$ "

changes the prompt so that it displays the user name (\u), followed by the dollar sign (or pound sign, if you're a superuser). You can use other characters to insert the current time, date, or working directory (\t, \d, and \w, respectively). Here's how to use these various options:

PS1="\t \$ "	Yields 09:15:24 $.
PS1="\u (\d) \$ "	Yields hermie (Wed Nov 4) $.
PS1="\u (\w) \$ "	Yields hermie (/home/hermie) $.

All you're actually doing here is setting the variable PS1 (prompt string number 1) to a special string of characters. The bash shell interprets the value of the PS1 variable each time it's ready to build the prompt string.

In the "Environment Variables" section, you'll learn more about special variables such as PS1 and how to set them automatically each time you log in.

WILDCARDS

Wildcards come in handy when you want to perform an operation on a group of files. As with DOS or Windows, if you want to delete all your files that start with "jan" and end with "txt," you can use the asterisk (*) wildcard character, as in **rm jan*txt**, to delete all such files (**rm** is the command you use to delete files).

The * character tells the shell to find any files that begin with "jan" and end with "txt" regardless of the number of characters between. It will even find files with no characters between, like **jantxt**. Thus, a file named **jan-96.txt** would be deleted, as would **jantxt**.

A more restrictive wildcard is the question mark, which matches any single character. Here are some examples of its use:

rm jan-8?.txt	Deletes jan-81.txt and jan-82.txt, but not jan-89b.txt
rm jan-95.???	Deletes jan-95.txt and jan-95.dat, but not jan-95.db

When you use wildcards, the shell finds all matching files and expands the command you entered, so the **rm jan-95.*** command would be the same as typing

```
rm jan-95.txt jan-95.dat jan-95.db
```

■ *PROGRAMMERS TAKE NOTE: In Linux, the shell performs wildcard interpretation, and the actual commands (programs) never see the wildcard characters. This provides a convenient and common way for all Linux programs to handle wildcards. In DOS, the program (not the shell) must have the intelligence to handle wildcards. The unhappy result there is that you never know which DOS commands will accept wildcards, and each program may interpret them differently—yuck!*

COMMAND HISTORY AND EDITING

Bash remembers what commands you've recently entered so that you can recall and issue them again easily. If you press the up-arrow key, bash places the contents of the previous command on the command line. Repeatedly pressing the up or down arrow navigates through the command history; you can even modify the text in the recalled commands with the left and right arrows, as well as the **INSERT** and **DELETE** keys, before pressing **ENTER** to issue the recalled command.

COMMAND COMPLETION: LINUX CAN EVEN READ YOUR MIND

If you're a lazy typist, you'll love this feature. Let's say you have a directory containing the following files:

```
cars-are-fun
cats-are-bad
dogs-are-good
birds-have-lips
```

Typing **rm cat** and then pressing the **TAB** key magically expands your command line to

```
rm cats-are-bad
```

matching a file in your current directory that starts with the word cat. The shell looks at what you've typed so far and then checks to see if there is a single file that starts with those characters. If there is, the shell finishes typing that file name for you. If there isn't such a file, nothing happens. If multiple files match, a beep will sound. You can then press **TAB** twice to see all the matches, or just keep typing the filename.

You still have to press **ENTER**, but if you remember this nifty feature, you can save a lot of keystrokes and pretend that the computer is actually reading your mind.

Aliases: Create Meaningful Synonyms for Commands

Defining an alias is another way to minimize your work at the keyboard, and you can also eliminate the need to remember long, awkward commands by creating synonyms that are more meaningful to you. Here are some examples:

```
alias dir='ls -l'
alias dogs='find . -name "*dog*" -print'
```

In this example, the first alias tells bash that when you enter **dir** on the command line, it should actually execute the **ls -l** command instead. If you're a hard-core DOS user, you could use **alias** to create DOS-like synonyms for many Linux commands.

The second alias lets you enter **dogs** instead of that long, ugly **find** command shown above. Don't worry about the **ls** and **find** commands right now. Just keep in mind that the **alias** command can save you some keystrokes and make it easier to remember a command.

Undoubtedly you will find other clever things to do with the **alias** command and add them to your **.profile** file so they will be available each time you log in. Your **.profile** file contains a series of commands that bash executes automatically when you log in, similar to **autoexec.bat** in the DOS world.

Redirecting the Input or Output of Linux Commands

Another useful bash feature is its ability to redirect the input and output of Linux commands. You can save the results of a command in a file instead of displaying the results on the screen, or you can feed data from a file to a program instead of entering data from the keyboard.

Let's look at redirection first. Imagine a fictitious command called **nocats** that prompts the user for a number and then waits for that many lines of text to be entered before processing them. (The program looks at each input line and prints only the ones that do not contain the word *cat*.)

You could feed the program by entering the data from the console (bold text is your typed input, normal text is console output):

```
nocats
3
Dogs are much better than those other household animals.
A cat would never beg for jerky treats.
Dogs are pretty stupid, but at least they stick around.
Dogs are much better than those other household animals.
Dogs are pretty stupid, but at least they stick around.
```

Or using a text editor, you could put all the input data in a file called **stuff** and feed the nocats program like this:

```
nocats < stuff
Dogs are much better than those other household animals.
Dogs are pretty stupid, but at least they stick around.
```

The less-than (<) symbol causes the program to get input from the **stuff** file instead of waiting for keyboard input. The greater-than (>) symbol, on the other hand, redirects output to a file instead of to the console. Thus, the command

```
nocats < stuff > bother
```

will cause the nocats program to read its input from one file (**stuff**) and write it to another (**bother**), without the keyboard or console entering the picture. Note that the nocats program doesn't know or care about all this redirection. It still thinks it is reading data from the keyboard and writing to the console—but the shell has temporarily reassigned the input and output to files instead of physical devices.

To append to an existing file instead of creating a new one, use two greater-than symbols (>>), as in this example:

```
zippity > somefile
doodah >> somefile
```

The **zippity** command runs first, and the output is placed in a new file called **somefile**. Then **doodah** runs, and its output is added (appended) to the **somefile** file.

■ *NOTE: Remember that piping with a single > symbol will wipe out existing data if the output file already exists.*

PIPES: PUMP A PROGRAM'S OUTPUT INTO ANOTHER PROGRAM

Linux provides you with a wide array of utilities to manipulate data. You can search, sort, slice, dice, and transform data stored in files in many different ways. A *pipe* (also called a pipeline) is a powerful shell feature that allows you to pump the output of one program directly into another.

For example, say you have a file with information about a group of people, including a name, age, zip code, and phone number for each person, that looks like this:

Roosevelt	Tommy	38	54579	555-1212
Nixon	Edward	19	37583	246-3457
Roosevelt	Freddie	47	11745	674-6972
Lincoln	Albert	26	26452	916-5763

If you wanted to find all the Roosevelts and sort them by zip code, you could do it like this:

```
grep Roosevelt people.txt > grep.out
sort +3 grep.out
rm grep.out
```

Since I haven't introduced the **grep** and **sort** commands yet, here's an English translation of what's happening above:

Look for lines that contain *Roosevelt* in the **people.txt** file and put them in a file named **grep.out**. Then sort the **grep.out** file on the fourth column and display the results on the console before deleting the **grep.out** file. (Yes, it is odd that the +3 flag tells sort to use the fourth column!)

But you could avoid creating and deleting the intermediate file (**grep.out**) by combining the operation into one command like this:

```
grep Roosevelt people.txt | sort +3
```

The vertical bar tells the shell that the output of the program on the left (grep) should become the input for the program on the right (sort). Behind the scenes, the shell may be issuing the exact same three commands as in the previous example, but you don't really care—you've combined three commands into one.

You can have any number of steps in a pipeline, and you can even combine pipes with redirection, as shown here:

```
grep Roosevelt people.txt | sort +3 > sort-results
```

Here, the same thing happens, except that the end result is stored in a file called **sort-results**.

Listing Processes

Linux is a multitasking operating system, which means that more than one task can be active at once. To find out what tasks are running on your system concurrently, use the command

```
ps -f
UID     PID PPID  STIME      TTY   TIME   COMD
hermie  24  1     00:35:28   tty1  0:01   bash
hermie  137 24    00:36:39   tty1  0:00   ps -f
```

The output here shows, for each active task, the UID (owning user), PID (process ID), PPID (parent process ID), STIME (when the task started), TIME (how long the task has been active), and CMD (the actual command line used to start the task). If you examine the PIDs and PPIDs, you can see that bash invoked the **ps -f** command, because the PPID of the latter matches the PID of the former.

Launching Tasks in the Foreground and Background

Suppose you have a long-running task (for example, compiling a large program) that you need to run, but you also want to get some other work done. Linux lets you start a task in the background and keep on doing other things from the command prompt. By adding the ampersand (&) to the end of any command, you can launch it in the background and get your command prompt back right away. For example,

```
cc hugepgm.c > outlist &
```

will start cc (the C compiler) as a background task, executing it in parallel with other tasks on your system.

■ **NOTE:** *It's a good idea to redirect the output of background tasks to a file, as shown here, since the background task still shares the console with foreground tasks. If you don't, the background task will splash any output it might produce all over your screen while you're editing a file or typing another command.*

If you start a long-running task and forget to add the ampersand, you can still swap that task into the background. Instead of pressing CTRL-C (to terminate the foreground task) and then restarting it in the background, just press **CTRL-Z** after the command starts, type **bg**, and press **ENTER**. You'll get your prompt back and be able to continue with other work. Use the **fg** command to bring a background task to the foreground.

You might wonder why you'd ever want to swap programs between the foreground and background, but this is quite useful if for example you're doing a long-running compile and you need to issue a quick command at the shell prompt. While the compilation is running, you could press **CTRL-Z** and then enter the **bg** command to put the compiler in the background. Then do your thing at the shell prompt and enter the **fg** command to return the compiler task to the foreground. The **CTRL-Z** trick also works with the Emacs text editor and the Pine email program. You can suspend either program and then return to your work in progress with the **fg** command.

Of course, in the X Windows environment, all these unnatural gyrations are not necessary. Just start another shell window and run the other command there. You can watch both processes running in separate windows at the same time, and you don't have to worry about adding ampersands, piping output to files, or keeping track of foreground versus background processes.

STOP THAT TASK!

Although it's unfortunate, some tasks are unruly and must be killed. If you accidentally entered the (fictitious) command

```
seek_and_destroy &
```

you'd have a background task doing potentially nasty things. Pressing the **CTRL-C** key would have no effect, since it can terminate only a foreground task. Before this rogue eats your system alive, issue the **ps -f** command to find out the process ID (PID) of the seek_and_destroy task:

```
ps -f
UID                PID        PPID       STIME        TTY      TIME      COMD
hermie             24         1          00:35:28     tty1     0:01      bash
hermie             1704       24         00:36:39     tty1     0:00
                   seek_and_destroy
```

Note that the offender has a PID of 1704 and then quickly issue the command

```
kill 1704
```

to terminate the background task.

You can terminate any active task with the **kill** command, which sends a "terminate gracefully" signal to the running task that allows it to do any necessary cleanup, close files, and so on before giving up the ghost. Occasionally, though, a task will not respond to the **kill** command, either because a program has become disabled or is coded specifically to ignore it. Time for the heavy artillery. Adding the **-9** flag to the **kill** command, as in

```
kill -9 1704
```

basically sends the "die you gravy-sucking pig" signal to the running task and forces it to shut down immediately without any chance to do cleanup. Use this flag only as a last resort, since it could cause work in progress (by the soon-to-be-killed task) to be lost.

ENVIRONMENT VARIABLES

Environment variables in the bash shell help you in several ways. Certain built-in variables change the shell in ways that make your life a little easier, and you can define other variables to suit your own purposes. Here are some examples of built-in shell variables:

PS1   Defines the shell's command-line prompt.

HOME   Defines the home directory for a user.

PATH   Defines a list of directories to search through when looking for a command to execute.

To list the current values of all environment variables, issue the command

---

env

---

or list a specific variable with the echo command, prefixing the variable name with a dollar sign (the second line shows the result of the echo command):

---

echo $HOME
/home/hermie

You've already learned how to customize your shell prompt with the PS1 variable. The HOME variable is one you shouldn't mess with, because lots of programs count on it to create or find files in your personal home directory.

UNDERSTANDING THE PATH VARIABLE

As in DOS, the shell uses the PATH variable to locate a command. PATH contains a list of directories separated by colons:

---

echo $PATH
/bin:/usr/bin:/usr/local/bin

When you enter a command, the shell looks in each of the directories specified in PATH to try to find it. If it can't find the command in any of those directories, you'll see a "Command not found" message.

If you decide to put your own programs in a bin directory under your home directory, you'll have to modify the path to include that directory, or the system will never find your programs (unless you happen to be in that directory when you enter the command). Here's how to change your PATH variable so it includes your personal bin directory:

PATH=$PATH:$HOME/bin

So if PATH was set to **/bin:/usr/bin:/usr/local/bin** beforehand, it would now have the value **/bin:/usr/bin:/usr/local/bin:/home/ hermie/bin**.

CREATING YOUR OWN SHELL VARIABLES

If you are a programmer, you'll find it handy to create your own shell variables. First issue the command

```
code=$HOME/projects/src/spew
```

and then, regardless of what directory you are in, you can issue

```
cd $code
```

to pop over quickly to the directory containing the source code for that way-cool spew program you're developing. (The **cd** command means "change directory.")

A variable assignment like this will work just fine, but its scope (visibility) is limited to the current shell. If you launch a program or enter another shell, that child task will not know about your environment variables unless you **export** them first.

Unless you know for sure that an environment variable will have meaning only in the current shell, it's a good idea to always use **export** when creating variables to ensure they will be global in scope—for example,

```
export PS1="\u \$ "
export code=$HOME/projects/src/spew
```

And be sure to add these commands to your **.bashrc** file so you won't have to retype them each time you log in.

HOW TO GET HELP

Need help figuring out what a command is supposed to do? In an operating system with strange-sounding commands like **awk**, **grep**, and **sed**, it's not surprising. The **man** command (short for manual) is a source of online help for most Linux commands. For example, you can enter

```
man grep
```

to learn all the secrets of the very useful **grep** command. (For a summary of the most-used Linux commands, see Chapter 6, "Important Linux Commands.")

If **man** claims no knowledge of the command in which you're interested, try **help** instead. This command will list all the built-in bash commands with a brief syntax summary.

Another help format called **info** is more powerful, since it provides hypertext links to make reading large documents much easier, but not all documentation is available in info format. There are some very complete **info** documents on various aspects of Red Hat (especially the portions from the GNU project).

To try it out, use the **info** command without any arguments. It will present you with a list of available documentation. Press **h** to read the help for first-time users, or use the TAB key to move the cursor to a topic link and then press ENTER to follow the link. Pressing **p** returns you to the previous page, **n** moves you to the next page, and **u** goes up one level of documentation. To exit info, press **q**.

THE GNOME HELP BROWSER

If you're running X Windows with the GNOME interface (the default when you install Red Hat Linux), you can access the **man** and **info** pages much more easily. Just click on the taskbar button with the big question mark (see Figure 4-4), and you'll launch the GNOME Help Browser (Figure 4-5). From there, you can browse a catalog of **man** or info pages, along with special help files for the GNOME interface.

Figure 4-4: *The GNOME taskbar with the ? button*

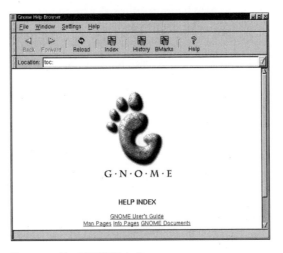

Figure 4-5: *The GNOME Help Browser*

THE LINUX FILE SYSTEM

When you installed Linux, one of the first things you did was create a file system. In the process, you carved out a chunk of hard disk and formatted it so that Linux could use it. You also created a hierarchical (treelike) structure for storing files, to impose some order on the file system to help both you and the Linux system find needed files.

In this chapter, you'll learn how to work with files and directories in a Linux system. You'll understand how the file system is structured to separate system data from personal data and how to navigate through it. We'll cover three ways to manipulate your files: using the command line, the Midnight Commander, and the graphical File Manager.

When you're done, you'll be creating, deleting, copying, renaming, listing, linking, and protecting your files like a pro. You'll also learn the Nine Deadly Keystrokes—or how to wipe out the entire file system without really trying. (But don't worry; this command can affect you only if you're logged in as **root**.)

Log in as **hermie** and try the examples in this chapter as you read through it. You'll find that the Linux file system is a lot like DOS, only more robust and flexible.

WHAT IS A LINUX FILE?

We've created a structured file system and filled it with a whole bunch of files—without knowing what Linux files are. Here's what files are in the Linux world and how they are named.

TYPES OF FILES

In most operating systems, a file is simply a blob of data stored on disk with a unique name. A file could be a list of names and numbers, a cheesecake recipe, or an executable program. But under Linux, *everything* is a file. In addition to data and executable files, Linux treats directories and even the various components of your computer as files.

This means there are files that represent your keyboard, console, printer, CD-ROM, and even your system's RAM. These special files are called devices, and they are found in the /**dev** directory (see Figure 5-1). (If you look in this directory later, you'll see files such as /**dev**/**fdo** [a floppy drive], /**dev**/**tty1** [a console], and others you may be able to identify by their names.) When Linux (or any Unix program) needs to talk to a physical hardware device, it does so by simply reading from or writing to one of these special files.

WHAT'S IN A FILE NAME?

Linux file names can be up to 256 characters long, but you really have to enjoy typing to get to that extreme. You can name a file **panda-corporation-financial-reports.y96** if you wish, but you'll probably find that shorter names (and intelligent use of directories) will save lots of time and keystrokes in the course of a day.

When naming files, you can use uppercase and lowercase letters, numbers, and certain special characters. It's a really good idea to stick with letters, numbers, and the dash, dot, and underscore characters to avoid trouble and confusion.

■ *NOTE: Don't use asterisks, backslashes, or question marks in Linux file names—these characters have special meaning to the shell and could cause your commands to do something quite different from what you intended. Also avoid using a dash as the first character of a file name, since most Linux commands will treat it as a switch.*

Files starting with a dot (.) are *hidden* files. They behave just like any other file, except that the **ls** (list files) command will not display them unless you explicitly request it to do so. Your **.bashrc** file is an example of a hidden file.

Also remember that Linux file names are case sensitive, which can be difficult to get used to if you have a DOS background. Linux allows you to have unique files named **goodstuff**, **GOODSTUFF**, and **GoodStuff** in the same directory.

It's best to *always* use lowercase in Linux unless you can think of a good reason to use uppercase or mixed case. Most Unix people use lowercase almost exclusively, but aside from this "cultural" point, there's another good reason to use lowercase. If you're sharing or accessing a DOS file system with Linux, DOS will not be able to see the files that have uppercase or mixed-case file names.

Unlike under DOS, the dot character (.) has no special meaning. You're not limited to the eight dot three (xxxxxxxx.yyy) style of naming because Linux treats the dot just like any other character; you can name a file **Some.Yummy.CHEESECAKE.Recipes** if you're so inclined.

Along these lines, Linux executables do not need or use a special extension such as .exe or .bat. Linux will happily run a program file named **zippity** just as readily as it will run **DOODAH.EXE**.

And here's another slight difference between Linux and DOS filesystems. Linux uses the forward slash (/) in path names, and DOS uses the backslash (\). Don't blame this little quirk on Linux though . . . the DOS filesystem was originally modeled after Unix! In fact, the popular rumor is that Bill Gates and Company implemented the DOS filesystem just differently enough from the Unix filesystem to avoid being criticized for stealing the idea. The same charge is made about the DOS batch file (.BAT) utility since it bears striking similarities to the Unix shell scripting languages, but I digress. . . .

DIRECTORIES

A Linux directory is a special file that acts as a container for other files and even other directories. You can create directories to hold groups of related files as an alternative to keeping all your files in one huge directory. A Linux file system is like a filing cabinet with a bunch of folders, each of which can contain subfolders and files.

After installing Linux and creating a new hermie user account, you'll end up with a file system hierarchy like the one shown here.

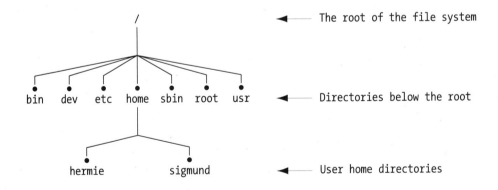

As you can see, the file system resembles an upside-down tree and is very similar to the treelike directory structure in DOS. The top level is denoted by a slash (/) and is called the root directory. Several system-related directories such as bin, dev, and etc appear below the root directory—here's a summary of their purpose in life:

/bin Contains the Linux system commands and programs (also called binaries). Pronounced "slash bin."

/dev Contains special device files that correspond to hardware components. Pronounced "slash dev."

/etc Contains configuration files for Linux and other installed software. Pronounced "slash et-see."

/home Contains the home directories (personal storage) foreach user on the system. Pronounced "slash home."

/sbin Contains more Linux binaries (special utilities not for general users). Pronounced "slash ess-bin."

/root The home directory for the root user; not to be confused with /. Some Linux systems use /**home**/**root** instead of /**root**. Pronounced "slash root."

/usr Contains system programs and other files for general users such as games, online help, and documentation. By convention, a user should not put personal files in this directory. Pronounced "slash user."

■ ***NOTE:*** *Unless you are an All-Knowing Linux Guru, you should never combine or delete any of the directories (or files therein) that appear just below the root directory. This could prevent your system from booting or operating properly.*

DIRECTORY LINGO

To navigate your Linux file system, there are several terms you should understand.

Current directory The directory you are in at a given time, sometimes called the current working directory. The **pwd** (print working directory) command will tell you the name of the current directory.

Subdirectory A directory within the current directory.

Parent directory The directory above the current one. Every directory except the top level has a parent. If you are in the /**usr**/**spool** directory, then /**usr** is the parent.

Home directory A user's personal directory. For example, if your user name is hermie, your home directory is /**home**/**hermie**. The user normally has complete control over all files stored in directories beneath the home directory, with one exception: If the root user copies a file to your home directory, root still owns and controls that file.

Root directory The top of the file system, denoted by a slash. Only subdirectories appear below this directory. Don't confuse this with /**root**, the home directory for the root user. When speaking, always refer to / as "the root directory" and to /**root** as "slash root."

Absolute file name A file name that is valid no matter where you are in the file hierarchy. In practice, this means it must start with a slash and specify the full path to the file. For example, /**home**/ **hermie**/**recipes**/**sludge_fudge** is an absolute file name, but **sludge_fudge** is not.

Relative file name A file name that specifies a file relative to the current directory. For example, if you were in hermie's home directory, /**home**/**hermie**/, you would reference that healthy fudge recipe as **recipes**/**sludge_fudge**.

TREE CLIMBING

You can move from one directory to another using the **cd** command. For example, if you are in your home directory (/**home**/**hermie**) and want to switch to the recipes directory (/**home**/**hermie**/**recipes**), the following command does the trick:

```
cd recipes
```

To switch back to your home directory, you could type

```
cd /home/hermie
```

but there are two shortcuts you will find useful. The first is the double-dot (..) notation, as in

---

`cd ..`

This will move you one level up, to the parent directory. You can even enter something like

---

`cd ../secrets`

---

to move up to the parent and then go back down to a directory that is at the same level as the current one. This double-dot notation is not specific to the **cd** command, though. You can use it with any Linux command that needs a file name as input. You might also see the single-dot (.) notation, which means "this directory." It wouldn't make much sense to enter **cd .** because you'd still be in the same directory, but there are other commands (notably, the **find** command, described in Chapter 6, "Important Linux Commands") where it's convenient to use the single dot as shorthand for the current directory name.

Another directory navigation shortcut involves using **$HOME**. No matter what directory you are in, the following command will return you to your personal recipes directory:

`cd $HOME/recipes`

And if you want to change to another user's home directory, you can use the tilde (~) notation. In the following examples, the tilde character is shorthand for "the home directory of." You must put the name of a user on your system immediately after the tilde. For example, **cd ~sigmund** means "change to sigmund's home directory"; **cd ~edbo/stuff** means "change to edbo's stuff directory".

The single-dot, double-dot, and tilde notations are useful in conjunction with the **cd** command, but they can also be used in any Linux command where you need to enter a file or directory name.

■ *TIP: One common mistake people make in navigating Linux directories is using a slash in front of file names when it is not needed. Suppose you have a bin directory under your home directory. If you were at /home/hermie and you entered cd/bin, you'd end up at the bin underneath the root directory—oops. (Linux understands the slash before bin as telling it to go to the root directory first and then to the bin directory just below the root.) The correct way to reach the bin directory under /home/hermie is to type from within your home directory (/home/hermie) cd bin. Don't use a leading slash unless you're sure you want to start at the top (root) of the file tree.*

LISTING FILES

The **ls** command lists all the files in a directory. Here are some examples:

`ls`	Lists the files in the current directory
`ls recipes`	Lists the files in another directory using relative addressing
`ls /usr/bin`	Lists the files in another directory using absolute addressing

By default, **ls** prints a simple, columnar list of your files; but it will list your files in many different formats if you add one or more flags on the command line. To use any of them, simply type the **ls** command at the prompt, followed by a space, and then add a switch by typing a hyphen followed by the flag, like this:

```
ls -F
```

Here are some of the most commonly used **ls** flags:

- **a** Lists all files, including hidden ones
- **l** Displays the file list in long format, includingfile details like size, time stamp, and owner
- **F** Adds a slash after the name for directories,an asterisk for executables, and an at sign (@) for linked files
- **r** Reverses the sort order (alphabetic or time)
- **t** Sorts the list by the time each file was created

Here's a look at the contents of a directory named animals, using some of these flags:

```
ls -F animals
  cat_info    cow_info    dog_info
  pig_info    slugs/      zippity*
```

In this case, **ls** returns just the file names in columnar format, but with a few marks, thanks to the -F flag. The slash suffix on **slugs** indicates that it is a directory, and **zippity** is identified as an executable.

```
ls -al animals
-rw-r--r--     1 hermie     users       1758    Mar 17 23:17 .hoohah
-rw-r--r--     1 hermie     users      45090    Mar 23 23:17 cat_info
-rw-r--r--     1 hermie     users      64183    Feb 14 22:07 cow_info
-rw-r--r--     1 hermie     users     115032    Jan 06 11:14 dog_info
-rw-r--r--     1 hermie     users        248    Jan 16 09:18 pig_info
drwxr-xr-x     1 hermie     users       1024    Feb 28 06:12 slugs
-rwxr-xr-x     1 hermie     users      45198    Jan 23 11:14 zippity
```

Here, **ls** has displayed all files in the animals directory, including the hidden **hoohah** file. In addition to the file name, the file's permissions, owner, group, size in bytes, and date and time of last modification are displayed. (More on permissions later in this chapter.)

```
ls -lrt animals
-rw-r--r--     1 hermie     users     115032    Jan 06 11:14 dog_info
-rw-r--r--     1 hermie     users        248    Jan 16 09:18 pig_info
-rwxr-xr-x     1 hermie     users      45198    Jan 23 11:14 zippity
-rw-r--r--     1 hermie     users      64183    Feb 14 22:07 cow_info
drwxr-xr-x     1 hermie     users       1024    Feb 28 06:12 slugs
-rw-r--r--     1 hermie     users      45090    Mar 23 23:17 cat_info
```

This time, the files are sorted by time stamp, in reverse order. If you have lots of files in a directory, this is a handy way to find out which are the oldest and newest. Also notice that the **-l**, **-r**, and **-t** switches were combined into **-lrt** in the preceding command. We could just as well have issued the command **ls -l -r -t animals**.

LISTING FILES WITH MIDNIGHT COMMANDER

Red Hat Linux comes with a handy utility called Midnight Commander (see Figure 5-1), which is a text-based utility that makes it easier to list and manipulate your files. To start Midnight Commander, enter the **mc** command. Midnight Commander shows you the file system tree in the left panel and the files from the selected directory in the right panel. Follow the prompts at the bottom of the screen to navigate directories, browse or edit a file, or perform other operations such as copy, move, and delete.

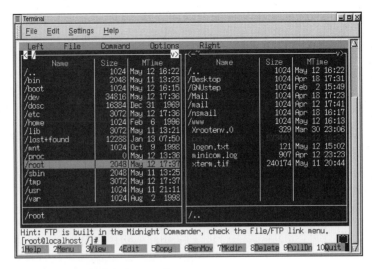

Figure 5-1: *The Midnight Commander program*

LISTING FILES WITH FILE MANAGER

If you're running X Windows with GNOME, the File Manager (Figure 5-2) is highly recommended over the shell prompt commands or Midnight Commander. File Manager, also known as GNOME Midnight Commander, is a graphical version of the text-based Midnight Commander

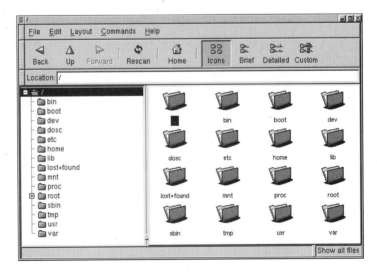

Figure 5-2: *The File Manager program*

program. When you start X Windows, the File Manager is already active and minimized on your desktop. Double-click on the folder icon at the top left of your screen to see the File Manager window. (Refer to Chapter 2, "GNOME: The Linux GUI," for more detailed usage information.)

DISPLAYING FILES

You know how to get a list of files. But what if you want to take a peek at a file's contents? Several commands, including **cat**, **more**, and **less**, can be used to display files. Let's see how they work in this example:

```
cat pig_info
Pigs make great pets, but they are not dogs or cats. Maybe
somewhere in between. I tend to believe that they have more
personality. They do require significant amounts of attention,
love, and scratches. But they aren't always snuggly in return.
```

The **cat** command (short for concatenate) shown in this example is like the DOS **type** command. In response to the command **cat pig_info**, the system simply splatters the file on the screen. If there is more data in the file than will fit on one screen, the contents whiz by before you can see it. The **more** command solves this problem by displaying the file screen by screen:

```
more dog_info
Affectionately known as the "Toller," the Nova Scotian Duck
Tolling Retriever was once called the Little River Duck Dog,
since it was developed in the Little River district of Yarmouth
County, Nova Scotia. This engaging dog is a specialist with
waterfowl. Tolling, or luring, is the practice of tricking ducks
into gunshot range. Hunters had long observed this behavior
—More—(01%)
```

The **more** command pauses when the screen fills up and waits for you to press the spacebar before it rolls out another screenful of text. A legend at the bottom of the screen tells you what percentage of the file has been displayed so far. You can press CTRL-C to quit **more** before reaching the end of the file.

The **less** command works like **more** except that it lets you move both forward and backward in the file while the command is running— use the **B** key on your keyboard to back up one screen and the spacebar to move forward and show the next screen.

Although all of these commands will let you view the contents of a file in different ways, none allow you to change the data in the file. If you want to view and update a file, use one of the text editors discussed in Chapter 7, "Text Editors."

DISPLAYING FILES WITH MIDNIGHT COMMANDER OR FILE MANAGER

If you like the Midnight Commander program, you can use the built-in View function to look at the contents of a file. Just press the **F3** key after selecting the desired file with the arrow keys. To exit the viewer, press **F3** again. Or if you're running X Windows with GNOME, the File Manager also has a built-in file viewer. Right-click on a file and select the **View** option (see Figure 5-3) to launch the file viewer in a new window (Figure 5-4).

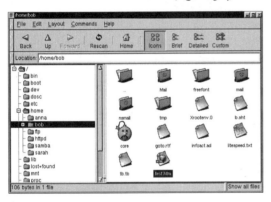 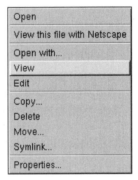

Figure 5-3: *Selecting a file to view*

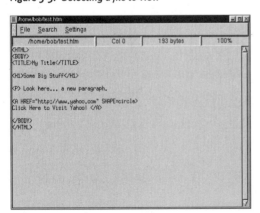

Figure 5-4: *Viewing the contents of an HTML file*

Copying Files

Copying files under Linux is similar to copying files under DOS. Here's an example using the **cp** (copy) command:

```
cp goulash recipes/hungarian
cp stuff stuff.bak
```

The first example copies the **goulash** file from the current directory and stores it in your recipes/hungarian directory. The second example creates a file called **stuff.bak** in the current directory that is identical to the source file **stuff**.

■ *NOTE: The **cp** command will overwrite files with the same name without warning. To be prompted before overwriting, use the **-i** flag, like so:*

```
cp -i goulash recipes/hungarian
cp: overwrite recipes/hungarian/goulash (y/n)?
```

Renaming Files

Use the **mv** command to rename a file or move it to another directory, like so:

```
mv stuff junk
mv junk trashcan
```

The first example renames the file **stuff** as **junk,** and the second moves the file **junk** into a directory called trashcan.

■ *NOTE: The **mv** command will wipe out files without warning. To be prompted before overwriting, use the **-i** flag, like so:*

```
mv -i stuff junk
mv: overwrite junk (y/n)?
```

CREATING FILES

If you want to create a new file rather than copy an existing one, use the **touch** command:

```
touch new.file
```

This creates a new, empty file.

If you issue the **ls -l new.file** command, you can verify that the file has a size of zero bytes. It might seem silly to create an empty file, but you can use them to verify that you have permission to create files in a certain directory, and some programs insist upon a control or log file even if it's empty. (The **touch** command will also update the time and date stamp on an existing file.)

If you'd rather create a new file with data in it—for example, a line of text—use the **echo** command:

```
echo "Remember to buy oatmeal raisin cookies." > reminder
```

This will create a file named **reminder** with just one line in it (the text in quotation marks). The **echo** command normally just prints a line to the screen, but here we've directed the output to a file. (This command also works in DOS.)

If you want to create a multiline file, use the **cat** command (similar to the DOS **type** command):

```
cat > fox.socks
Through three cheese trees three free fleas flew.
While these fleas flew, freezy breeze blew.
Freezy breeze made these three trees freeze.
Freezy trees made these trees' cheese freeze.
That's what made these three free fleas sneeze.
^D
```

The first line in this example tells Linux what to name the new file (**fox.socks**). The typed lines that follow will become the contents of this new file. Pressing **CTRL-D** tells Linux that the file is done, and the **cat** command transfers your typing to the new file.

DELETING FILES

Ready to do a little damage? The **rm** command removes a file (assuming you have permission to do so) without even saying hasta la vista. Be sure you really want to delete your files before you use **rm**, because once the files are gone, they're not coming back. For example,

---

`rm wallet`

---

immediately deletes the file named **wallet** in the current directory without prompting. If you want to be prompted before the deletion, use the **-i** flag.

> ■ *NOTE: There is one little safety feature in rm—it won't delete a directory (unless you use the -r flag).*

One other **rm** flag is **-f,** which translates roughly to "Don't ask me any questions—just delete the files." While **rm** normally asks for confirmation before deleting a write-protected file, the **-f** (force) flag overrides this prompt.

Be careful with the **rm** command, since the multiuser nature of Linux does not allow for undelete as in DOS. As soon as you let go of the space occupied by a file, the operating system is likely to use it for something else.

CREATING DIRECTORIES

If you have a bunch of related files scattered in your home directory, why not create a directory for them? Use the **mkdir** command as follows:

`mkdir cooking`

This creates a new directory named cooking in the current directory, into which you can move all those recipes for easy retrieval.

DELETING DIRECTORIES

If you created a directory named spelunking six months ago, and now you're not so keen on crawling through slimy caves, the **rmdir** command may be able to help:

```
rmdir spelunking
```

This command removes the specified directory, but only if it's empty. If the directory contains files or subdirectories, you'll have to delete them using **rm** first.

One alternative to painstakingly removing all the contents of a directory that you just want to make disappear is to use the **rm -r** command. The **-r** flag gives **rm** license to kill directories, their files, and even their subdirectories. Be very sure you understand what's about to happen before using a command like this:

```
rm -r spelunking
```

Let's just say that careless use of the **-r** flag might end your spelunking hobby prematurely.

USING WILDCARDS

Wildcards come in quite handy when you want to operate on more than one file at a time. You can use wildcards with any of the commands in this chapter to list, copy, rename, or delete groups of files or directories.

The asterisk (*) character will match any number of characters in a file name, so consider these examples in light of the animals directory we used earlier.

```
ls -l c*
-rw-r--r--    1 hermie    users      45090 Mar 23 23:17 cat_info
-rw-r--r--    1 hermie    users      64183 Feb 14 22:07 cow_info
mv *inf* ../docs
rm -f *
```

The first command lists only those files that begin with the letter "c." The second will move files with the term *inf* anywhere in the name to another directory. The third command will delete all (nonhidden) files from the current directory.

■ **NOTE:** *The expansion of the wildcard is done by the shell, not the command you are running. This means that when you enter the command*

```
rm -f *
```

the shell expands the wildcard by replacing it with all files that match and actually ends up executing this command:

```
rm -f cat_info cow_info dog_info pig_info slugs zippity
```

This might seem a bit arcane, but it's actually important. Since the shell handles the wildcards in Linux, you don't have to worry about which commands accept wildcards and which don't. This is quite different from DOS, where only certain commands work with wildcards.

Here's a little pop quiz: What will be left in the animals directory if you execute the **rm** command in the preceding example? Try it and then use the **ls -al** command—you may be surprised at the answer.

DON'T TRY THIS AT HOME

At the beginning of this chapter, I promised to reveal the Nine Deadly Keystrokes that could wipe out your entire file system. Given what you know now about the **rm** command and the structure of the Linux file system, perhaps you can see that the command

```
rm -rf /
```

would be something to avoid at all costs if you were logged in as **root**. But don't let this scare you—it's just a reminder to be careful when deleting files. You can avoid nasty surprises like this by running the **pwd** and **ls** commands before you delete anything. (Use **ls** on the same file or directory that you're going to delete.) Then you'll always be sure what directory you're in and what files are about to be deleted.

And in general, it's a good idea to log in as **root** only when you're performing system administration tasks such as adding new users or installing software. Create another account and use it for all your normal, everyday Linux tasks.

Controlling Access to Your Files with Permissions and Owners

If you share a Linux (or Unix) system, you will undoubtedly have private files that you want to keep private, as well as files that you want to be public. You can control access to your files by setting the permission flags and ownership for your files.

How to Tell What Access Your Files Have

When we discussed using the **ls** command, you may have been wondering about that gibberish in the first few columns of the **ls -l** command (stuff like -rw, r—, and so on). Here's an example of output from the **ls -l** command showing the contents of a directory:

Permissions	User	Group	Size	Date	Name
-rw-r-----	1 hermie	users	64183	Feb 14 22:07	cow_info
-rw-r-----	1 hermie	users	115032	Jan 06 11:14	dog_info
-rw-r--r--	1 hermie	users	248	Jan 16 09:18	pig_info
-rw-r--r--	1 hermie	users	45090	Mar 23 23:17	cat_info
-rwx--x---	1 hermie	users	45198	Jan 23 11:14	zippity
drwxr-x---	1 hermie	friends	1024	Feb 28 06:12	slugs

For each file you see listed a set of permissions; the owning user; a group name; and the size, creation date, and name of the file. We'll focus on the permission first by dissecting the file-access permissions for the **cow_info** file. Specifically, these permissions are shown in the string of characters preceding the file in the first column: **-rw-r-----**. Note that the permissions data is made up of ten characters, each of which has meaning.

To understand how to read file permissions, let's start by splitting apart those ten characters for **cow_info**:

Directory?		User's Access	Group Access	Others' Access
-		r w -	r - -	- - -
		| | |	| | |	
Readable	----+ | |		| | +---- Not executable	
Writable	-------+ |		| +------ Not writable	
Not executable	---------+		+-------- Readable	

The character in the first position, a hyphen (-), indicates that this is a file and not a directory. Directories are marked with a d, as in **drwxr-x---** (this precedes the directory slugs).

The next three characters (**rw-**) tell us whether the file's owner (**hermie**) can read, write, and execute the file. An r in the first position means that the file can be read; a w in the second position means that the file can be written to (updated); and an x in the third position means that the file can be executed (run). In all three cases, if a hyphen appears in place of an r, w, or x, that specific privilege is removed. For example, rw- means that the file can be read and written to, but not executed.

The next sets of three characters define read, write, and execute access for the users in a particular group (the users group, in this case), along the same lines as above. For example, the characters **r--** that appear in these positions for **cow_info** tell us that the users group can read this file but can't write to or execute it.

The final set of three characters—all hyphens, in this case—defines access for those who are not the owner or in the listed group. This one's easy: No one outside the listed group has any kind of access to this file.

■ **NOTE:** *Groups are a convenient way to give a set of users the same access to a bunch of files. Only a superuser can add to or remove users from groups. To find out what groups you belong to, use the* **groups** *command.*

In sum, access to the **cow_info** file is controlled like so: The user (hermie) can read and update the file, but cannot execute it. People in the users group can only read the file, and everybody else on the system gets no access at all.

Here's another example:

```
-rwx--x---   1 hermie   users     45198 Jan 23 11:14 zippity
```

The characters that precede the file name **zippity** tell us that this file is readable, writable, and executable by hermie; only members of the users group can execute it; and others outside the users group have no access to it.

■ **NOTE:** *You can give execute permission to any file, but it doesn't make sense to do so unless the file is actually a program.*

Look at the listing for slugs:

```
drwxr-x---   1 hermie   friends    1024 Feb 28 06:12 slugs
```

You can see first that it's a directory (signified by the d in the first position). User hermie has read and write access, which in the case of a directory translates into the ability to list files and to create and delete files. Hermie also has execute access, which in the case of a directory means the ability to use **cd** to change to it. Those in the friends group can list files in the directory and use **cd** to make it the current directory, but others have no access whatsoever to the directory.

- *■ **NOTE:** Unless you are administering a large Unix system with lots of users, groups are not very important. In these examples, users is just the name of a group that all users belong to by default in a Linux system. If your primary group is users, all files you create will show that as the group name, unless you use the **chgrp** command to change it. If you're curious, use the **man chgrp** command to find out more.*

USING CHMOD TO CHANGE A FILE'S PERMISSIONS

Fine; you can decipher the permissions for a file or directory, but what if you want to change them? Maybe you've decided that the **pig_info** file is a little too sensitive for just anybody to view, or that you should allow all users to execute the zippity program. The **chmod** (change mode) command can take care of that.

The general form of the **chmod** command is

```
chmod <permission flags> <file or directory name(s)>
```

To tell **chmod** the new permissions for a file, you can use any combination of these permission flag characters:

WHO IT APPLIES TO	ACCESS CHANGE	ACCESS TYPE
(Pick One or More)	**(Pick One)**	**(Pick One or More)**
u For the owner	+ Grant access	r For read access
g For the owner	- Deny access	w For write access
g For the group		x For execute access
o For all others		

Here are some examples:

`chmod o-r pig_info`	Remove read access from all others
`chmod g+rw pig_info`	Grant read and write access to group
`chmod ugo+x zippity`	Grant execute access to everybody

In effect, you're saying "change the mode for *these people* by *adding/removing* their access to *read/write/execute* the file named *whatever*." Just pick the proper combination of flags in each of the three columns, depending on what type of access you want for the file.

■ **NOTE:** *If you give **chmod** a directory name instead of a file name, the permissions have slightly different meanings. For a directory, read access means that you can list the files with the **ls** command; write access allows you to create or delete files; and execute access gives you the ability to change to that directory with the **cd** command.*

TRANSFERRING OWNERSHIP OF A FILE USING CHOWN

If you are logged in as root, you can transfer ownership of a file or directory (if you move it into another user's directory) using the **chown** command.

To tell **chown** what to do, just give it the new owner and the file name, like this:

```
chown sigmund zippity
```

This will make sigmund the owner of **zippity.** Once you've transferred ownership, sigmund will be able to set the file's permissions (with **chmod**) if he wants to.

IMPORTANT LINUX COMMANDS

Working from a Linux command line is not always intuitive, especially since there are hundreds of different commands with a myriad of switches and flags to make things even more confusing. You certainly don't need to know all of them to make good use of your Linux system, but there is a certain set of indispensable tools with which you should be familiar.

We've covered a handful of commands in previous chapters that let you work with the shell and your file system. The commands covered in this chapter will complement what you've learned and give you some essential tools to manage your Linux environment. (You'll also be able to use these commands on other Unix-based systems.) You'll pick up other important commands in Chapter 7, "Text Editors," and Chapter 8, "Slicing and Dicing," but you should first master this starter set to build the skills that will help you perform common Linux tasks more easily.

IF YOU NEED HELP, ASK THE MAN

Assuming you can remember the right command for a particular job, it's tougher still to remember all the switches associated with that command. The **man** command (short for manual) will help you on both counts by displaying pages from online manuals and telling you which commands may be relevant to the task at hand.

Say you want to change your password, but you don't know the command to do it. You can use the **man** command plus the keyword flag, **-k**, to search by keyword password for relevant commands:

```
man -k password
passwd     passwd (1)      - change login password
pwck       pwck (1m)       - password/group file checkers
vipw       vipw (1b)       - edit the password file
```

You can probably deduce that **passwd** is the correct command. But before blindly issuing any Linux command, you should know the proper syntax and understand what the command might do to you first. Using **man** with a command name will display all you need to know (probably more) about a command. For example, entering

```
man passwd
```

will display

```
passwd(1)        User Commands         passwd(1)
NAME
    passwd - change login password and attributes
SYNOPSIS
    passwd [ name ]
    passwd [ -d | -l ] [ -f ] [ -n min ] [ -w warn ]
           [ -x max ] name
    passwd -s [ -a ]
    passwd -s [ name ]

DESCRIPTION
    The passwd command changes the password or lists
    attributes associated with the user's login name.
--More--(5%)
```

(The **man** command pauses after each screenful and waits for you to press the spacebar before continuing.) The word *More* at the bottom of each page indicates how much of the help has so far been displayed. The terms in square brackets are optional parameters (**-d, -l, -f**, for example); vertical bars indicate that the terms on either side are mutually exclusive—you can use only one at a time.

For more information on getting help with Linux commands, see the section at the end of Chapter 4, "Living in a Shell," that discusses the GNOME Help Browser. The Help Browser operates in the X Windows environment and offers point-and-click access to several sources of help information.

USE PASSWD TO CHANGE YOUR PASSWORD

You can use the **passwd** command to change your log-in password, and as you can tell from the **man** output shown in the preceding section, you have quite a few options. Here are some of the most common:

passwd	Change your own password
passwd sleepy	Change sleepy's password
passwd -d sleepy	Delete sleepy's password

When you enter one of these commands to change a password, you will be prompted for the old (current) password and a new password. Your new password should be at least six characters long and not too easy for someone else to guess. Oh, and writing it down on a scrap of paper taped to your monitor is not recommended either. :-)

If you share your Linux system with multiple users, or if you have a dial-in modem attached, password security for each account is particularly important. But if you're the only one who will ever lay a finger on your system, you might want to delete your password, thus removing the need to enter it each time you log in. It's your call, but you never know when your five-year-old will wander by the keyboard!

By the way, you might get the idea from the preceding commands that users can go around changing each other's passwords at will, but that's not the case. Only a superuser (such as root) can change or delete another user's password.

SWITCH USERS WITH SU

Even if you have no schizophrenic tendencies, sometimes you'll want to become someone else while using Linux. For example, if you're logged in as **hermie** and you need to do something quickly that requires superuser authority, just enter the command

```
su - root
```

In response to the **su** (switch user) command, you'll be prompted for the root account password. If you enter the password correctly, your prompt will change from a dollar sign to a pound sign (to reflect your status as root), and you will assume the powers of the root user. Issue the command

```
exit
```

to return to your previous identity. You can also use **su** to become any user on the system, not just root. For example, to become sigmund, you would enter this command:

```
su - sigmund
```

Don't forget the minus sign when you use **su** to temporarily become another user. Without it, the login profile for that user is not executed—so it's not really the same as logging in because your environment variables and aliases would not change.

This would be like starting DOS without running the **autoexec.bat** file—things wouldn't work the same because your personal setup commands (PATH and so on) would not run.

But why would you want to use **su** when you can have multiple log-ins via virtual consoles (see Chapter 4, "Living in a Shell")? Because it's sometimes quicker or more convenient to switch between users using **su**, and because you may have no virtual consoles available—you may be using all of them or, if you're logged in to the machine via a modem, virtual consoles may not be available to you.

TELL ME WHO IS LOGGED IN

If you want to know which users are currently logged in to your Linux system, which console they're using, and the date and time they logged in, issue the **who** command. You'll see output something like this:

```
who
root              tty1              Nov 2 17:57
hermie            tty3              Nov 2 18:43
sigmund           tty2              Nov 2 18:08
```

In the output shown here, the term *tty* stands for teletype. In the olden days of computing, a terminal was just a keyboard with an attached printer, so you read everything off the teletype.

If you've logged in with multiple virtual consoles and changed your identity on any of them, you may have some trouble figuring out who you are—or at least what user is logged in to the console you're using. If you find yourself in such an identity crisis, try this variant of the **who** command:

```
who am i
```

WHAT'S TODAY'S DATE?

Use the **date** command to print the current date and time. If you add the **-u** flag, the results will be for the Greenwich mean time zone. And if you log in as a superuser, you can even change the date or time with the **-s** flag. Now, that's power! Here are some examples:

date	Print the date and time
`Sat Nov 2 20:09:43 EST 1996`	
date -u	Print the GMT date and time
`Sun Nov 3 01:09:45 GMT 1996`	
date -s 0503	Set the clock to 5:03 AM

GRAPHICAL CLOCKS

Figure 6-1: *Simple clock in the GNOME taskbar*

If you're running X Windows with the GNOME interface, you'll see a simple digital clock with time and date in the far-right panel of the taskbar, as shown in Figure 6-1.

You can also start a graphical clock to keep track of the time and date without entering any commands. Choose **Gnome Foot • Panel • Add Applet • Utility • Another Clock.** (See Figure 6-2.)

Figure 6-2: *"Another Clock" applet in the GNOME taskbar*

You can also try "Afterstep Clock" instead of "Another Clock." Either option will place a clock in the GNOME taskbar. If you prefer a clock on the desktop (see Figure 6-3) instead of the taskbar, enter the command

```
xclock
```

from a shell-prompt (terminal) window.

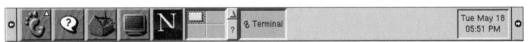

Figure 6-3: *A clock on the desktop*

Figure 6-4: *The Time and Date tool*

You can also use a graphical tool (see Figure 6-4) to set the system clock, if you are logged in as root. Choose **Gnome Foot • System • TimeTool.**

Is There an echo in Here?

The **echo** command displays a message on the screen and is primarily useful for programmers writing shell scripts (see Chapter 9, "Rolling Your Own—Linux Programming"). But anyone can use **echo** to show the value of environment variables. Here are some examples:

```
echo $PATH
/usr/bin:/usr/local/bin
echo My name is $USER - Home directory=$HOME.
My name is hermie - Home directory=/home/hermie.
```

The **echo** command is very similar to the DOS command of the same name, except that the DOS **echo** command cannot display environment variables—it just displays a message.

What Good Is a spell Checker?

Always run your important documents through a spell checker. It will plane lee mark four you're revue, miss steaks ewe mite knot sea. However, it probably won't do much for poor grammar or sentences like that one! Linux has a rudimentary spelling checker, which you can invoke like this:

spell important.txt	Perform a regular spell check on important text
spell -b important.txt	Perform a spell check using British spelling rules

If the spell checker finds words that do not appear in its dictionary, it will display them on the console.

Running a spell checker from the command line may seem a bit old-fashioned if you're accustomed to modern word processors. You can also perform a spell check using the graphical Gedit editor. Start the editor with the command

```
gedit
```

from a shell-prompt window, load the file to be checked, and then choose **Plugins • Spell Check**; the spell check dialogs (see Figure 6-5) will show you words that may be spelled incorrectly, along with alternatives you can select.

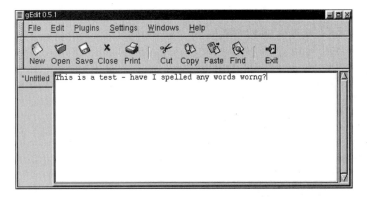

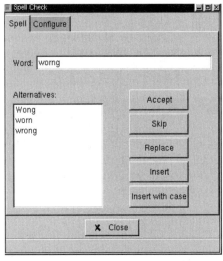

Figure 6-5: *Spell checking with gEdit*

CONFIGURING YOUR SYSTEM FOR PRINTING

Red Hat Linux comes with a nice graphical printer configuration utility that will create the necessary system files to set up your printer. After logging in as root and starting X Windows, choose **Gnome Foot • AnotherLevel Menus • Administration • Printer Tool** and then follow these steps:

1. Click the "Add" button; the Printer Type window appears. (See Figure 6-6.)

2. Pick "Local Printer" and then click **OK;** a second pop-up window appears. (See Figure 6-7.)

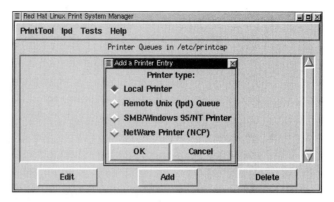

Figure 6-6: *The Printer Type Window*

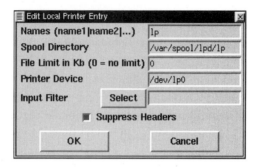

Figure 6-7: *Default values for local printer*

The fields should be prefilled with automatically generated default values. If they are not:

- In the "Names" field, enter **lp.**

- In the "Spool Directory" field, enter **/var/spool/lpd/lp.**

- In the "File Limit" field, enter **0** (zero).

- In the "Printer Device" field, enter **/dev/lpo.**

  3. Click the "Select" button next to the "Input Filter" field—a third pop-up window appears. (See Figure 6-8.)

  4. Choose your printer type from the list on the left.

- In the Resolution field, choose **180x180** (for draft quality) or **360x360** (for higher quality). Some printers offer other choices for higher or lower resolutions. Pick the one you think will suit you best and experiment. You can always come back here and change

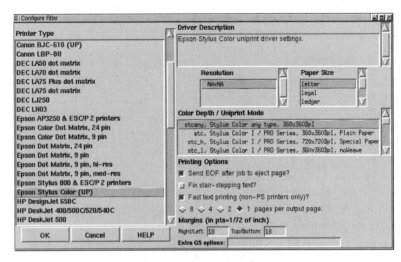

Figure 6-8: *Click the "Select" button to choose your printer type*

the resolution. If your printer selection does not allow you to select a Resolution value (it shows only **NAxNA**), look below and select an option from the "Color Depth/Uniprint Mode" list.

- In the "Paper Size" field, choose "letter."

- Check the "Send EOF" box and click **OK** (the second pop-up window returns).

- Select the "Suppress Headers" box and click **OK**.

    5. Now restart the Linux printer subsystem by selecting "lpd" from the action bar and clicking on "restart lpd."

That's it; now you can try a little printing.

PUT IT IN PRINT

Now that your system is ready for printing and your important document is free of spelling errors, why not print a copy for posterity? In Linux, the print command is **lpr,** so you might enter a command like this:

```
lpr paperless-office.txt
```

The **lpr** command makes a copy of your file and stuffs it in the system's print queue (a process called spooling), so you can change or delete the original file without harming your printout.

The **lpr** command will accept two optional flags:

-**r**   Delete the file after printing.

-**s**   No spooling (don't make a temporary copy for printing).

The **-r** flag tells the system to delete the file after printing, and **-s** tells the system to print directly from the original file instead of spooling to the print queue. Of course, if you specify the **-s** flag, you can't modify or delete the original file while it's printing, but this option can save a bit of time (since no copy is made) when the original file is big.

Here are some examples using the **-r** and **-s** flags:

`lpr -r humongous`	Delete the file **humongous** after printing.
`lpr -s humongous`	Print the file **humongous** without spooling.
`lpr -r -s humongous`	Print the file **humongous** without spooling and then delete it.

■ *NOTE: Some printers under Linux exhibit a staircase effect as shown here, with each line starting in the column where the last line ended, instead of starting in the first column:*

```
this is line one
            this is line two
                        this is line three
```

*If this happens with your printer, see the **Printing-Usage-HOWTO** file in the **doc/HOWTO** directory on the CD.*

CUSTOMIZING YOUR PRINTOUTS

The **lpr** command is a no-frills way to print your files. It doesn't do any fancy formatting; it just dumps your file on the printer. If you'd like to format your printout (paginate, add a title, set margins, or control the page length), you can use the **pr** command in conjunction with **lpr**. By default, **pr** will add page numbers and a title consisting of the file's name and the date and time it was last modified. But you can do lots of other fancy formatting as well. Here are some of the options that **pr** supports:

-d	Double-space the printout.
-h <*my title*>	Specify a title for the page header (the default is the file name).
-L*n*	Set the page length to *n* lines (the default is 66).
-O*n*	Set the margin to *n* characters (the default is 8).
-T	Suppress the page header.
-2 | **-3** | **-4**	Print output in two, three, or four columns (as in a newspaper).

Typically, the output from **pr** is sent only to your printer (by piping the output to **lpr,** as shown in the following examples), but if you leave off the **lpr** step, you'll see the output on the screen instead. Here are some examples using the **pr** command to print a file named **panda97.txt**—for example, with no options specified, just adding page numbers and the default title (file name and date):

```
pr panda97.txt | lpr
```

Here we've specified a more meaningful title for the printout:

```
pr -h "Financial Report" panda97.dat | lpr
```

And now we've set the page length to 55 lines, set the margin to 5 spaces, and added double-spacing:

```
pr -h "Financial Report" -l55 -o5 -d panda97.dat | lpr
```

STOP THE PRESSES!

If you send a file to the printer by mistake, you might be able to snatch it from the print queue before it's too late. First use **lpq** to find the job number:

```
lpq
Rank Owner  Job  Files            Total Size
1st  hermie 17   really-humongous 2317678 bytes
```

In the example shown above, the job number is 17. Once you know the job number, enlist the assistance of **lprm** to remove that file from the queue as follows (using job 17 as an example):

```
lprm 17
```

PRINTING POSTSCRIPT FILES

PostScript is a complex formatting language that certain laser printers can interpret to produce really nice-looking documents. But if you send a PostScript file to a printer that doesn't understand the PostScript language, your printout will be pages of incomprehensible gibberish. And unless you shelled out megabucks for your laser printer, chances are it won't print a PostScript file.

■ *TIP: You can tell a PostScript file by the file name and the contents. If the file name ends with .ps and the first line of the file starts with the percent sign (%), you can be sure it's PostScript.*

It gets worse. Most of the documentation for Linux comes in PostScript format, which suggests that you may not be able to print it unless you have PostScript capability. But all is not lost. The version of Linux included with this book has a nifty program called Ghostscript that can read a PostScript file and either display it on the screen or print it on your printer, even if the printer doesn't have built-in PostScript support.

To view a PostScript file on the screen, enter a command like this (**qwerty.ps** is a sample file name):

```
gv qwerty.ps
```

■ *NOTE: You must start X Windows (with the startx command) before running the gv command.*

Assuming you followed the preceding instructions to set up your printer, you can print a PostScript file with the **lpr** command, just like any other file. The system will invoke Ghostscript behind the scenes and send the file to your printer.

DRAG-AND-DROP PRINTING

If you're running X Windows with GNOME, you can print files by dragging them from the File Manager window to the Printer applet—but first, you have to add the applet to your taskbar. Choose **Gnome Foot • Panel • Add Applet • Utility • Print**. From the File Manager window, drag a plain text file and drop it on the "Printer Applet" icon. (See Figure 6-9.) The file should begin to print.

Figure 6-9: *GNOME Printer Applet*

USE CAT TO JOIN FILES

The **cat** command's primary function is to concatenate, or join, files, but you can also use it to display a file on the screen. The **cat** command takes one or more files that you specify, smashes them together, and then sends the resulting file to the standard output device (without changing any of the original files).

The standard output device is your screen, but by using the greater-than (>) operator, you can redirect **cat**'s output to another file. Here are some examples:

cat food	Display the **food** file on the screen.
cat scratch fever	Join the files **scratch** and **fever** and then display the result on the screen.
cat eats bird > DetailsAt11	Join the files **eats** and **bird** and save them in the file **DetailsAt11**.

Note that the original files that **cat** joins are not modified. For example, say the file **eats** contained these lines:

```
The Owl and the Pussy-Cat went to sea
In a beautiful pea-green boat.
```

Also say the file **bird** contained these lines:

```
They took some honey, and plenty of money
Wrapped up in a five-pound note.
```

After the preceding command, neither file would change, but a new file called **DetailsAt11** would be created, containing all four lines:

```
The Owl and the Pussy-Cat went to sea
In a beautiful pea-green boat.
They took some honey, and plenty of money
Wrapped up in a five-pound note.
```

SEARCH FOR FILES WITH find

Linux's tree-structured file system is great for organizing your files, but a plethora of directories and subdirectories can make it easy to lose track of specific files. To search for a file named **cookie**, you can use the **find** command, like this:

```
find / -name "cookie" -print
```

This command tells **find** to start looking in the root directory of the file system (/) for files named (**-name**) **cookie** and then to print (**-print**) the full name of each file it finds.

Actually, you don't need the **-print** flag on Red Hat Linux, but on most Unix systems, if you leave off the **-print** flag, **find** will merrily search and then throw the results in the bit bucket. (This is a fictitious device attached to all computers. When the operating system deletes a file or discards data, it is said to be thrown in the bit bucket.)

This is a departure from the rule of thumb that Linux commands will print their output on the screen unless you specify otherwise.

Starting from the root directory may take a long time, since **find** will search every single directory on the system. You can shorten the search time by telling **find** where to start searching if you know that the file you want lies along a certain path. Here are a few examples:

find . -name "cookie" -print	Start looking in the current directory.
find ~sigmund -name "cookie" -print	Start looking in sigmund's home directory.
find /etc -name "cookie" -print	Start looking in the /**etc** directory.

If you can't remember the exact name of the file you're after, but you have some sort of clue about it (for example, it has the word *cow* in it), you can use wildcards to search:

`find . -name "cow*" -print`	Look for files beginning with *cow*.
`find . -name "*cow" -print`	Look for files ending with *cow*.
`find . -name "*cow*" -print`	Look for files with *cow* anywhere within them.

Finding the right files is one thing, but doing something useful with the found files would be a big plus. You can use the **-exec** flag to apply a command to each of the found files. The following example will send all the files it finds to the printer (**lpr**):

```
find . -name "*.txt" -exec lpr {} \;
```

The set of brackets ({}) is a placeholder that represents the name of each file found, and the slash-semicolon (\;) is a bit of magic that signals the end of the command. So if you had files in the current directory named **sample1.txt** and **sample2.txt**, the **find** command would issue the following commands for you:

```
lpr sample1.txt
lpr sample2.txt
```

You can apply any command you like to the found files.

Using **find** with the **-exec** flag is a convenient way to copy, move, print, and even delete groups of files that may be scattered across many different directories. A word of caution, though: If you're going to apply some potentially dangerous command (like **rm**) to your files, use the **-ok** flag instead of **-exec**. It works the same way, except it prompts you to confirm each command before executing it. Here's an example:

```
find . -name "*.txt" -ok mv {} junkdir \;
mv sample1.txt junkdir    ok? (y/n)
mv sample2.txt junkdir    ok? (y/n)
```

The **find** command found two matching files, constructed the commands shown here by substituting a file name for the brackets, and then asked for confirmation before executing the commands.

USING THE GRAPHICAL FILE FINDER

If you're running X Windows with GNOME, you can search for files with the GNOME Search Tool. Choose **Gnome Foot • Utilities • Gnome Search Tool** to launch the Search tool (see Figure 6-10). Enter a start directory and a file name (with optional wildcards) and click "Start" to view the results.

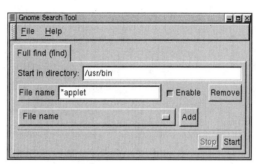

Figure 6-10: *The GNOME Search tool*

WHAT'S THE DIFFERENCE BETWEEN TWO FILES?

If, when you use **find,** you discover two files with suspiciously similar names, you might want to know whether they really contain the same information. The **diff** command will compare two files and give you the lowdown on just how different they are. Here's an example of how you would use the **diff** command and the output you might get from it:

```
diff cookies.old cookies.new
5c5
< One cup vanilla extract
---
> One teaspoon vanilla extract
7d6
< Six ounces chopped liver
21a22
Note: The previous version of this recipe had a few errors!
```

The output is actually a description of how to transform the old file into the new one. Here, **diff** is telling you three things:

- The fifth line of the file has undergone a change. The **5c5** message says to replace line 5 of the old file with line 5 of the new file. Both the old and new text are displayed, separated by a line of three dashes. (The less-than (<) notation means "remove this line," and the greater-than (>) sign means "add this line.")

- Line 7 of the old file does not appear in the new file. The **7d6** message says to delete line 7 from the old file, and the files will then be in sync, starting at line 6 of the new file. The text to be deleted is displayed on the next line.

- A line was added to the new file. The **21a22** message says to add a new line after line 21 of the old file. The text to be added is displayed on the final line of the output.

Two useful flags you can specify when comparing files are **-b** (ignore blanks) and **-i** (ignore case). You can use them separately or in combination. The ignore blanks feature is especially useful when you're comparing the source code for two programs, since indentation changes are rarely significant. For example, here's how you might compare two program files, **ur2cool.c** and **ur2cool.backup**:

```
diff -b -i ur2cool.c ur2cool.backup
```

Don't worry if you have some difficulty understanding the output of the **diff** command. It's cryptic because it was designed to be used by computers, not humans. (Some source-code control systems used by programmers use **diff** to keep a record of the changes made to a program over time.)

Do pay attention, though, to the less-than and greater-than indicators to see at a glance what was added or deleted; and be happy if you manage to get a general feeling for the ways the files differ.

REMIND ME AT SIX

Linux provides a really handy way to schedule future events so they run automatically. You can use the **at** command to schedule reminders or administrative tasks or to run a command later when the computer won't be busy. After you specify the time (and optional date) for your event, **at** prompts you for the command to run. After entering your command, press **CTRL-D** to finish. Here are some examples:

```
at 8:15am Jul 14
echo "Remember to call Ruth about the Amalgamated Contract!"
^D
at midnight Friday
cp project/source backup
^D
```

To find out what events you have already scheduled with **at**, enter the following:

```
at -l

1 1999-07-14 08:15 a
2 1999-07-16 00:00 a
```

To cancel an event scheduled with **at**, use the **atrm** command and a job number (which you can find in the first column of the **at -l** results). For example, to cancel job number 2 you would enter:

```
atrm 2
```

LINK FILES TOGETHER

You can link files together in two ways: with hard links or symbolic links.

CREATING A HARD LINK

The **ln** command lets a file on your disk be accessed with more than one file name by *hard-linking* a new file name to it. When you hard-link a file, you create a new file name and connect it with the original file. Hard-linking can let two users share the same file or provide a more convenient way of referencing files buried deep in a series of directories.

Here's an example. Suppose hermie and sigmund are working on the Top Secret Snowgun Project, and the formula for the Snowgun is stored in **/home/hermie/projects/snowgun/formula.txt**. Sigmund doesn't want to type that long, ugly file name every time he needs to update the file, so he creates a hard link to the file, like this:

```
ln /home/hermie/projects/snowgun/formula.txt sgformula
```

The preceding command links the file name **sgformula** to the file **formula.txt** contained at the end of that directory string. There's still only one copy of the snowgun formula (**formula.txt**) on the disk, but now sigmund can access it quickly with the name **sgformula** (assuming hermie gives him write permission to the file). Interestingly, if hermie deletes his **projects/snowgun/formula.txt** file, Linux will not remove the file from the file system because sigmund still has a link to it.

Think of the **ln** command as a way of creating a kind of nickname for a file. By the way, there is no parallel to this file-linking concept in the DOS world—you'd have to create a second copy of the file and keep the various copies in synch manually to get a similar result.

CREATING A SYMBOLIC LINK

The type of link we just created is called a hard link. There's another type called a *symbolic link*. Symbolic links (also called *symlinks*) work like hard links, but you can do a bit more with them. If you want to create a link to a directory (as opposed to a file), you must create a symlink. Symlinks are also required when linking to a file on a different disk partition or on a network.

To create a symbolic link, add the **-s** parameter to the **ln** command, like this:

```
ln -s /dev/fd0 A:
ln -s /etc/httpd/conf web
```

The first example allows you to access the floppy drive as drive A, just like in DOS, and the second creates a directory entry called **web** that can be used instead of /**etc**/**httpd**/**conf**.

WRAPPING UP

Learning Unix would be hard if you tried to master everything it has to offer all at once. But then so would DOS, and especially Windows. In fact, Windows' configuration files are more complex than Unix's. When you first learned DOS, there were only a dozen or so commands that you needed to understand—you could learn the rest as needed. It's the same with Unix. You need learn more only if you want to get more out of Unix.

Also, though you may not realize it, DOS is a kind of subset of Unix. DOS adopted from Unix the idea of a hierarchical file system, as well as the concepts of filters and piping. Moreover, each command that you learned in DOS has a direct parallel in Unix. (See Appendix B, "DOS and Unix Equivalencies.")

Take a little time to play with each of the commands discussed in this chapter, and you'll be well on your way to becoming a proficient Linux user. If you want to dig deeper, use the **man** command to get more detailed information on any command. I've listed the most common usage and options for these commands, but there's more if you care to explore.

TEXT EDITORS

F or most people, a text editor is the most basic and often-used computer tool. If you want to write a letter, send email, or compose a computer program, you use a text editor to enter your prose and save it in a file.

Although they perform the same basic functions, a text editor and a word processor (such as Word or WordPerfect) are slightly different in nature. In general, a text editor is like a very basic word processing program—it doesn't offer fancy stuff like fonts, underlining, and boldface. A text editor is useful for entering, updating, and storing text, but you need a word processor to create really sharp-looking documents.

Aside from their differing looks and abilities, text editors and word processors store data in different formats. Text editors store files in plain-text (ASCII) format, which means the files can be read by any other text editor or program, whereas word processors store them in specially coded formats that can be read only by that program. (Actually, most of the popular word processors can read files created by other programs, but you don't always get the same formatting.) In the DOS/Windows environment, the Edit and Notepad programs are simple text editors, whereas Microsoft Word is a true word processor.

This chapter focuses on three nongraphical Linux text editors (vi, Emacs, and Pico) and two that run under X Windows (Gnotepad+ and gEdit), which can be used to create and modify files. You'll get an introduction to each one here, and then you can decide which one is best for you.

THE VI EDITOR

The vi editor comes with every version of Linux or Unix. It's a terribly unfriendly beast of an editor, but you should know about it because someday you're likely to find yourself on a system where you have no other choice but to use it. A friend of mine calls vi the Heart of Evil, but that might be just a bit harsh—you decide.

Using vi is similar to using other editors in that you can see your file on the screen (this is not the case with a line editor, for example), move from point to point in the file, and make changes. But that's where the similarities end. Cryptic commands, a frustrating user interface, and the absence of prompts can all drive you up a wall. Still, if you focus on a few basics, you'll get the job done.

COMMAND AND INPUT MODE

The hardest thing to understand about vi is the concept of modes. When using vi, you're always in either Command or Input mode. Unfortunately, there's no clue as to which mode is currently active. In Command mode, you can move the cursor, search for characters, and delete existing text. But to enter or edit new text, you have to switch to Input mode.

When you start vi, you're in Command mode. To enter Input mode, type the letter **a** (lowercase only) to signal that you want to add text after the cursor position. Press **ESC** to switch back to Command mode at any time.

Here's how to create a file from scratch using vi. To start, create a new file named **cow.joke** by typing

```
vi cow.joke
```

You'll see a screen that looks like Figure 7-1.

```
|
~
~
~
~
~
~
~
~
"cow.joke" [New file]
```

Figure 7-1: *The vi editor screen*

ADDING NEW TEXT TO YOUR FILE

Your cursor (the vertical bar at the top of Figure 7-1) is in the upper-left corner of the screen, and the message at the bottom tells you that a new file called **cow.joke** was just created. The tilde characters in the first column are just placeholders for empty lines.

Now press the letter **a** to enter Input mode and type the lines shown in Figure 7-2. Press **ENTER** at the end of each line to go on to the next.

```
Jane: Knock, knock...
Bill: Who's there?
Jane: The Interrupting Cow.
Bill: The Interrupting Cow wh...
Jane: MOOOOOO!
|
~
~
~
~
"cow.joke" [New file]
```

Figure 7-2: *Creating a file with vi*

SAVING YOUR WORK

So far, so good—let's save this little masterpiece. You're still in Input mode, so press **ESC** to enter Command mode; then type **ZZ** (to put your file to sleep). You won't see any Z's on the screen, but after you've entered the second Z, your file will disappear, your Linux command prompt will return, and you'll see this message, indicating that your file was successfully saved:

```
"cow.joke" 6 lines, 113 characters.
```

Congratulations—you've just survived your first encounter with vi. You know that the **a** command switches to Input mode, **ESC** gets you back to Command mode, and **ZZ** saves the file, but you'll have to expand this limited repertoire to get any real work done.

COMMON VI COMMANDS

Have a look at this list of common vi commands (there are many more, but these will at least allow you to get some basic work done). Then we'll do one more exercise before moving on.

■ *NOTE:* *As with all of Linux, vi commands are case sensitive.*

POSITIONING THE CURSOR

→	Move cursor one space right.
←	Move cursor one space left.
↑	Move cursor up one line.
↓	Move cursor down one line.
CTRL-F	Move forward one screen.
CTRL-B	Move backward one screen.
$	Move cursor to end of line.
^	Move cursor to beginning of line.
:1	Move to first line of file.
:$	Move to last line of file.
/	Search for a character string.
?	Reverse search for a character string.
x	Delete the character at the cursor position.
dd	Delete the current line.
p	Paste data that was cut with x or dd commands.
u	Undo.

ENTERING INPUT MODE

a	Add text after the cursor.
i	Insert text before the cursor.
R	Replace text starting at the cursor.
o	Insert a new line after the current one.

Entering Command Mode

ESC	Switch from Input mode to Command mode.

Exiting or Saving Your File

:w	Write file to disk, without exiting editor.
zz	Save the file and exit.
:q!	Quit without saving.

Trying Out Some vi Commands

Here's another example to try out some of the vi commands. Enter the following command to fire up vi again, and you should see the file as we left it in Figure 6-2:

```
vi cow.joke
```

Changing Text

Let's change Bill's name to Biff on the second line. To do so, use the arrow keys to position your cursor on the third character of line 2 (the letter "l" in Bill); then press **x** twice (to delete the two l's). Now press **i** (to enter Input mode) and then type **ff** to complete the change from Bill to Biff.

■ *TIP: Be careful about pressing the arrow keys while you're in Input mode. in some versions of vi you can position the cursor only in Command mode. Yuck.*

You could also have used the **R** command to do this job of replacing text, so use it to change the other Bill now. Press **ESC** to enter Command mode; then type **/Bill** to search for the word *Bill*. The cursor should move to line 4, right to where Bill is located.

Now position your cursor on the third character (the letter "l"), press **R** to replace the characters, and type **ff**. Both Bills should now be Biffs.

Adding and Deleting Lines

Here's how to add or delete a line. Press **ESC** to enter Command mode; then press the **o** key to add a new line. You're in Input mode again, so you can type whatever you like on this new line. But that would ruin the joke, so delete this new line by pressing **ESC** and then entering the **dd** command. The line you just added should go away.

Quitting without Saving Your Changes

Hmmm. . . . "Biff" just doesn't have that wholesome ring to it, so let's forget about all the changes we've made in this editing session and exit vi without saving the file. Make sure you're in Command mode, enter the **:q!** command, and then press **ENTER**. Your Linux prompt should return, and the **cow.joke** file will be just as it was before.

Parting Words about vi

Using vi can be frustrating, but it really isn't rocket science once you get used to the concept of the two modes and get the hang of when it's okay to move your cursor or enter text. If you're ever unsure about which mode you're in, simply press **ESC** once or twice, and you can be sure you're in Command mode.

There are some powerful (but arcane) commands that diehard vi users use to get things done quickly in this relic-of-the-sixties text editor. The **man vi** command will tell you a lot more about vi if you decide you want to become proficient.

The Usenet newsgroup comp.editors is a good place to discuss vi or ask questions. You can find the vi FAQ (Frequently Asked Questions) file on the Web at http://www.faqs.org/faqs/editor-faq/vi/.

The Emacs Editor

The Emacs editor is not part of Linux, but since it is one of the GNU utilities, it's on the CD that comes with this book. If you selected all the suggested packages when you installed Linux, Emacs should already be on your system. If not, you can install it by mounting the CD and running the **gnorpm** command after starting X Windows.

The Emacs editor is a lot easier to use than vi. There are no silly modes to trip you up—when you want to enter text, you just position the cursor and type. Gee, what a great idea. It also has built-in help.

But while Emacs is a vast improvement over vi, you'll still have to remember quite a few commands to be productive, and you'll probably get a little lost. If vi is a relic of the sixties, Emacs sports the cutting-edge technology of the early eighties. If you get into a situation where Emacs seems to be stuck, or if you don't know what to do, press **CTRL-G** and things will return to normal. (The **CTRL-G** key cancels the current operation in Emacs.)

Let's try creating a file from scratch using Emacs. To start, enter this command:

```
emacs bulb.joke
```

In response, you should see a screen that looks like Figure 7-3.

ADDING NEW TEXT TO YOUR FILE

Your cursor (the vertical bar in Figure 7-3) is in the upper-left corner of the screen, and the message at the bottom tells you that a new file called **bulb.joke** was just created. The body of the file is blank (no tildes as in the vi editor).

To enter new text, just start typing! There's no need to press any special keys first. Go ahead and enter the text shown in Figure 7-4. (Press **ENTER** at the end of each line.)

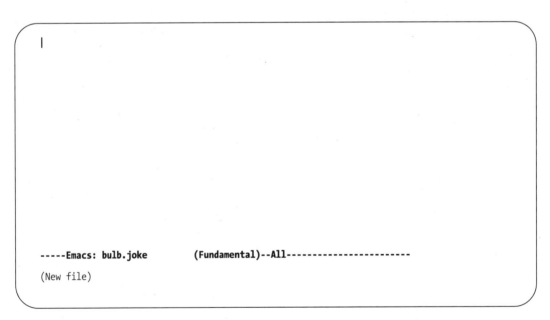

```
-----Emacs: bulb.joke        (Fundamental)--All-----------------------
(New file)
```

Figure 7-3: *Starting the Emacs editor*

```
Q: How many surrealists does it take to change a light bulb?

A: Two-one to hold the giraffe, and the other to fill the

   bathtub with brightly colored machine tools.




--**-Emacs: bulb.joke        (Fundamental)--All------------------------
```

Figure 7-4: *Entering text with Emacs*

SAVING YOUR WORK

To save your work without leaving Emacs, press **CTRL-X** (for exit) and then **CTRL-S** (for save). A message at the bottom of the screen should confirm that the file was written to disk. It's a good idea to save your work every few minutes, just so you don't lose it all if the system suddenly crashes.

To save your file and exit Emacs, press **CTRL-X** and then **CTRL-C**. A prompt like this should appear at the bottom of the screen:

```
Save file bulb.joke? (y, n, !, ., q, C-r or C-h)
```

Type the letter **y** to save your file and exit the editor. After leaving Emacs, you'll be back at the Linux command prompt. (I'll discuss the other choices later.)

COMMON EMACS COMMANDS

Have a look at this list of Emacs commands, and then we'll do one more exercise before moving on.

POSITIONING THE CURSOR

→	Move cursor one space right (also **CTRL-N**).
←	Move cursor one space left (also **CTRL-P**).
↑	Move cursor up one line (also **CTRL-F**).
↓	Move cursor down one line (also **CTRL-B**).
CTRL-V	Move forward one screen (also **PGUP**).
ESC-V	Move backward one screen (also **PGDN**).
ESC-<	Move to beginning of file.
ESC->	Move to end of file.
ESC-F	Move cursor to next word.
ESC-B	Move cursor back one word.
HOME	Move cursor to beginning of line (also **CTRL-A**).
END	Move cursor to end of line (also **CTRL-E**).
DELETE	Delete character at cursor (also **CTRL-D**).
CTRL-K	Delete to end of line.
CTRL-Y	Undelete the last thing you deleted.
CTRL-X U	Undo the last command.
CTRL-S	Perform a search (forward).
CTRL-R	Perform a search (backward).
CTRL-H	View online help.
CTRL-H T	View Emacs tutorial.

EXITING OR SAVING YOUR FILE

CTRL-X CTRL-S	Save your file and exit.
CTRL-X CTRL-C	Quit without saving.

Unlike vi commands, Emacs commands are not case sensitive, so whether you enter **CTRL-H** or **CTRL-h,** for example, you'll get the same result. There are many other Emacs commands, but the starter set shown here should be enough to get you rolling.

TRYING OUT SOME EMACS COMMANDS

Here's another example to let you try out some of these Emacs commands. Enter **emacs bulb.joke** to fire up Emacs again, and you should see the file as we left it in Figure 7-4.

Changing Text and Moving through Your Document

To change text that's already in the file, you first need to reach it. You can move through your file in various ways. The arrow keys provide the simplest way, and they work just like you'd expect them to—they move you character by character through your file.

If you want to jump to the beginning or end of the current line, use the **HOME** and **END** keys, respectively. You can jump from word to word using **ESC**-F and **ESC**-B, or you can scroll page by page using **CTRL**-V (next page) and **ESC**-V (previous page). On some keyboards, the **PGUP** and **PGDN** keys work, too.

Text that you enter is inserted to the left of the cursor, and any text to the right of cursor is pushed to the right as you type. You can use the **DEL** key (or **CTRL**-D) to delete one character at a time, or press **CTRL**-K to delete all characters from the cursor to the end of the line.

Searching for Text

When you're working in a big file, you'll often want to locate a certain string of text. You can either scroll through the file until your eye catches it, or you can use **CTRL**-S to search using Emacs' less-than-elegant search tool.

As soon as you press **CTRL**-S, you can start to enter the text you want to find, but don't type too fast! As you enter your search string, Emacs immediately moves the cursor to a word in the file that matches what you've entered so far, so if you type too fast, you may miss something.

Try it. Starting at the top of the file, press **CTRL**-S and then type the letter **b**. The cursor should jump to the word *bathtub* right away. If you now type an **r** after the b, Emacs searches for *br*, and the cursor should jump to the word *brightly*. You can search backward, too, by using **CTRL**-R instead of **CTRL**-S.

Adding and Deleting Lines

Let's practice adding and deleting lines now. To add a new line to your file, move the cursor to the end of a line (press **END** or use the right-arrow key), then press **ENTER**. A new blank line should appear after the current line. Pressing **ENTER** with the cursor at the beginning or end of a line adds a new blank line before the current line; pressing **ENTER** with the cursor anywhere else on a line splits the line at that point.

To delete a line, move to the beginning of the line (with the **HOME** key) and press **CTRL**-K. The line will become blank, but it will not go away. To delete the blank line from the file, press **CTRL-K** again or press the **DEL** key.

Cutting and Pasting with Emacs

If you ever want to move a block of text from one spot in your file to another, you can use **CTRL-K** (kill) along with **CTRL-Y** (yank) to get the job done. When you press **CTRL-Y**, the last thing you "killed" with **CTRL-K** will be yanked back into the file. So to move a block of text, just kill one or more lines with **CTRL-K**, then put your cursor at the spot where you'd like to place the text and press **CTRL-Y** to yank it back.

For example, here's how to move the first line of the **bulb.joke** file to the end. With your cursor on the first character of the first line, press **CTRL-K** twice. (Line 1 disappears.) Press the down arrow twice to move your cursor to the third line of the file, which is now blank. Press **CTRL-Y** once to paste the deleted line at line 3 and then press **CTRL-Y** again.

You should now have two copies of the deleted line at the end of your file, which should look like Figure 7-5.

```
A: Two--one to hold the giraffe, and the other to fill the
   bathtub with brightly colored machine tools.
Q: How many surrealists does it take to change a light bulb?
Q: How many surrealists does it take to change a light bulb?




--**-Emacs: bulb.joke      (Fundamental)--All----------------------
```

Figure 7-5: *Entering text with Emacs*

Quitting without Saving Your Changes

To leave Emacs without saving your changes, press **CTRL-X** and then **CTRL-C**. A prompt like this will appear at the bottom of the screen:

```
Save file bulb.joke? (y, n, !, ., q, C-r or C-h)
```

Press **n** and then answer **yes** when Emacs asks:

```
Modified buffers exist; exit anyway? (yes or no)
```

Your Linux prompt will return, and the **bulb.joke** file will be just as it was before you started editing.

Parting Words about Emacs

We haven't even scratched the surface of what you can do with the Emacs editor. As its name suggests, you can write your own macros to add functionality to the editor or to automate repetitive editing tasks.

Take the time to go through the Emacs tutorial (accessed by pressing **CTRL-H T**) to get an idea of all the things you can do with it. Although it's not easy to learn all the various CTRL and ESC commands, if you're a programmer (or even if you dabble), Emacs' customizability makes it your best bet as a text editor.

The Usenet newsgroup comp.emacs is a good place to discuss Emacs or ask questions. You can find the Emacs FAQ file online at ftp://rtfm.mit.edu/pub/usenet/comp.emacs.

THE PICO EDITOR

Pico, short for Pine Composer, started life as the built-in editor for the Pine email program. Lots of people use Pico as a text editor because they also use the friendly Pine program for email.

The Pico text editor doesn't have a lot of fancy features, but it's a welcome alternative to the vi or Emacs editors because learning it is quick and easy. Cursor movement and text entry are straightforward, and—best of all—you don't have to learn any arcane commands: all commands are listed in a handy menu at the bottom of the screen.

To start Pico, enter a command like this:

```
pico bulb.joke
```

In response, you should see the file **bulb.joke** displayed on your screen in Pico, ready for editing, as shown in Figure 7-6.

```
UW PICO(tm) 4.3                                    File: bulb.joke


Q: How many surrealists does it take to screw in a light bulb?
A: Two--one to hold the giraffe, and the other to fill the
   bathtub with brightly colored machine tools.







                         [ Read 3 lines ]
^G Help   ^O WriteOut  ^R Read File ^Y Prev Pg  ^K Cut Text   ^C Cur Pos
^X Exit   ^J Justify   ^W Where is  ^V Next Pg  ^U UnCut Text ^T To Spell
```

Figure 7-6: *The Pico editor*

GETTING AROUND IN PICO

Before we explore Pico commands, here's a summary of how to navigate your way around a file in Pico.

POSITIONING THE CURSOR

→	Move cursor one space right (also **CTRL-N**).
←	Move cursor one space left (also **CTRL-P**).
↑	Move cursor up one line (also **CTRL-F**).
↓	Move cursor down one line (also **CTRL-B**).
DELETE	Delete character at cursor (also **CTRL-D**).

CTRL-Y	Move backward one screen (**F7**).
CTRL-V	Move forward one screen (also **F8**).
CTRL-A	Move cursor to beginning of line.
CTRL-E	Move cursor to end of line.

With the exception of the CTRL-Y (page down) command, text entry and cursor handling are identical to that of the Emacs editor, so we won't cover that again here.

THE PICO MENU

When you start Pico you'll see this menu of commands:

```
^G Help   ^O WriteOut  ^R Read File ^Y Prev Pg  ^K Cut Text   ^C Cur Pos
^X Exit   ^J Justify   ^W Where is  ^V Next Pg  ^U UnCut Text ^T To Spell
```

Here's a list of what they mean. Note that the circumflex (^) stands for CTRL.

PICO COMMANDS

CTRL-G	Display help screens.
CTRL-O	Write file to disk.
CTRL-R	Read another file.
CTRL-K	Cut line or marked text.
CTRL-C	Display cursor position.
CTRL-X	Exit from Pico.
CTRL-J	Reflow the paragraph.
CTRL-W	Search for text.
CTRL-U	Paste (uncut) text.
CTRL-T	Run spelling checker.

TRYING OUT SOME PICO COMMANDS

Now let's try out some Pico commands.

SAVING AND EXITING

Saving your file is easy with Pico—just press **CTRL-O** to write your file to disk and remain in the editor, or press **CTRL-X** and respond **y** to the **Save Modified Buffer?** prompt to save and exit.

If you want to exit from Pico without saving your file, press **CTRL-X** and respond **n** to the **Save Modified Buffer?** prompt.

INSERTING ANOTHER FILE

To insert another file into the one you're currently editing, position the cursor where you want to insert the file, press **CTRL-R,** and enter the name of the file you wish to insert at the prompt that appears on your screen:

```
Insert file from home directory: _____
^G Get Help   ^T To Files
^C Cancel
```

If you can't remember the name of the file to insert, press **CTRL-T** to display a list of all your files. If you ultimately decide not to insert it, press **CTRL-C** to cancel.

CUTTING AND PASTING WITH PICO

If all you want to do is cut and paste a line of text, you can use **CTRL-K** to delete the current line and **CTRL-U** to paste it somewhere else. Pico also lets you cut and paste blocks of text. Put your cursor on the word *light* on the first line of the **bulb.joke** file and press **CTRL-^** (the circumflex is the shifted **6** key).

Nothing happens right away, but as you move the cursor, it highlights a block of text. Move the cursor to the end of the word *giraffe* on the next line—your file should look like Figure 7-7.

Once you've marked a block of text, **CTRL-K** acts a bit differently from before. Instead of deleting the entire line where the cursor is located, it deletes the highlighted block. You can then use **CTRL-U** to paste the deleted block elsewhere.

```
UW PICO(tm) 4.3                                   File: bulb.joke


Q: How many surrealists does it take to screw in a light bulb?

A: Two--one to hold the giraffe, and the other to fill the
   bathtub with brightly colored machine tools.
```

Figure 7-7: *Marking text for cutting and pasting*

> ■ *TIP: You don't have to paste the deleted text right away, or ever. **CTRL-K** can be used simply as a handy way of deleting unwanted text. (Deleted text goes to an invisible clipboard, and it disappears once you delete more text.)*

PICO BELLS AND WHISTLES

Pico has a few nifty features you might not expect to find in a simple text editor. For example, **CTRL-J** will justify the sentences in the current paragraph. Type a bunch of short sentences on separate lines and try it. If you don't like the results, **CTRL-U** will undo the operation.

Pico also has a built-in spelling checker you can call up with **CTRL-T** from within a file. If Pico doesn't find any dubious words in the current document, nothing much happens except that the message "Done checking spelling" appears at the bottom of the screen.

And if you'd like to know exactly where you are within a file (on which line and at which character), or if you'd like a quick character or line count, press **CTRL-C** and look in the message area at the bottom of the screen for something like this:

```
line 2 of 4 (50%), character 65 of 173 (37%)
```

PARTING WORDS ABOUT PICO

Pico is my personal favorite in text editors because it's easy to use and starts quickly. Pico is under constant development at the University of Washington. For more information, you can visit the Pine Information Center on the Web at http://www.washington.edu/pine. You can even download the latest version of Pico for Linux there.

THE GNOTEPAD+ EDITOR

The Gnotepad+ program (see Figure 7-8) is a text editor for the X Windows environment. It's similar to the Notepad program found on Microsoft Windows systems, but it has many added features, including these:

- Multiple files in multiple windows
- Unlimited undo and redo capabilities

- Recent-document menu

- Document autosave

- Ability to save window size and position

- Configurable toolbars and document tabs

You may find it convenient to use a graphical text editor, since it allows you to manipulate text using the mouse, and Gnotepad+ offers two toolbars with buttons that can speed up common operations such as opening and closing files, printing, text entry, and cutting and pasting.

To start Gnotepad+, enter the command

gnp

from a shell prompt, or select the **GNOME Foot • Applications • Gnotepad+** menu item. You can also add a Gnotepad+ button to your GNOME taskbar by choosing **Gnome Foot • Panel • Add new launcher**. Specify **gnp** as the program name, and pick an icon you like.

Additionally, you can define Gnotepad+ as the default editor to be started when you double-click a text file in File Manager. Choose **Gnome Toolbox • Gnome Edit Properties** and specify **gnp** as the program name.

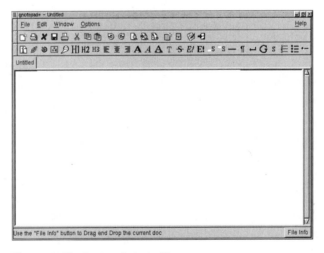

Figure 7-8: *The Gnotepad+ text editor*

USING GNOTEPAD+

Using Gnotepad+ is very simple—just start typing. If you make a mistake, use the **BACKSPACE** or **DELETE** key. You can always use the mouse to position the text cursor or mark text for cut-and-paste operations. If you've used Windows Notepad or any graphical word processor, you will have no trouble with Gnotepad+.

Let's quickly run through the drop-down menus corresponding to the File, Edit, Window, and Options menu items.

The File menu (see Figure 7-9) has the expected file open, close, save, and print functions, with a few extras. The "Open Recent" function displays a list of recently edited files so you can quickly reopen one of them. The "View HTML" function applies only to HTML source-code files; it shows you a quick-but-rough view of how the HTML will look as a Web page, or it launches the Netscape browser to render the page.

The Edit menu (see Figure 7-10) offers all the usual cut, copy, and paste functions, along with unlimited Undo, Redo, and Replace options. Also of note is the "Insert Shell Output" option, which allows you to run a Linux command and pipe its output directly to the open

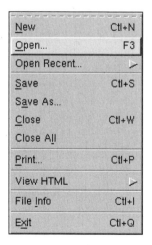

Figure 7.9: *The Gnotepad+ File menu*

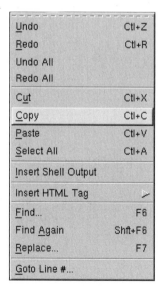

Figure 7-10: *The Gnotepad+ Edit menu*

file at the cursor location; an example might be capturing a list of the file names in a certain directory by piping in the results of an **ls** command. The "Insert HTML Tag" option displays a list of HTML tags and will insert the selected tag at the cursor location (this is equivalent to using the HTML button bar, described later in this section).

The Window menu (see Figure 7-11) helps you manage multiple open files. You can use the "Doc List" option to display a list of currently open documents. The "Messages" option is not terribly useful to most usersæit displays a log of actions taken during the editing session.

The Options menu (see Figure 7-12) allows you to configure the operation of the editor to suit your own preferences. The "Message Bar" option toggles the message line at the bottom of the screen on or off. Leave it on, unless you really need a tiny bit of extra viewable screen space. The "Wordwrap" option toggles word wrapping at the end of a line; oddly, the default setting is off. The "Doc Tabs" and "Toolbar" options allow you to fiddle with the appearance and placement of the document tabs and toolbars that normally appear at the top of the screen. (Document tabs are useful when you have multiple open files and are used to quickly switch among them.) The "Preferences" option allows you to specify settings that will be applied each time the editor is started, such as toolbar appearance, fonts, screen colors, and autosave frequency.

USING GNOTEPAD+ FOR HTML FILES

Gnotepad+ has a special toolbar that is designed to speed up the creation of HTML files (the language used to code Web pages). Each button on the toolbar inserts HTML tag(s) in the document at the cursor

Figure 7-11: *Gnotepad+ Edit menu*

Figure 7-12: *The Gnotepad+ Options menu*

location. Place the mouse pointer over a button on the lower toolbar, and a small pop-up help window will show what that button does.

In Figure 7-13, I've created a very basic HTML file using just ten mouse clicks. All of the HTML tags (the uppercase text enclosed in < > symbols) were entered automatically, and I had to type only the text that will appear on the Web page.

MORE ABOUT GNOTEPAD+

Gnotepad+ is free software developed and distributed under the GNU General Public License, which means you can view the source code and contribute your own updates to the developer. The program is written and maintained by Andy Kahn, who has a Gnotepad+ Web site at http://ack.netpedia.net/gnp/.

THE gEDIT EDITOR

The gEdit editor (see Figure 7-14) is a another text editor designed for the X Windows GNOME environment. It supports user-written plug-ins, which allow gEdit to be extended to support new features while keeping the size of the core program small. It also supports multiple documents and, of course, standard text-editor functions such as search

Figure 7-13: *Creating an HTML file with Gnotepad+*

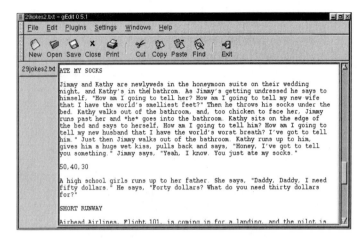

Figure 7-14: *The gEdit editor*

and replace, a toolbar, printing, cutting, copying, and pasting. If you are a programmer, you may find gEdit preferable to Gnotepad+ because of the programming plug-ins available for gEdit.

To start gEdit, enter the command

gedit

from a shell prompt, or select the **GNOME Foot • Applications • gEdit** menu item. You can also add a gEdit button to your GNOME taskbar by choosing **Gnome Foot • Panel • Add new launcher**. Specify **gedit** as the program name, and pick an icon you like.

USING GEDIT

Using gEdit is not much different than using Gnotepad+ or other graphical editors. Instead of boring you with yet another "here's how to use this editor" sermon, let's focus on some of the more interesting plug-ins available for gEdit. The plug-ins menu is shown in Figure 7-15.

The **Spell Check** plug-in (see Figure 7-16) looks for misspelled words and displays possible alternatives. For some reason, I couldn't get the "Replace" button to replace the incorrect word in the file with the selected alternative. Your mileage may vary.

The **Reverse** plug-in reverses the text in the current document. The only thing good about this is that you can unreverse the text by running it again. Actually, this plug-in is meant to serve as a tutorial for people interested in writing plug-ins. You can find more about writing plug-ins at the gEdit Web site mentioned at the end of this section.

The **Project Manager** plug-in allows you to manage programming projects, displaying a tree of the C source-code files and the header include files used by the source file. Double-clicking on the source file or a header file will open it into gEdit.

The **View in Browser** plug-in renders and displays the current HTML document.

The **Encryption** plug-in encrypts or decrypts the current document using the ROT13 encryption algorithm, which is a simple character-substitution scheme. Don't use this for serious encryption needs. Instead, use the PGP program discussed in Chapter 11, "Compression, Encoding, and Encryption." Better yet, write a PGP plug-in for gEdit and share it with the world!

The **Email** plug-in will email the current document to any email address. A dialog box lets you fill in the From, To, and Subject lines before sending.

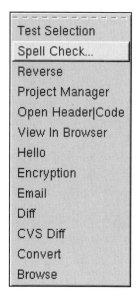

Figure 7-15: *The gEdit Plugins menu*

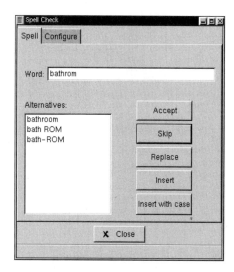

Figure 7-16: *The gEdit Spell Check plug-in*

The **Diff** and **CVS Diff** plug-ins are for programmers who want to compare two files using the **diff** command. (See Chapter 6, "Important Linux Commands," for more about the **diff** command.)

MORE ABOUT GEDIT

The gEdit editor is free software developed and distributed under the GNU General Public License, which means you can view the source code and contribute your own updates to the developers. There is a gEdit Web site at http:/gedit.pn.org/.

SLICING AND DICING

One of the nice things about Linux is that it comes with a bunch of tools to help you manipulate files and data without writing programs. For example, if you want to search inside a bunch of files, pull out all lines that contain a certain keyword, sort those lines, eliminate duplicates, and then print just the third column of each line, it's really not much trouble using the tools described in this chapter.

Writing a C program to do that would not be a trivial exercise, even for an experienced programmer. But you can use these slicing-and-dicing tools like building blocks to manipulate data and produce reports without a computer science degree.

Following is a description of how each tool works, and at the end of the chapter, you'll find some tips on how to combine them into even more powerful commands.

THE HEAD COMMAND

The **head** command displays the first few lines at the top of a file. It can be useful when you want a quick peek at a large file, as an alternative to opening the file with a text editor. By default, **head** will show the first ten lines of a file, but you can also tell it how many lines to display. Here are a couple of examples:

`head some.file`	Show first ten lines of **some.file**
`head -5 some.file`	Show first five lines of **some.file**

THE TAIL COMMAND

The **tail** command displays the last few lines of a file. Like **head**, it can save you time because it's a lot quicker than calling up a file with a text editor and scrolling all the way down to the bottom. By default, tail will show the last ten lines of a file, but you can also tell it how many lines to display:

`tail some.file`	Show last ten lines of **some.file**
`tail -3 some.file`	Show last three lines of **some.file**

Here's a practical example of how to use the **tail** command. Many Linux programs put diagnostic messages in the **/var/syslog/messages** file when they run, so this file can get pretty large after a while. To see if your most recent command issued any messages, look at the tail end of this file by entering the **tail /var/syslog/messages** command.

THE SORT COMMAND

The **sort** command sorts a file according to fields—the individual pieces of data on each line. By default, **sort** assumes that the fields are just words separated by blanks, but you can specify an alternative field delimiter if you want (such as commas or colons). Output from **sort** is printed to the screen, unless you redirect it to a file.

If you had a file like the one shown here containing information on people who contributed to your presidential reelection campaign, for example, you might want to sort it by last name, donation amount, or location. (Using a text editor, enter those three lines into a file and save it with **donor.data** as the file name.)

```
Bay Ching 500000 China
Jack Arta 250000 Indonesia
Cruella Lumper 725000 Malaysia
```

Let's take this sample donors file and sort it according to the donation amount. The following shows the command to sort the file on the second field (last name) and the output from the command:

```
sort +1 -2 donors.data
Jack Arta 250000 Indonesia
Bay Ching 500000 China
Cruella Lumper 725000 Malaysia
```

The syntax of the **sort** command is pretty strange, but if you study the following examples, you should be able to adapt one of them for your own use. The general form of the sort command is

```
sort <flags> <sort fields> <file name>
```

The most common flags are as follows:

-f   Make all lines uppercase before sorting (so "Bill" and "bill" are treated the same).

-r   Sort in reverse order (so "Z" starts the list instead of "A").

-n   Sort a column in numerical order.

-t*x*   Use *x* as the field delimiter (replace *x* with a comma or other character).

-u   Suppress all but one line in each set of lines with equal sort fields (so if you sort on a field containing last names, only one "Smith" will appear even if there are several).

Specify the sort keys like this:

+*m*   Start at the first character of the *m*+1th field.

-*n*   End at the last character of the *n*th field (if -*N* omitted, assume the end of the line).

Looks weird, huh? Let's look at a few more examples with the sample **company.data** file shown here, and you'll get the hang of it. (Each line of the file contains four fields: first name, last name, serial number, and department name.)

```
Jan Itorre 406378 Sales
Jim Nasium 031762 Marketing
Mel Ancholie 636496 Research
Ed Jucacion 396082 Sales
```

To sort the file on the third field (serial number) in reverse order and save the results in **sorted.data**, use this command:

```
sort -r +2 -3 company.data > sorted.data
Mel Ancholie 636496 Research
Jan Itorre 406378 Sales
Ed Jucacion 396082 Sales
Jim Nasium 031762 Marketing
```

Now let's look at a situation where the fields are separated by colons instead of spaces. In this case, we will use the **-t:** flag to tell the **sort** command how to find the fields on each line. Let's start with this file:

```
Itorre, Jan:406378:Sales
Nasium, Jim:031762:Marketing
Ancholie, Mel:636496:Research
Jucacion, Ed:396082:Sales
```

To sort the file on the second field (serial number), use this command:

```
sort -t: +1 -2 company.data
Nasium, Jim:031762:Marketing
Jucacion, Ed:396082:Sales
Itorre, Jan:406378:Sales
Ancholie, Mel:636496:Research
```

To sort the file on the third field (department name) and suppress the duplicates, use this command:

```
sort -t: -u +2 company.data
Nasium, Jim:031762:Marketing
Ancholie, Mel:636496:Research
Itorre, Jan:406378:Sales
```

(Note that the line for Ed Jucacion did not print because he's in Sales and we asked the command (with the **-u** flag) to suppress lines that were the same in the sort field.)

There are lots of fancy (and a few obscure) things you can do with the **sort** command. If you need to do any sorting that's not quite as straightforward as these examples, try the **man sort** command for more information.

THE UNIQ COMMAND

The **uniq** command reads the input file and compares adjacent lines. Any line that is the same as the one before it will be discarded. In other words, duplicates are discarded, leaving only the unique lines in the file.

Let's say you're a publisher with an inventory of all your books in the **my.books** file shown here:

```
Atopic Dermatitis for Dummies
Atopic Dermatitis for Dummies
Chronic Rhinitis Unleashed
Chronic Rhinitis Unleashed
Chronic Rhinitis Unleashed
Learn Nasal Endoscopy in 21 Days
```

To remove all the duplicates from the list of books, use this command:

```
uniq my.books
Atopic Dermatitis for Dummies
Chronic Rhinitis Unleashed
Learn Nasal Endoscopy in 21 Days
```

If you want to print only the book titles that are *not* duplicated (to find out which books you have one copy of), add the **-u** flag, like this:

```
uniq -u my.books
Learn Nasal Endoscopy in 21 Days
```

Conversely, you might want to exclude the titles that appear only once. If so, add the **-d** flag, like this:

```
uniq -d my.books
Atopic Dermatitis for Dummies
Chronic Rhinitis Unleashed
```

Now let's take inventory. To summarize the list of books and add a count of the number of times each one appears in the list, add the **-c** flag, like this:

```
uniq -c my.books
2 Atopic Dermatitis for Dummies
3 Chronic Rhinitis Unleashed
1 Learn Nasal Endoscopy in 21 Days
```

Note that the **uniq** command does not sort the input file, so you may want to use the **sort** command to prepare the data for **uniq** in advance. (See the end of this chapter for an example.)

Here's a recap of the flags you can use with the **uniq** command:

-u Print only lines that appear once in the input file.

-d Print only the lines that appear more than once in the input file.

-c Precede each output line with a count of the number of times it was found.

THE CUT COMMAND

The **cut** command takes a vertical slice of a file, printing only the specified columns or fields. Like the **sort** command, the **cut** command defines a field as a word set off by blanks, unless you specify your own delimiter. It's easiest to think of a column as just the *n*th character on each line. In other words, "column 5" consists of the fifth character of each line.

Consider a slight variation on the **company.data** file we've been playing with in this chapter:

```
406378:Sales:Itorre:Jan
031762:Marketing:Nasium:Jim
636496:Research:Ancholie:Mel
396082:Sales:Jucacion:Ed
```

If you want to print just columns 1 to 6 of each line (the employee serial numbers), use the **-c1-6** flag, as in this command:

```
cut -c1-6 company.data
406378
031762
636496
396082
```

If you want to print just columns 4 and 8 of each line (the first letter of the department and the fourth digit of the serial number), use the **-c4,8** flag, as in this command:

```
cut -c4,8 company.data
3S
7M
4R
0S
```

And since this file obviously has fields delimited by colons, we can pick out just the last names by specifying the **-d:** and **-f3** flags, like this:

```
cut -d: -f3 company.data
Itorre
Nasium
Ancholie
Jucacion
```

Here is a summary of the most common flags for the **cut** command:

-c [*n* | *n,m* | *n-m*]   Specify a single column, multiple columns (separated by a comma), or range of columns (separated by a dash).

-f [*n* | *n,m* | *n-m*]   Specify a single field, multiple fields (separated by a comma), or range of fields (separated by a dash).

-d*c*   Specify the field delimiter.

-s   Suppress (don't print) lines not containing the delimiter.

THE GREP COMMAND

The **grep** command selects and prints lines from a file (or a bunch of files) that match a pattern. Let's say your friend Bill sent you an email recently with his phone number, and you want to call him ASAP to order some books. Instead of launching your email program and sifting through all the messages, you can scan your in-box file, like this:

```
grep 'number' /var/mail/hermie
can call No Starch Press at 800/420-7240. Office hours are
noted that recently, an alarming number of alien spacecrafts
among colleagues at a number of different organizations
```

Here, **grep** has pulled out just the lines that contain the word *number*. The first line is obviously what you were after, while the others just happened to match the pattern. The general form of the **grep** command is this:

```
grep <flags> <pattern> <files>
```

The most useful **grep** flags are shown here:

-i Ignore uppercase and lowercase when comparing.

-v Print only lines that do *not* match the pattern.

-c Print only a count of the matching lines.

-n Display the line number before each matching line.

When **grep** performs its pattern matching, it expects you to provide a *regular expression* for the pattern. Regular expressions can be very simple or quite complex, so we won't get into a lot of details here. Here are the most common types of regular expressions:

abc   Match lines containing the string "abc" anywhere.

^abc   Match lines starting with "abc."

abc$ Match lines ending with "abc."

a..c   Match lines containing "a" and "c" separated by any two characters (the dot matches any single character).

a.*c   Match lines containing "a" and "c" separated by any number of characters (the dot-asterisk means match zero or more characters).

Regular expressions also come into play when using vi, sed, awk, and other Unix commands. If you want to master Unix, take the time to understand regular expressions.

Here is a sample **poem.txt** file and some **grep** commands to demonstrate regular-expression pattern matching:

```
Mary had a little lamb
Mary fried a lot of spam
Jack ate a Spam sandwich
Jill had a lamb spamwich
```

To print all lines containing *spam* (respecting uppercase and lowercase), enter

```
grep 'spam' poem.txt
Mary fried a lot of spam
Jill had a lamb spamwich
```

To print all lines containing *spam* (ignoring uppercase and lowercase), enter

```
grep -i 'spam' poem.txt
Mary fried a lot of spam
Jack ate a Spam sandwich
Jill had a lamb spamwich
```

To print just the number of lines containing the word *spam* (ignoring uppercase and lowercase), enter

```
grep -i 'spam' poem.txt
3
```

To print all lines *not* containing *spam* (ignoring uppercase and low-ercase), enter

```
grep -i -v 'spam' poem.tx
Mary had a little lamb
```

To print all lines starting with *Mary*, enter

```
grep '^Mary' poem.txt
Mary had a little lamb
Mary fried a lot of spam
```

To print all lines ending with *ich*, enter

```
grep 'ich$' poem.txt
Jack ate a Spam sandwich
Jill had a lamb spamwich
```

To print all lines containing *had* followed by *lamb,* enter

```
grep 'had.*lamb' poem.txt
Mary had a little lamb
Jill had a lamb spamwich
```

If you want to learn more about regular expressions, start with the **man regexp** command. There's also a good book called *Mastering Regular Expressions,* by Jeffrey Friedl, published by O'Reilly & Associates.

THE SED COMMAND

You can use the **sed** command to change all occurrences of one string to another within a file, just like the search-and-replace feature of your word processor. The **sed** command can also delete a range of lines from a file. Since **sed** is a stream editor, it takes the file given as input and sends the output to the screen, unless you redirect output to a file. In other words, **sed** does not change the input file.

The general forms of the **sed** command are as follows:

Substitution sed 's/*<oldstring>*/*<newstring>*/g' *<file>*
Deletion   sed '*<start>*,*<end>*d' *<file>*

Let's start with a substitution example. If you want to change all occurrences of *lamb* to *ham* in the **poem.txt** file in the **grep** example, enter this:

```
sed 's/lamb/ham/g' poem.txt
Mary had a little ham
Mary fried a lot of spam
Jack ate a Spam sandwich
Jill had a ham spamwich
```

In the quoted string, the "s" means substitute, and the "g" means make a global change. You can also leave off the "g" (to change only the first occurrence on each line) or specify a number instead (to change the first *n* occurrences on each line).

Now let's try an example involving deletion of lines. The values for **start** and **end** can be either a line number or a pattern to match. All lines from the *start* line to the *end* line are removed from the output. This example will delete starting at line 2, up to and including line 3:

```
sed '2,3d' poem.txt
Mary had a little lamb
Jill had a lamb spamwich
```

This example will delete starting at line 1, up to and including the next line containing *Jack:*

```
sed '1,/Jack/d' poem.txt
Jill had a lamb spamwich
```

The most common use of **sed** is to change one string of text to another string of text. But I should mention that the strings that **sed** uses for search and delete are actually regular expressions. This means you can use pattern matching, just as with **grep**. Although you'll probably never need to do anything like this, here's an example anyway. To change any occurrences of **lamb** at the end of a line to **ham**, and save the results in a new file, enter this:

```
sed 's/lamb$/ham/g' poem.txt > new.file
```

Since we directed output to a file, **sed** didn't print anything on the screen. If you look at the contents of **new.file** it will show these lines:

```
Mary had a little ham
Mary fried a lot of spam
Jack ate a Spam sandwich
Jill had a lamb spamwich
```

Use the **man sed** command for more information on using **sed**.

THE AWK COMMAND

The **awk** command combines the functions of **grep** and **sed**, making it one of the most powerful Unix commands. Using **awk**, you can substitute words from an input file's lines for words in a template or perform calculations on numbers within a file. (In case you're wondering how **awk** got such an offbeat name, it's derived from the surnames of the three programmers who invented it.)

To use **awk**, you write a miniature program in a C-like language that transforms each line of the input file. We'll concentrate only on the **print** function of **awk**, since that's the most useful and the least confusing of all the things **awk** can do. The general form of the **awk** command is

```
awk <pattern> '{print <stuff>}' <file>
```

In this case, *stuff* is going to be some combination of text, special variables that represent each word in the input line, and perhaps a mathematical operator or two. As **awk** processes each line of the input file, each word on the line is assigned to variables named $1 (the first word), $2 (the second word), and so on. (The variable $0 contains the entire line.)

Let's start with a file, **words.data**, that contains these lines:

```
nail hammer wood
pedal foot car
clown pie circus
```

Now we'll use the print function in **awk** to plug the words from each input line into a template, like this:

```
awk '{print "Hit the",$1,"with your",$2}' words.data
Hit the nail with your hammer
Hit the pedal with your foot
Hit the clown with your pie
```

Say some of the data in your input file is numeric, as in the **grades.data** file shown here:

```
Rogers 87 100 95
Lambchop 66 89 76
Barney 12 36 27
```

You can perform calculations like this:

```
awk '{print "Avg for",$1,"is",($2+$3+$4)/3}' grades.data
Avg for Rogers is 94
Avg for Lambchop is 77
Avg for Barney is 25
```

So far, we haven't specified any value for **pattern** in these examples, but if you want to exclude lines from being processed, you can enter something like this:

```
awk /^clown/'{print "See the",$1,"at the",$3}' words.data
See the clown at the circus
```

Here, we told **awk** to consider only the input lines that start with *clown*. Note also that there is no space between the pattern and the print specifier. If you put a space there, **awk** will think the input file is '{print and will not work. But all this is just the tip of the **awk** iceberg— entire books have been written on this command. If you are a programmer, try the **man awk** command.

THE FIND COMMAND

The **find** command locates files in many different ways. Unlike the rest of the commands in this chapter, **find** does not look at the contents of a file—it only helps you find files that meet certain criteria, such as name, size, age, and type. The general form of the **find** command is

The starting point is the name of the directory where **find** should start looking for files. The **find** command examines all files in this directory (and any subdirectories) to see if they meet the specified search criteria. If any do, **find** performs the specified action on each found file. Here are some of the most useful search criteria options:

-name *pattern*	Find files with names that match the pattern.
-size [+|-] *n*	Find files larger or smaller than a certain size.
-atime [+|-] *n*	Find files accessed before or after a certain date.
-mtime [+|-] *n*	Find files modified before or after a certain date.
-type *filetype*	Find only regular files or only directories.

And here are the actions that can be applied to found files:

-print	Print just the names of matching files.
-ls	Print the names, dates, sizes, and so on of matching files.
-exec *command*	Execute a command with the file name as input.
-ok *command*	Same as -exec, but asks for confirmation first.

That all might look a bit confusing, so here are some examples to bring things down to earth. To find files (starting in the current directory) with names ending with *.data* and to print their names, try this

```
find . -name '*.data' -print
company.data
donor.data
grades.data
sorted.data
words.data
```

To find files larger than 40K and print the file names and details (use a minus sign instead of a plus sign to find files smaller than a certain size), issue this command:

```
find . -size +40k -ls
-rw-rw-r-- hermie users   56720 Jan 16 12:42 bigfile
-rw-rw-r-- hermie users  415206 Feb 27 21:37 largefile
-rw-rw-r-- hermie users  315428 Jan 07 05:23 hugefile
```

To find files ending with *.dat* that are smaller than 100K, enter

```
find . -name *.txt -size -100k -ls
-rw-rw-r-- hermie users   26720 Feb 06 23:52 recipes.txt
-rw-rw-r-- hermie users     506 Feb 18 18:45 poem.txt
```

To find files that have not been accessed for over 30 days and delete them (by sending their names to the **rm** command), enter

```
find . -atime +30 -exec rm {} \;
```

To find directories (starting in the **junk** directory) and conditionally delete them (by sending their names to the **rmdir** command), enter

```
find junk -type d -ok rmdir {} \;
```

Pipe Fitting

Throughout this chapter, we've discussed how to manipulate a file with many different tools. But you can use each of these tools in a more powerful way by combining them into pipelines. Back in Chapter 4, "Living in a Shell," you learned how to pump the output from one command to another by redirecting the input or output of those commands.

Following are several examples that show how to combine the power of the tools described in this chapter.

- To find files that have not been accessed for over 30 days and print the first five lines of each:

```
find . -atime +30 -exec head -5 {} \;
```

- To find out if a process named netscape is running:

```
ps | grep netscape
```

- To print only the second and third lines of a file:

```
head -3 some.file | tail -2
```

Note that the usage changes slightly when a command is in the second or subsequent stages of a pipeline. No input file is specified because the previous stage feeds the command.

At the beginning of this chapter, I said that it would be no problem to search within a bunch of files, pull out all lines that contain a certain keyword, sort those lines, eliminate duplicates, and then print just the third column of each line. Here's proof that you can do it all on one line:

```
grep 'stuff' *.data | sort +1 -2 | uniq | cut -f3
```

Seems almost too easy, doesn't it? Beats the heck out of writing a program several hundred lines long if you want to run it only once! Now let's use the rest of the commands from this chapter in another pipeline. Start by creating the file **odds.ends** containing the lines shown here:

```
Ford Cat 47
IBM Lion 152
Xerox Slug 31
Zenith Bear 26
Intel Cat 133
Hershey Lynx 28
Apple Panda 74
```

Then execute the following command. (The backslash at the end of a line tells the shell that you are continuing a command on the next line.) Can you figure out what the output will be?

```
head -5 odds.ends | sed s/Cat/Tigger/g | \
awk /Tigger/'{print "Buy",$1,"from",$2,"at",$3}' | \
tail -1
```

The correct answer is "Buy Intel from Tigger at 133"—can you prove it?

ROLLING YOUR OWN: LINUX PROGRAMMING

Even if you think you're not a programmer, Linux has some features to make your life a bit easier. Anytime you have a repetitive task that involves entering Linux commands or changing the contents of a file, you should think about automating it with a program.

If you've ever written a word processor macro or a spreadsheet formula, you're a programmer. By taking advantage of Linux's built-in programming features, you can automate repetitive tasks and build simple interactive applications without a degree in computer science.

This chapter covers basic shell script programming and introduces you to other, more powerful programming tools available in Linux, such as Perl and the C and C++ programming languages.

BASIC SHELL PROGRAMMING

The Bash shell is your main port of entry to Linux, since the shell interprets everything you enter on the command line before passing it along to the operating system for execution. But in addition to providing the niceties of command resolution, wildcard handling, and piping, Bash has its own powerful built-in programming language.

A *shell* script is a program written for Bash. The simplest shell script is a sequence of Linux commands, but when you add the power of variables and flow control, you can do a lot more with it. Shell scripts are similar to DOS batch files (those files that end in **.bat**), but shell scripts are more powerful and actually easier to create.

Shell scripts are interpreted, which means that the shell reads each line and acts on it immediately. This process differs from that of a formal programming language like C or C++, where the program is compiled and optimized for faster execution. So there's a tradeoff—it's easier to create quick little shell scripts, but if the task at hand requires serious number crunching or complicated logic, a compiled language is better.

■ *NOTE: All of the shell script syntax and examples in this chapter will work in both the Bash and Korn (pdksh) shells. The C shell (tcsh) has subtle differences in many areas, so scripts written for one shell may not work in another. If you decide to use the C shell instead of Bash, use the **man tcsh** command for more information on writing shell scripts for that environment.*

CREATING A SHELL SCRIPT

To create a shell script, use a text editor and enter your Linux commands as if you were typing them at the command prompt. For example, try this:

```
cd /tmp
echo "Removing temp files..."
ls -al
rm junk*
```

If you save those four lines in a file named **deltemp**, you will have a simple shell script that automates the process of switching to the **/tmp** directory, listing all the files there, and deleting the ones that start with the word *junk*.

EXECUTING A SHELL SCRIPT

So how do you run this little wonder of technology? In DOS, all you have to do is name a file with a .bat extension and it'll be recognized as an executable file—but not so with Linux. Since Linux attaches no meaning to file extensions, you have to mark the file as executable by using the **chmod** command, like this:

```
chmod +x deltemp
```

The **x** marks the file as executable; if you list the permissions for the **deltemp** file afterward, you will see the **x** in position four, confirming this:

```
ls -l deltemp
-rwx------   1 hermie other   55 Feb 19 14:02 deltemp
```

If you want other users to be able to run this script, give them both read and execute permission, like so:

```
chmod ugo+rx deltemp
ls -l deltemp
-rwxr-xr-x   1 hermie other   55 Feb 19 14:04 deltemp
```

Now the permissions show that any user can view or execute the **deltemp** script, but only you can modify it. To run the script, just enter its name at the command prompt, prefixed with *./* as shown here:

```
./deltemp
```

■ **NOTE:** *If the current directory is in the PATH environment variable, you can omit the ./ before the name.*

But there's one important thing you should know about running shell scripts this way. When you enter the shell script name and tell Bash to run it, a subshell is created for the execution of the script. This subshell inherits all the shell environment variables, including the current directory, but you lose any changes made to that environment when the script terminates.

What's the practical meaning of this? Well, you might expect that the current directory would be **/tmp** after you've run the **deltemp** script, but it's not. You'll still be in hermie's home directory. And if we had set an environment variable inside the script, its value would be good only during the execution of the script. Here's an example to demonstrate this point. Create an executable **setvar** script with these lines:

```
PS1='My Prompt: '
echo $PS1
```

Now watch how the values of the current directory and the PS1 variable change:

```
$ PS1='Bash Me! '
$ echo $PS1
Bash Me!                    PS1 before setvar.
$ setvar
My Prompt:                  PS1 during setvar.
$ echo $PS1
Bash Me!                    PS1 after setvar.
```

It looks like this script is absolutely useless for the intended purpose of setting the environment variable. But a little trick will make it work the way you want. Run the script by prefixing the name with a dot and a space, like so:

```
. setvar
```

This tells Bash to run the **setvar** script in the current shell environment, instead of creating a temporary subshell. Verify for yourself that the command prompt does in fact change to "My Prompt:" after running this script.

VARIABLES AND QUOTING

A variable in a shell script is a means of referencing a numeric or character value. And unlike formal programming languages, a shell script doesn't require you to declare a type for your variables. Thus, you could assign a number to the variable **stuff** and then use it again in the same script to hold a string of characters. To access the value (contents) of a variable, prefix it with a dollar sign.

```
stuff=5
stuff='chocolate truffles'
```

Don't put any spaces before or after the equal sign, or you'll get an error. And if you want to assign a string that contains spaces, you will need to put quotation marks around the string.

This is a good time to note that there are several distinct ways to use quotations marks in a shell script. Let's look at the differences among single quotation marks, double quotation marks, and the backslash character and then follow up with some examples.

- *Single quotation marks*, as in the preceding example, will always get you exactly what's inside the quotation marks—any characters that might otherwise have special meaning to the shell (like the dollar sign or the backslash) are treated literally.

- Use *double quotation marks* when you want to assign a string that contains special characters the shell should act on.

- The *backslash* is used to escape (treat literally) a single character (such as $ or *) that might otherwise be treated as a special character by the shell.

Now let's look at some examples that show when to use each method of quoting.

```
howdy='Good Morning $USER !'
echo $howdy
Good Morning $USER !

howdy="Good Morning $USER !"
echo $howdy
Good Morning hermie !
```

In the first case, the value of the **howdy** variable would probably not be what you wanted. The single quotation marks caused Bash to not treat **$USER** as a variable. In the second case, the results look much better. The double quotation marks allowed Bash to substitute the value of **$USER**, which is set automatically when you log in, in the string.

Here's another example that demonstrates a common error:

```
costmsg="Price is $5.00"
echo $costmsg
Actual result: Price is .00
```

We thought enough to quote the string, but the dollar sign tells Bash to use the value in the **$5** variable, which is not what we wanted. We can easily solve the problem by prefixing the dollar sign with a backslash, as shown here:

```
costmsg="Price is \$5.00"
echo $costmsg
Actual result: Price is $5.00
```

ARGUMENTS AND OTHER SPECIAL VARIABLES

Arguments are the values you pass to a shell script. Each value on the command line after the name of the script will be assigned to the special variables **$1, $2, $3**, and so on. The name of the currently running script is stored in the **$0** variable.

Here are some other special variables you will find useful in script writing:

$#   The number of arguments

$*   The entire argument string

$?   The return code from the last command issued

So let's try some examples working with arguments and other special variables. Create an executable script called **testvars** containing these lines:

```
echo "My name is $0"
echo "First arg is: $1"
echo "Second arg is: $2"
echo "I got a total of $# arguments."
echo "The full argument string was: $*"
```

Now if you run this script, here's what you'll see:

```
./testvars birds have lips
My name is testvars
First arg is: birds
Second arg is: have
I got a total of 3 arguments.
The full argument string was: birds have lips
```

FLOW CONTROL

So far, all of our sample scripts have been just a sequence of commands executed one after the other. We haven't added any **if/then/else** logic or used looping constructs to control the flow of the program.

■ *NOTE:* *If you've never written or seen a computer program in your entire life, the rest of this chapter will probably seem a bit foreign. But try to follow the examples; then test and modify them on your own to get the hang of it.*

CONDITIONAL OPERATIONS

Let's look at the **if/then/else** construct in a Bash shell script and see how to control the flow of a script with conditional logic. The general form of **if/then/else** is shown here, with the actual syntax shown in boldface and the parts you must supply in normal type:

```
if [ condition is true ]
then
        execute these commands
else
        execute those commands
fi
```

The **else** clause is optional, but you must end the construct with the **fi** command. You can also have nested **if** clauses by using the **elif** command like this:

```
if [ condition1 is true ]
then
        execute these commands
elif [ condition2 is true ]
then
        execute these commands
else
        execute those commands
fi
```

So what kind of conditions can we test for? If you're dealing with numbers, here are the conditional expressions you can use. In other words, any of these expressions can go inside the brackets on the **if** or **elif** statement:

num1 -eq num2	True if **num1** equals **num2**.
num1 -ne num2	True if **num1** is not equal to **num2**.
num1 -lt num2	True if **num1** is less than **num2**.
num1 -gt num2	True if **num1** is greater than **num2**.
num1 -le num2	True if **num1** is less than or equal to **num2**.
num1 -ge num2	True if **num1** is greater than or equal to **num2**.

If you're comparing character strings, these are the valid conditional expressions:

str1 = str2	True if **str1** and **str2** are identical.
str1 != str2	True if **str1** and **str2** are not identical.
-n str1	True if **str1** is not null (length is greater than zero).
-z str1	True if **str1** is null (length is zero).

You can also test certain file conditions, such as whether or not files exist, the type of file, and so on. Here are the conditional expressions for files:

-f somefile	True if **somefile** exists and is an ordinary file.
-d somefile	True if **somefile** exists and is a directory.
-s somefile	True if **somefile** contains data (the size is not zero).
-r somefile	True if **somefile** is readable.
-w somefile	True if **somefile** is writable.
-x somefile	True if **somefile** is executable.

And finally, here are the logical operators, for performing tests that involve *and*, *or*, and *not* conditions.

cond1 -a cond2	True if both **cond1** and cond2 are true.
cond1 -o cond2	True if either **cond1** or cond2 is true.
! cond1	True if **cond1** is false.

Some if/then/else Examples

Here are some examples using the conditional expressions just listed. Note that the spaces on either side of the square brackets are *not* optional!

```
if [ $carprice -gt 20000 ]
then
        echo 'Too rich for my blood.'
else
        echo 'Can you get that model in blue?'
fi


if [ $maker = 'Buick' ]
then
        echo 'Have you driven a Ford lately?'
fi

if [ -r $1   -a   -s $2 ]
then
        echo "The $1 file is readable and contains data."
fi
```

The case Statement

Bash provides a **case** statement that lets you compare a string with several possible values and execute a block of code when it finds a match. Here's an example of the **case** command, with the syntax shown in boldface and the parts you would supply in normal type:

```
case $1 in
        -a)
                commands;;
        -f)
                commands;;
        *)
                commands;;
esac
```

In this example, if the value of **$1** was **-a**, the first block of commands would execute. If the value of **$1** was **-f**, the second block of commands would execute. Otherwise, the third block of commands, following the asterisk clause, would execute. (Think of the asterisk as meaning "match anything.")

You can put as many commands as you need in place of *commands* in the sample, but be sure to end the block with a double semicolon. Only the first matching block of commands will execute in a **case** statement, and you must signal the end of the construct with the **esac** command.

Looping

Shell scripts written in Bash can implement *looping*, or iteration, with the **while, until,** and **for** constructs. In each case, a block of code is executed repeatedly until a loop exit condition is satisfied. The script then continues on from that point.

The while Statement

In a **while** loop, the block of code between the **do** and **done** statements is executed so long as the conditional expression is true. Think of it as saying, "Execute *while* this condition remains true." Here's an example:

```
while [ "$*" != "" ]
do
        echo "Argument value is: $1"
        shift
done
```

This trivial example prints the value of each argument passed to the shell script. Translated to English, the **while** condition says to continue so long as the input argument string is not null. You could also code the **while** statement as

```
while [ -n "$*" ]
```

but I think the first method is much easier to read and understand.

You might think that this loop would continue to print the first argument (**$1**) forever and ever, since you don't expect the value of the **$*** variable (the list of arguments from the command line) to change during the course of running the script. You'd be right, except that I slipped the **shift** command into the body of the loop.

What **shift** does is discard the first argument and reassign all the **$n** variables—so the new **$1** variable gets the value that used to be in **$2**, and so on. Accordingly, the value in **$*** gets shorter and shorter each time through the loop, and when it finally becomes null, the loop is done.

The until Statement

The **until** construct works almost exactly the same as **while**. The only difference is that **until** executes the body of the loop so long as the conditional expression is false, whereas **while** executes the body of the loop so long as the conditional expression is true. Think of it as saying, "Execute *until* this condition becomes true."

Let's code the previous example using an **until** loop this time and making it a little fancier by adding a *counter* variable:

```
count=1
until [ "$*" = "" ]
do
  echo "Argument number $count : $1 "
  shift
  count=`expr $count + 1`
done
```

Again, you could have coded the **until** statement as

```
until [ -z "$*" ]
```

but I recommend not using the **-n** and **-z** operators because it's harder to remember what they do.

The only new concept here is the strange-looking line that increments the counter:

```
count=`expr $count + 1`
```

The **expr** command signals to the shell that we're about to perform a mathematical calculation instead of a string operation. And the doo-dads that look kind of like single quotation marks are not—they're the **backtick** (`) character, found to the left of the number 1 key on most keyboards. By enclosing an expression in backticks, you tell the shell to assign the result of a Linux command to a variable, instead of printing it to the screen.

■ *NOTE: The spaces on either side of the plus sign are required.*

THE FOR STATEMENT

The **for** statement is yet another way to implement a loop in a shell script. The general form of the **for** construct is shown here:

```
for item in list
do
        something useful with $item
done
```

Each time through the loop, the value of the **item** variable is assigned to the *n*th item in the list. When you've processed all the items in the list, the loop is done. Here's an example similar to the **until** and **while** loops you saw earlier in this chapter:

```
for $item in "$*"
do
        echo "Argument value is: $item"
done
```

Debugging Shell Scripts

Sometimes shell scripts just don't work the way you think they should, or you get strange error messages when running your script. Just remember: The computer is always right. It's easy to omit a significant blank, quotation mark, or bracket, or to mistakenly use a single quotation mark when you should have used double quotation marks or a backtick.

When you get unexpected behavior from a shell script and you're thinking "I just know this is coded right . . . the computer is wrong!" — remember: The computer is always right. But fortunately, there is help. By prefixing your shell invocation with **bash -x,** you can turn on tracing to see what's really happening. Let's say we have this **listarg** script:

```
count=1
until [ "$*" = "" ]
do
  echo "Arg $count : $1 "
  shift
  count=$count+1
done
```

At first glance, it looks golden, but for some reason the counter is not incrementing properly. Try running it with the command

```
bash -x listarg abc def
```

and look at the trace output as the shell executes. The lines prefixed with a plus sign show the progress of the running script, and the lines without the plus sign are the script's normal output.

```
+ count=1
+ [ abc def =  ]
+ echo Arg 1 : abc
Arg 1 : abc
```

```
+ shift                                      Hmmm . . .
+ count=1+1
+ [ def =  ]
+ echo Arg 1+1 : def
Arg 1+1 : def                                Not Good!
+ shift
+ count=1+1+1
+ [  =  ]
```

Instead of printing **Arg 2 : def**, we got **Arg 1+1 : def**. But the trace output line reading **count=1+1** nails the problem. You forgot to use the **expr** command, so the shell is treating this as a string concatenate instead of a mathematical calculation.

■ *NOTE: You can always press CTRL-C to stop a running shell script. This is handy if you accidentally create a script with an infinite loop (one that will never end by itself).*

PROGRAMMING SCRIPTS WITH PERL

Perl is an interpreted language that is very popular in the Unix community because it has a rich and powerful feature set, but is still easy to use. Perl borrows heavily from other languages such as C and awk and is especially useful for processing text, generating reports, and handling Common Gateway Interface (CGI) requests submitted via Web browsers.

Perl has been ported to many non-Unix environments, including DOS, OS/2, Macintosh, VMS, and Windows NT. The fact that a Perl program can run with little or no modification on many different platforms is another reason for its popularity. In this section, I'll introduce you to basics of Perl and point you to some resources where you can learn more.

PERL BASICS

To create a Perl script, use a text editor to enter Perl commands, save the file with a **.pl** extension (such as **sample.pl**), and then use **chmod** to mark the file as executable. The extension is not required, but it's a common Unix convention and will help you identify your Perl source files without looking inside.

Here's a very simple Perl script:

```
#!/usr/bin/perl
print "I am here. \n";
```

The mysterious first line starting with "pound splat slash" is required for all Perl scripts to run; it tells the system where to find the Perl interpreter. Hopefully, you've already figured out that this program prints a message followed by the newline character.

Unlike the **echo** command in Bash scripts, Perl's **print** command doesn't automatically send a carriage return and line feed. If you forget the **\n** sequence, the next **print** command will start on the same line. Also note that all Perl statements must end with a semicolon.

VARIABLES AND QUOTING

A variable in a Perl script is a means of referencing a numeric or character value. As in Bash scripts, Perl doesn't require you to declare a type for your variables. Perl figures out by context whether the value should be treated as a number or a character string and will even perform character-to-numeric value conversions when necessary. To assign or access the value (contents) of a variable, prefix it with a dollar sign. Spaces before or after the equal sign are optional, but if you want to assign a variable that contains character data, you must put quotation marks around the string.

```
$num=5;
$stuff = "chocolate truffles";
$user = $ENV{USER};
```

In these examples, Perl assigns 5 to the numeric variable **$num**, "chocolate truffles" to the variable **$stuff**, and the value of the USER environment variable to **$user**.

This is a good time to note that there are several distinct ways to use quotation marks in a Perl script. Let's look at the differences among single quotation marks, double quotation marks, backticks, and the backslash character and then follow up with some examples.

- *Single quotation marks*, as in the preceding example, will always get you exactly what's inside the quotation marks—any characters that might otherwise have special meaning (like the dollar sign or the backslash) are treated literally.

- Use *double quotation marks* when you want to assign a string that contains special characters that need to be interpreted.

- The *backslash* is used to *escape* (treat literally) a single character (such as $ or *) that might otherwise be treated as a special character.

- Use *backticks* to indicate that the string is a Linux command that should be executed, with the results assigned to a variable.

Now let's look at some examples that show when to use each method of quoting:

```
$user = $ENV{USER};
print 'Good Morning $user';
Yields: Good Morning $user
```

```
$user = $ENV{USER};
print "Good Morning $user";
Yields: Good Morning hermie
```

In the first case, the results would probably not be what you wanted. The single quotation marks caused Perl to not treat **$user** as a variable. In the second case, the results look much better. The double quotation marks allowed Perl to substitute the value of **$user** in the string.

Here's another example that demonstrates a common error:

```
$costmsg = "Price is $5.00";
print "$costmsg";
Yields: Price is .00
```

We thought enough to quote the string, but the dollar sign tells Perl to use the value in the **$5** variable, which is as yet undefined. We can easily solve the problem by prefixing the dollar sign with a backslash, as shown here:

```
$costmsg = "Price is \$5.00";
print "$costmsg";
Actual result: Price is $5.00
```

Finally, here's an example using backticks to execute a Linux command and capture the results in a Perl variable:

```
$currdir = `pwd`
print "Current directory is $pwd";
Yields: Current directory is /home/hermie
```

ARGUMENTS AND OTHER SPECIAL VARIABLES

Arguments are the values you pass to a Perl script. Each value on the command line after the name of the script will be assigned to the special variables **$ARGV[0]**, **$ARGV[1]**, **$ARGV[2]**, and so on. The number of arguments passed to the script is stored in the **$#ARGV** variable, and the full argument string is in the variable **@ARGV**. The name of the currently running program is stored in the **$0** variable.

Let's try some examples working with arguments and other special variables. Create an executable script called **testvars.pl** containing these lines:

```
#!/usr/bin/perl
print "My name is $0 \n";
print "First arg is: $ARGV[0] \n";
print "Second arg is: $ARGV[1] \n";
print "Third arg is: $ARGV[2] \n";
$num = $#ARGV + 1; print "How many args? $num \n";
print "The full argument string was: @ARGV \n";
```

Now if you run this script, here's what you'll see:

```
./testvars dogs can whistle
My name is testvars.pl
First arg is: dogs
Second arg is: can
Third arg is: whistle
How many args? 3
The full argument string was: dogs can whistle
```

Just a few notes about that example. I did say that the **$#ARGV** variable contained the number of arguments, but I lied—sort of. Since the arguments are numbered starting at zero, you have to add one to the value of **$#ARGV** to get the actual number of arguments. It's a bit weird, but if you're a fan of the C language, it'll all seem quite normal.

Also note that the **@ARGV** variable doesn't start with a dollar sign. That's because it's an *array* variable, as opposed to the regular *scalar* variables we've worked with so far. An array can be thought of as a list of values, where each value is addressed by a scalar (dollar sign) variable and an index number in square brackets, as in **$ARGV[0]**, **$ARGV[1]**, and so on. Don't worry too much about arrays for now— that's a topic for more study on your own.

FLOW CONTROL

A Perl script that's just a sequence of commands executed one after the other isn't very exciting. Let's look at how to use **if/then/else** logic and looping constructs to control the flow of a Perl program.

CONDITIONAL OPERATIONS

The general form of an **if/then/else** construct is shown here, with the actual syntax shown in boldface and the parts you must supply in normal type:

```
if ( condition is true ) {
        execute these commands
}
else {
        execute those commands
}
```

The **else** clause is optional, but you can also have nested **if** clauses by using the **elsif** construct like this:

```
if ( condition is true ) { execute these commands }
elsif { execute those commands }
elsif { execute those commands }
else  { execute those commands }
```

So what kind of conditions can we test for? For number and string comparisons, here are the conditional expressions you can use. In other words, any of these expressions can go inside the parentheses of the **if** or **elsif** statement:

NUMBERS	STRINGS	RESULT
$a == $b	$a eq $b	True if **$a** is equal to **$b**.
$a != $b	$a ne $b	True if **$a** is not equal to **$b**.
$a > $b	$a gt $b	True if **$a** is greater than **$b**.
$a < $b	$a lt $b	True if **$a** is less than **$b**.
$a >= $b	$a ge $b	True if **$a** is greater than or equal to **$b**.
$a <= $b	$a le $b	True if **$a** is less than or equal to **$b**.

Using the wrong comparison operator is a common Perl coding error, and is frustrating to debug. For example, if you use the == operator to compare two strings, you will not get the expected result.

To test certain file conditions (whether or not files exist, the type of file, and so on), use these conditional expressions:

CONDITIONAL EXPRESSION	RESULT
-e $somefile	True if **somefile** exists.
-f $somefile	True if **somefile** exists and is a plain file.
-d $somefile	True if **somefile** exists and is a directory.
-s $somefile	True if **somefile** contains data (the size is not zero).
-r $somefile	True if **somefile** is readable.
-w $somefile	True if **somefile** is writable.
-x $somefile	True if **somefile** is executable.

And finally, here are the logical operators, for performing tests that involve *and*, *or*, and *not* conditions:

OPERATOR	RESULT
$a && $b	True if both **$a** and **$b** are true.
$a and $b	Same as above.
$a || $b	True if either **$a** or **$b** is true.
$a or $b	Same as above.
! $a	True if **$a** is false.
not $a	Same as above.

Some if/then/else Examples

Here are some examples using the conditional expressions just listed. Note that the spaces on either side of the parentheses and braces are optional, and the placement of them is largely a matter of style.

```
if ( $carprice > 20000 )
   { print 'Too rich for my blood.'; }
else
   { print 'Can you get that model in blue?'; }

if ( $maker eq "Buick" )
{ print 'Have you driven a Ford lately?'; }

if ( -r $myfile  &&  -s $myfile )
{
print "The $myfile file is readable and contains data."
}
```

The case Statement

Most languages provide a **case** or **switch** statement that lets you compare a string with several possible values and execute a block of code when a match is found. Perl does not, but it does provide a way to implement this procedure. Here's an example of the **SWITCH** construct, with the syntax shown in boldface and the parts you would supply in normal type:

```
SWITCH: {
  if ( $A eq "ls" )   { system("ls"); last SWITCH };
  if ( $A eq "pwd" )  { system("pwd"); last SWITCH };
  if ( $A eq "date" ) { system("date"); last SWITCH };
  print "None of the args were very interesting. \n";
}
```

In this example, if the value of **$A** was **ls**, the first block of commands would execute. If the value of **$A** was **pwd**, the second block of commands would execute. Otherwise, the rest of the commands in the **SWITCH** clause would execute. The **last SWITCH** command tells Perl to short-circuit the rest of the stuff in the **SWITCH** clause, so as soon as one of the conditions is satisfied, the others are ignored.

Looping

Shell scripts written in Bash can implement *looping*, or iteration, with the **while, until,** and **for** constructs. In each case, a block of code is executed repeatedly until a loop exit condition is satisfied. The script then continues on from that point.

The while Statement

In a **while** loop, the block of code between the { and } braces is executed so long as the conditional expression is true. Think of it as saying, "Execute *while* this condition remains true." Here's an example:

```
while (@ARGV) {
  print "ARG: $ARGV[0] \n";
  shift @ARGV;
}
```

This trivial example prints the value of each argument passed to the shell script. Translated to English, the **while** condition says to continue so long as the input argument string is not null. You might think that this loop would continue to print the first argument **$ARGV[0]** forever and ever, since you don't expect the value of the **@ARGV** variable (the list of arguments from the command line) to change during the course of running the script. You'd be right, except that I slipped the **shift** command into the body of the loop.

What **shift** does is discard the first argument and reassign all the **$ARG** variables—so the new **$ARGV[0]** gets the value that used to be in **$ARGV[1]** and so on. Accordingly, the value in **@ARGV** gets shorter and shorter each time through the loop, and when it finally becomes null, the loop is done.

THE UNTIL STATEMENT

The **until** construct works almost exactly the same as **while**. The only difference is that **until** executes the body of the loop so long as the conditional expression is false, whereas **while** executes the body of the loop so long as the conditional expression is true. Think of it as saying, "Execute *until* this condition becomes true."

Let's code the previous example using an **until** loop this time and make it a little fancier by adding a *counter* variable:

```
$count=1;
until ( ! @ARGV ) {
  print "Argument number $count : $ARGV[0] \n";
  shift;
  $count++;
}
```

The only new concept here is the strange-looking line that increments the counter. The **$count++** syntax is equivalent to **$count=$count+1**, but the former is more common in Perl and C language programming. You can also decrement a value using the **$count--** syntax.

THE FOREACH STATEMENT

The **foreach** statement provides yet another way to implement a loop in a Perl script. The general form of the **for** construct is shown here:

```
foreach $item ( in-some-array )
{
  do something with $item
}
```

Each time through the loop, the value of the **$item** variable is assigned to the next item in the array. When you've processed all the items in the array, the loop is done. Here's an example similar to the **until** and **while** loops you saw earlier in this chapter:

```
foreach $var (@ARGV)
{
  print "NEXT ARG: $var \n";
}
```

Dealing with Files

One common operation in Perl is to open a text file and process it line by line. You might be creating a report or just sifting through the file to find certain strings. This example opens a file whose name is stored the **$file** variable and then prints each line that starts with the pound sign:

```
open MYFILE, $file or die "Can't open $file: $! \n";
while (<MYFILE>) {
 if (/^#/) { print "MATCH: $_"; }
}
```

A few things may need explaining here. The **open** command assigns a file handle (in this case, **MYFILE**) to the file named in the **$file** variable. You can use any file handle or variable names you like in the **open** command. If the file cannot be opened for some reason (it doesn't exist, it isn't readable, and so on), then the program will terminate (courtesy of the **die** command) with a message like this:

```
Can't open panda.txt: No such file or directory
```

The special variable **$!** contains the reason for the failure and was substituted into the error message. If the file is opened successfully, the program continues, and the <**MYFILE**> construct will return the next line from the file in the **$_** variable. (You'll find that a lot of Perl functions use this special **$_** variable.) When the end of the file is reached, <**MYFILE**> will return a null value, causing the loop to terminate.

Pattern Matching in Perl

One mystery remains: What's this (/^#/) stuff all about? Remember the **grep** command, back in Chapter 8, "Slicing and Dicing," and the discussion of regular expressions? If you think about it, the little Perl program in the previous example acts a lot like **grep,** since it sifts through each line and prints it if a pattern is matched.

In Perl, the forward slashes indicate that a pattern match is to be performed. The regular expression inside the slashes defines the search pattern, and **$_** is the variable that the search is performed on. In our case, the **^#** inside the slashes means to match only lines that begin with the pound sign.

So if we make the previous example a bit more generic, allowing it to get the search pattern and file name from the command line, it will behave almost exactly like the **grep** utility:

```
open MYFILE, $ARGV[1] or die "Can't open $ARGV[1]: $! \n";
while (<MYFILE>) {
 if (/$ARGV[0]/) { print "MATCH: $_"; }
}
```

Learn More about Perl

We've barely scratched the surface of what you can do with the Perl language. Try the **man perl** command to get more information on Perl, read *Programming Perl* by Larry Wall (O'Reilly & Associates), the inventor of the Perl language, or visit the Perl Institute Web site at http://www.perl.org.

Other Linux Programming Languages

Shell scripts are fine for many tasks, but if you need to do lots of number crunching, string manipulation, or complicated logic flow, look into one of the other languages briefly mentioned in this section.

The C Language

C is a general-purpose programming language originally written to help in the development of Unix. Most of the Linux operating system is written in C.

C is one of the most widely used programming languages (in spite of its awkward syntax) and is available on just about any computing platform you can imagine. Since it was designed for portability to other environments (it has source code compatibility), it is very popular with software developers.

The C compiler that comes with Linux is the GNU C compiler, created by the Free Software Foundation. To invoke the GNU C compiler, use the **gcc** command.

Here's a very simple C program that will print **Hello, World!** on your screen:

```
#include <stdio.h>
main ()
{
  printf ("Hello, World! \n");
}
```

Type those lines in a file named **hello.c** and then compile it like this:

```
gcc -o hello hello.c
```

This tells the compiler to compile **hello.c** and create an executable output file named **hello**. To run the program, enter the command **hello** at the prompt.

THE C++ LANGUAGE

C++ is an object-oriented programming language based on C that is fast becoming the language of choice for large software development projects. C++ compilers are available on a great many platforms and, of course, on Linux as well. To invoke the GNU C++ compiler, use the **g++** command.

It is far beyond the scope of this book to delve into the syntax of the C and C++ languages, but you can find stacks of C or C++ language reference books in any computer bookstore. For more information on using C and C++ with Linux, visit the Linux Documentation Project at http://metalab.unc.edu/LDP and look for the Linux Programmer's Guide and the **GCC HOWTO** file.

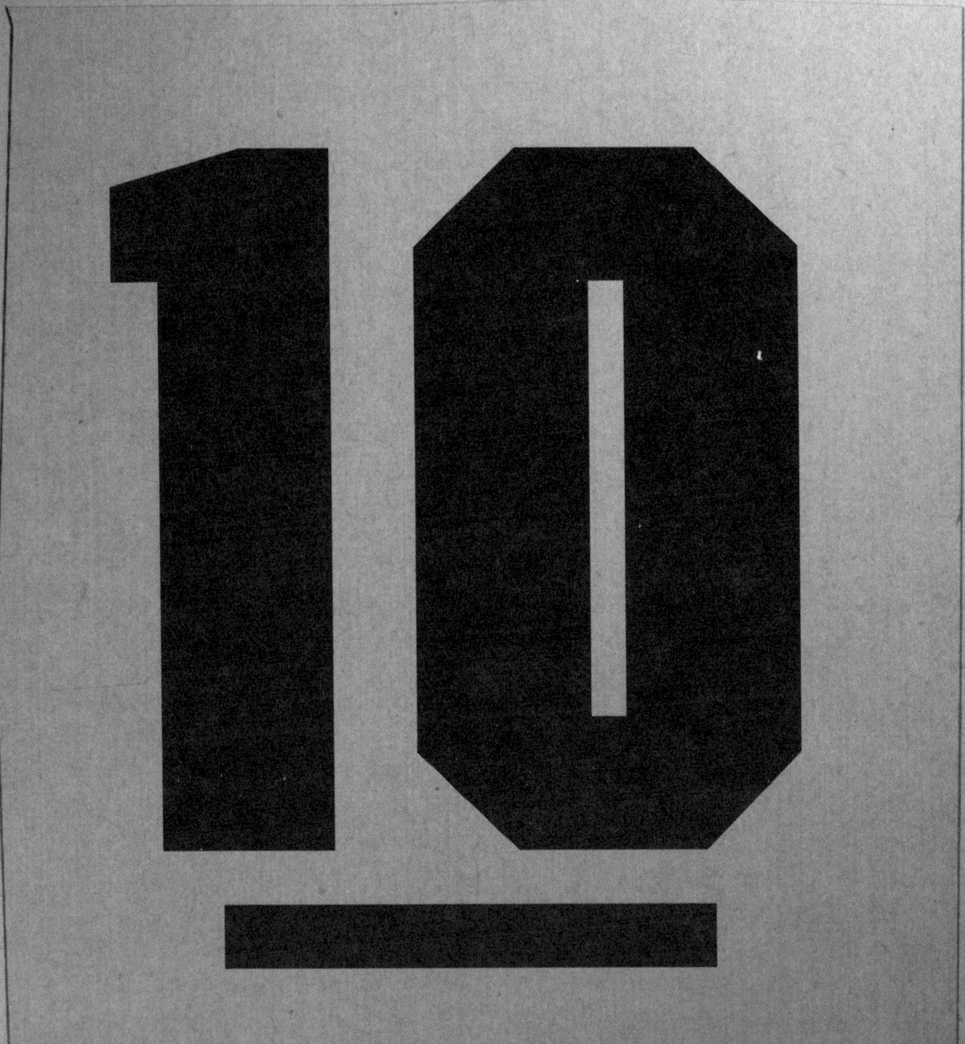
10

MANAGING YOUR EMAIL

There's a lot of hype about the multimedia aspects of the Internet, but the true killer app in the online world has always been email. More than anything else, people get online to communicate with other human beings—not other computers. In this chapter, you'll get a brief introduction to Internet email and learn about the tools you can use on a Linux system to send and receive email.

EMAIL ADDRESSES

To send email, you have to know the email address of the person who is to receive your message. An email address consists of two parts, a *user name* and a *domain name*, separated by the at (@) sign. And unlike almost everything else in the Unix world, email addresses are *not* case sensitive.

For example, if your email address is **hermie@fritz.com**, then hermie is the user name and **fritz.com** is the domain name. Most domain names end in a three-letter code, such as com, edu, or gov, which indicates something about the user's location (whether they're at a company, university, government office, and so on):

com Company or business

edu College or university

gov Government office

mil Military institution

net Network node (usually an Internet service provider)

org Organization (professional societies, nonprofit groups, and so on)

us Usually a school, library, or local government office in the U.S.

As this book goes to press, the domain registration process is being completely revamped, so you may soon see new top-level domains such as biz, web, info, and others.

Here are some examples of email addresses using the various domain names:

ICU@hq.bigbro.COM   A user at a large company (headquarters)

JaneDoe@CS.harvard.edu	A computer science student at Harvard University
Hacker7@WhiteHouse.gov	Hackers at the White House?
D.Nukem@ftriley.army.mil	A user at a military site
BobRankin@ulster.net	Yours truly :-)
elmo@IEEE.org	A member of the IEEE society
library@hometown.ny.us	A local library somewhere in New York State in the United States

The exceptions to this rule are non-U.S. addresses that end in a two-digit country code and are usually (but not always) preceded by "ac" (for a university) or "co" (for a company): for example,

Peter@nms.ac.uk	A student at a British university
aldeana@business.ntu.edu.au	A student at an Australian university
rkoltz@audg.gov.ab.ca	A government employee in Alberta, Canada
takemori@bs.mcts.co.jp	A user at a Japanese company
christoph.wolfe@metronet.de	A user at a German company

NETIQUETTE

It's sometimes so simple to communicate electronically that you forget that users on the other end of the wire can't necessarily pick up on your message's emotions and nuances the way they might in a handwritten letter or in spoken conversation. They may even misinterpret a joke as an insult—and many people do. It's especially important to keep this danger in mind when you're participating in group discussions such as Internet mailing lists.

The moral? Be extra careful to make your email messages clear. If you're telling a joke that could be construed as a fact or a harsh, personal comment, say so! Don't use the excuse of being able to hide behind your terminal as a license to be rude. And be extra-sensitive to the fact that the Internet is a *global* audience, and not all users have a strong command of English.

Smileys (sometimes called emoticons), or textual representations of emotions that people commonly use in their email, are one way to express feelings in the otherwise emotionless world of email. When you see a collection of dashes, parentheses, and other punctuation marks (like :-) or :-(for example) that don't seem to make sense, try turning your head sideways, and the meaning should come into focus right away.

One final point on netiquette, DON'T SHOUT! Even though email addresses are not case sensitive, the people who read email often are. And the use of ALL CAPITAL LETTERS in email is considered shouting. It'll also brand you (deservedly or not) as a clueless newbie who can't find the right key to turn off the caps.

SENDING EMAIL WITH LINUX

The most basic way to send email on a Linux system is with the **mail** command. The **mail** program is a command-line interface for sending and receiving electronic mail. It works, but it's not pretty. Later in this chapter, you'll learn about Pine, a much friendlier email interface, but you should know how to use **mail** since it's guaranteed to be available on any Unix system.

Let's say you're logged in as **root** and you want to send a message to hermie. Start the process by typing

```
mail hermie
```

The system will respond with a "Subject:" prompt. Type the subject for your note, press **ENTER**, and then write your message, line by line. When you're done with your missive, press **ENTER** to get to a blank line, then **CTRL-D** to send it.

Here's a sample mail session. (The stuff you type is shown in bold, and the system prompts are normal intensity.)

```
# mail hermie
Subject: Gone Fishing
I've decided to kick back this afternoon and go fishing.
So if this crazy Linux system rolls over and dies,
I suggest you do likewise.
^D
EOT
```

After you press **CTRL-D,** the system responds with the cryptic EOT message, which could mean "End of Text," or "Eat Only Twinkies," or whatever you like.

You may notice an apparent contradiction in the preceding example since the email address of the recipient does not contain an @ sign and a domain name. If the sender and recipient are on the same system, it's all right to give just the user name as the email address.

YOU'VE GOT MAIL!

If you log in as **hermie** now (pressing **ALT-F2** to access another virtual console would be convenient), you'll be greeted with the following cheery little message:

```
You have new mail.
```

You can receive and read your incoming email by using the **mail** command again.

Here's a sample **mail** session (text in bold is what you would enter):

```
$ mail
Mail version 5.6 6/1/95.  Type ? for help.
"/var/spool/mail/hermie":  1 message 1 new
>N  1 root@fritz.com     Mon Feb 10 14:58   "Gone Fishing"
 N  2 D.Rhodes@spam.net  Mon Feb 10 15:37   "Make Money Fast!"
 N  3 Chris@qwerty.com   Mon Feb 10 15:37   "Tennis, Anyone?"
& 1
Message 1:
Date: Mon, 10 Feb 1997 14:58:12 -0500
From: root@fritz.com
To: hermie@fritz.com
Subject: Gone Fishing
Saved 1 message in /home/hermie/mbox
Held 2 messages in /var/mail/spool/hermie
I've decided to kick back this afternoon and go fishing.
So if this crazy Linux system rolls over and dies,
I suggest you do likewise.
& q
```

Let's look at what just happened. After you entered the **mail** command, the system informed you of the version of the mail program that is running and told you how to get help for it.

The next line tells you that there is one new message in your mailbox, and that your incoming mail is stored in the file **/var/spool/mail/ hermie**. (Each user on the system has a mail file in the **/var/spool/mail** directory.) When new mail arrives, Linux tacks it onto the end of the recipient's mail file.

■ **NOTE:** *You should never directly edit your mail file—always use* **mail** *or another email program to handle your mail. (If you're editing your mail file when a new message arrives, it will be lost.) But it's quite all right to scan your mail file with* **grep** *or some other utility that doesn't try to modify it. (You might want to apply* **grep** *to your mail to find a particular string, such as the email address of a person who has corresponded with you.)*

The next line,

```
>N  1 root@fritz.com    Mon Feb 10 14:58   "Gone Fishing"
```

---

is referred to as a header line, and it tells you a number of things. The **>** tells you which message is the current one—the one you're working with.

The **N 1** indicates that you're dealing with message 1 and that it's flagged as a new message. (Later, the flag could be **U** for unread or **O** for an old message.) The rest of the line tells you who the message is from, when it was sent, and the Subject line.

The ampersand (&) on the following line is the mail prompt. In this example, we entered a **1** to display the first message, and the message text is shown on the lines that follow. Unfortunately, we can't tell from the context whether to roll over and die or just go fishing.

EXITING THE MAIL PROGRAM

The **q** command entered at the next **mail** prompt ends the session and returns you to the shell prompt. But take note of the messages that were printed on your way out: namely, "Saved 1 message in /home/hermie/mbox" and "Held 2 messages in /var/mail/spool/ hermie." For some odd reason, **mail** does not think it's a good idea to keep the mail you've already read in the **/var/spool/mail/hermie** file, so it moves read mail to a separate file called **mbox** in your own home directory.

To access the messages in the **mbox** file, you have to use the command

```
mail -f mbox
```

Kind of annoying, ain't it? But at least the mail program looks and acts the same regardless of which mail file you're working with.

OTHER MAIL COMMANDS

Let's get back into the mail program and have some fun with the two messages that we didn't read before with this scenario (again, bold type represents your input):

```
mail

Mail version 5.6 6/1/95.  Type ? for help.
"/var/spool/mail/hermie":  1 message 1 new
>U  1 D.Rhodes@spam.net   Mon Feb 10 15:37   "Make Money Fast!"
 U  2 Chris@qwerty.com    Mon Feb 10 15:37   "Tennis, Anyone?"
& 2
Message 2:
Date: Mon, 10 Feb 1997 15:37:52 -0500
From: Chris@qwerty.com
To: hermie@fritz.com
Subject: Tennis, Anyone?
Wanna whack a few a 4:30 today?  -Chris
& reply
Subject: Re: Tennis, Anyone?
Sure, I'll see you on the lower courts at 4:30.
^D
EOT
& header
 U  1 D.Rhodes@spam.net   Mon Feb 10 15:37   "Make Money Fast!"
>O  2 Chris@qwerty.com    Mon Feb 10 15:37   "Tennis, Anyone?"
& delete 1
& q
Saved 1 message in /home/hermie/mbox
```

We've introduced several new commands here, so let's take a closer look at the five operations that were performed in this mail session:

- As soon as I started the mail program, the mail headers were displayed, showing that both messages are marked **U** for unread. I displayed message 2 by entering a **2** at the prompt.

- The **reply** command responded with an appropriate Subject line for message 2, "Subject: Re: Tennis, Anyone?," and waited for me to enter the text of my message to Chris. Pressing **CTRL-D** makes EOT appear and sends my reply.

- The **header** command displays the message headers. I've used it here to show the difference in the status flags. The > indicates that message 2 is current, and the message is marked as **O** for old.

- I deleted the first message with **delete 1** without even reading it, since the Subject line was rather dubious.

- And as a parting gesture, the **q** command told me that another message was squirreled away in that **mbox** file. At this point, if I issued the **mail** command again, the system would respond:

```
No mail for hermie
```

Poor hermie. He needn't drink Draino, though—he can always send himself some more mail. ;-)

THE PINE MAIL SYSTEM

Pine is an email handler that is much friendlier than the plain ol' **mail** command. Pine sports a full-screen interface and a context-sensitive list of commands on each screen. Even though it's text-based (no GUI) it's very easy to use and has enough features to satisfy almost any user. I personally use Pine in a Unix environment, even though I access the Internet from a Windows machine.

In case you're wondering why an email system would be named after a tree, here's the scoop. Pine was originally based on another email program called Elm (short for "ELectronic Mail"), written by Internet pioneer Dave Taylor. The name Pine was first an acronym for "Pine Is Not Elm," but today the official title is Program for Internet News and Email. (Revisionists: 1, Geeks: 0—film at 11.)

STARTING PINE

To fire up the Pine program, use the following command, and you'll see the Pine main menu screen:

```
% pine

PINE 4.10      MAIN MENU                    Folder: INBOX   3 Messages
   ?  HELP                      -  Get help using Pine
   C  COMPOSE MESSAGE           -  Compose and send/post a message
   I  MESSAGE INDEX             -  View messages in current folder
   L  FOLDER LIST               -  Select a folder OR news group to view
   A  ADDRESS BOOK              -  Update address book
   S  SETUP                     -  Configure or update Pine
   Q  QUIT                      -  Exit the Pine program

Copyright 1989-1999. PINE is a trademark of the U. of Washington


     ?  Help                              P  PrevCmd        R  RelNotes
     O  OTHER CMDS   > [ListFldrs]        N  NextCmd        K  KBLock
```

Typically, I press **I** to jump right into my INBOX, but Pine also offers several options: pressing **C** to send a message, **L** to see a list of my saved mail folders, or **A** to manage my address book. (We'll touch on those options later.)

If you want to bypass this opening screen, you can add the **-i** flag to your **pine** command and go directly to the INBOX screen.

THE PINE INBOX

The INBOX folder is where you'll spend most of your time in Pine. Following is a sample screen showing three messages. Pine displays a message number, the date sent, the real name of the sender (if available), the size (in bytes), and the Subject line of each message in your INBOX.

The first message is flagged with an **A**, which indicates that I've already read and answered it. The other two are each flagged with an **N** because they are new messages. Messages that have been read but not answered are blank in the flag column.

So what about the plus (+) signs in front of certain messages? These tell me that these messages were addressed directly to me (your address appears in the To field, even though you don't see that field here). Email that comes from a mailing list manager or junk mail that comes from a spammer will typically have a generic (or bogus) To: address.

Unlike **mail**, Pine doesn't keep your incoming and previously read messages in totally different places. All your messages show up on this screen, whether they are brand-new or six months old.

```
PINE 4.10  MESSAGE INDEX              Folder: INBOX  Message 1 of 3


+ A 1   Feb  8  Joe Kramer         (1,116)  Let's do lunch
  N 2   Feb 10  Dave Rhodes        (7,264)  MAKE MONEY FAST!!!
+ N 3   Feb 11  davey@surfer.com   (1,220)  My new Toyota...


          [Folder "INBOX" opened with 3 messages]


? Help         < FldrList    P PrevMsg   - PrevPage     D Delete     R Reply

O OTHER CMDS > [ViewMsg]     N NextMsg   Spc NextPage    U Undelete   F Forward
```

MANAGING YOUR MAIL WITH PINE

You can display the current message (which is either underlined or in reverse video) by pressing > or the **ENTER** key while viewing the FOLDER INDEX screen. Here's an example of what you'll see when you view a message in Pine:

```
PINE 4.10   MESSAGE TEXT              Folder: INBOX  Message 1 of 3  ALL
                Date: Sat, 8 Feb 1997 13:57:22 -0800
                From: Joe Kramer <JoeK@asdf.com>
                To: hermie@fritz.com
                Subject: Let's do lunch

                Hey, howzabout we do a "power lunch" on Monday to work out the
                details of that Amorphous contract?  Call me at 555-0317...

? Help         < MsgIndex    P PrevMsg    - PrevPage     D Delete     R Reply
O OTHER CMDS > ViewAttch     N NextMsg    Spc NextPage    U Undelete   F Forward
```

From either this MESSAGE TEXT screen or the FOLDER INDEX screen, you can press one of the following keys to act on the current message. (Pine doesn't care about upper or lower case when entering commands.)

R   Reply to the current message.

D   Delete a message. (Messages don't actually go away when you ask to delete them—they're just flagged with a **D** and expunged later when you exit Pine, just in case you change your mind and don't want the message deleted.)

U   Undelete a message (remove the **D** flag).

If you press **O** to display more Pine commands, the legend at the bottom of the screen changes to the following:

```
  ? Help         M Main Menu   L ListFldrs   C Compose    % Print      S Save
  O OTHER CMDS   Q Quit Pine   G GotoFldr    W WhereIs    T TakeAddr   E Export
```

From here, you can use the following:

C   Compose a new message.

<   Return to the FOLDER INDEX screen.

W   Search for text in the current message.

%   Print the message.

T   Add the sender to your address book.

S   Save the message in a folder.

PINE MAIL FOLDERS

Folders are good for organizing your email. When you press **S** to save a message in a folder, Pine asks you to choose a folder. If that folder already exists, Pine copies the message to that folder and marks it as "Deleted" in your INBOX. If the folder doesn't exist, Pine asks if you want to create it.

You might want to save all messages from a mailing list in a folder with the same name as the list, or have a folder called URGENT for high-priority items. I create folders for people with whom I communicate on a regular basis, so my INBOX stays uncluttered and I can still find an old message when I need it.

You can use the **L** command to display a list of all your folders and then view the messages in a selected folder. The same FOLDER INDEX and MESSAGE TEXT screens are used whether you're dealing with the INBOX folder or another folder that you created.

PINE FOR POWER USERS

Pine is a great tool for managing your email because it's fast, easy to learn, and easily configurable. But it also has many advanced features for power users. Once you've become proficient at basic mail handling, try some of these features. (All are accessed from the FOLDER INDEX screen.)

SEARCHING
Use the **W** ("where is") command to search the FOLDER INDEX screen for messages with a certain word in the Subject line. You can also use the **W** command when you're viewing a message to search for text in the message body.

SORTING
Use the **$** command to sort your messages in a variety of ways, including by subject, sender, size, and arrival time.

ADDRESS BOOK
Use the **T** command to "take" the sender's address and store it in your Pine address book. You can also assign a nickname to the address and use the nickname instead of the full address when composing a new message.

HEADERS
Use the **H** command to view the normally hidden message header lines. At first glance, it's a lot of gobbledygook, but the Received lines will tell you the path a message traveled to reach your system. This can be handy for identifying forged sender addresses. Press **H** again to turn off the display of the header lines.

FORWARD AND BOUNCE

The **F** command lets you forward messages to other users. The message composition screen appears as usual, with the forwarded message pasted into the message text area. You can add your own comments before sending.

The **B** command will "bounce" a message to another user with no opportunity to add comments. If the recipient's mail system complies with standards, it will appear as if the message came from the original sender—not from you. This is handy when you get mail that was obviously meant for someone else and you want to quietly redirect it.

EXPORT AND PIPE

The **E** command will export a message to a file in your home directory. This is useful if someone sends you a file that you want to save and edit, or if you receive a uuencoded or encrypted message. (See Chapter 11, "Compression, Encoding, and Encryption," for more on decoding and decryption.)

The **|** (vertical bar) command will pipe a message directly to any command or program. For example, you could use this feature to pipe a message to a program that strips off mail headers and formats notes for printing.

ATTACHMENTS

Pine has excellent support for attached files. You can attach a binary file such as a program, image, or word processor document to an outgoing message using the **CTRL-J** command while the cursor is on the Attachment: line in the message composition screen. Pine encodes the attached file using MIME (Multi-purpose Internet Mail Enhancements), which is a widely used standard understood by most modern email programs.

Pine can also decode incoming MIME-attached files and either save them to disk or automatically launch the appropriate viewer tools. I used Pine to send Microsoft Word files back and forth to my publisher in the course of writing this book.

ROLES

Pine allows you to play different roles, depending on who you are replying to. For example, if you are replying to a message addressed to

sales@widgets.com, you may be acting as a customer service rep. That role may require that you use a different return address and/or a different signature.

Roles are optional, but if you set up roles, they work like this: Each role has a set of patterns that are used to decide which role is used and a set of actions that are taken when that role is used. When you reply to a message, the From, To, and Subject fields of the original message are compared to your role patterns. If a match is found, the matching role's actions are taken. These actions could include changing the From line, inserting a special template into the message body, or using an alternative signature file. There's a comprehensive section in the Pine help if you're interested in learning more about roles.

HTML EMAIL AND HOTLINKS

With the most recent release of Pine, you can now view HTML email messages directly without exporting them to a file and viewing them with a browser. Pine does a pretty good job of rendering the HTML, minus the color and special fonts.

Pine can also recognize URLs (Web hotlinks) in your email and launch a browser to view them, but you have to explicitly enable this feature to make it work. From the Pine main menu, press **S** (for Setup) and then **C** (for Config). Find the Viewer Preferences section and turn on these two options:

```
[X]   enable-msg-view-urls
[X]   enable-msg-view-web-hostnames
```

Then go all the way down to the bottom of the Config screen and set the following:

```
url-viewers  = /usr/bin/lynx
```

or

```
url-viewers  = /usr/bin/netscape
```

Now when you view a message, the up and down arrow keys will highlight the URLs in the message. Just press **ENTER**, and the browser you defined will launch and display the Web page at the selected URL.

HELP

The built-in help for Pine is excellent, so if you're interested in learning more, just press the **?** key from any screen. You can also visit the Pine Information Center online at http://www.washington.edu/pine for additional help or to download new versions of Pine.

GUI EMAIL PROGRAMS FOR LINUX

If you prefer a graphical interface to send and receive email, you have several options to select from while running the X Windows GUI for Linux.

The **exmh** program comes with Red Hat Linux and has most of the features found in Pine (see Figure 10-1). It seems a bit clunky though—there are lots of unfamiliar terms on the screen, and it takes a while to get used to the nonstandard user interface.

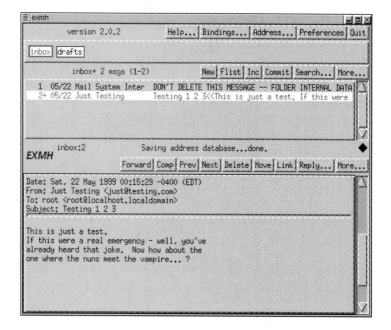

Figure 10-1: *The exmh email client*

The Netscape browser (see Figure 10-2) has built-in email capabilities, just like the Windows version. Click on "Communicator" and then select "Messenger" to start the email client (see Figure 10-3).

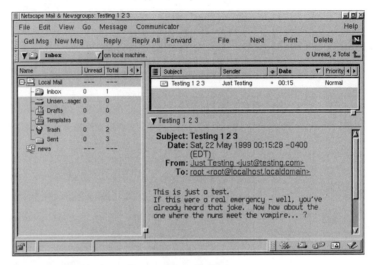

Figure 10-2: *The Netscape Messenger email client*

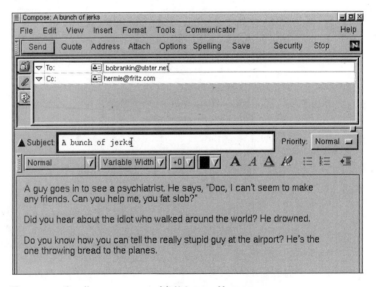

Figure 10-3: *Sending a message with Netscape Messenger*

COMPRESSION, ENCODING, AND ENCRYPTION

The Unix environment offers you several ways to transform your files. Depending on your needs, you can shrink files, smash them, or scramble them—and then return them to their original size and shape.

This chapter will give you an understanding of the tools available for compressing, archiving, encoding, and encrypting your files and show you when to use each.

PUTTING ON THE SQUEEZE: COMPRESSING AND ARCHIVING

When you compress a file, you reduce it to a fraction of its original size so you can more efficiently store it or transmit it to another person. Compressed files travel faster and take up less space in file libraries, but you can't open or execute a compressed file without first decompressing it.

When you smash a bunch of files together into a single file, you're creating an archive. (You don't necessarily compress the files, though.) Archives are useful because they create a package of files that belong together, which makes it easier to distribute a group of related files—for example, the files that make up a program. Because archive files are not always smaller than the sum of their parts, you will sometimes use a compression tool on an archive, resulting in a compressed archive.

Although zip is the most common compression format under DOS and Windows, Unix commonly uses files created with the **tar** and **gzip** commands. You'll certainly run into files with names like these:

`something.tar`	An archive file created with **tar**
`something.gz`	A compressed file created with **gzip**
`something.tar.gz`	A compressed archive file
`something.tgz`	Same as **something.tar.gz**

Although the **gzip** program is built into all Linux systems, it may not be part of some Unix systems, in which case, an older tool called **compress** is used. Files created by **compress** have names like this (note the capital "Z"):

something.Z	A compressed file
something.tar.Z	A compressed **tar** file

■ *TIP: If you find yourself on a Unix system that doesn't have **gzip**, you can download the source code (available free) and compile it yourself. See the GNU Project home page at http://www.gnu.org/ to find out how to get the source code.*

The sections that follow show you how to create and undo compressed files and archives.

THE TAR COMMAND

The **tar** (tape archive) command bundles a bunch of files together and creates an archive (commonly called a *tar file* or *tarball*) on a tape, disk drive, or floppy disk. The original files are not deleted after being copied to the tar file.

To create an archive using **tar**, use a command like this, which bundles all the files in the current directory that end with .doc into the **alldocs.tar** file:

```
tar cvf alldocs.tar *.doc
```

Here's a second example, which creates a tar file named **panda.tar** containing all the files from the **panda** directory (and any of its subdirectories):

```
tar cvf panda.tar panda/
```

In these examples, the **c**, **v**, and **f** flags mean create a new archive, be verbose (list files being archived), and write the archive to a file. You can also create tar files on tape drives or floppy disks, like this:

tar cvfM /dev/fd0 panda	Archive the files in the panda directory to floppy disk(s).
tar cvf /dev/rmt0 panda	Archive the files in the panda directory to the tape drive.

The /**dev**/**fdo** entry is Linux-ese for "floppy drive zero" (your A drive under DOS), and /**dev**/**rmto** means "removable media tape zero," or your primary tape drive. The **M** flag means use multiple floppy disks—when one disk is full, **tar** prompts you to insert another.

To automatically compress the tar file as it is being created, add the **z** flag, like this:

```
tar cvzf alldocs.tar.gz *.doc
```

In this example, I added the **.gz** suffix to the archive file name, because the **z** flag tells **tar** to use the same compression as the **gzip** command.

To list the contents of a tar file, use the **t** (type) flag in a command, like this:

tar tvf alldocs.tar   List all files in alldocs.tar.

To extract the contents of a **tar** file, use the **x** (extract) flag in a command, like this:

tar xvf panda.tar   Extract files from panda.tar.

This will copy all the files from the **panda.tar** file into the current directory. When a tar file is created, it can bundle up all the files in a directory, as well as any subdirectories and the files in them. So when you're extracting a tar file, keep in mind that you might end up with some new subdirectories in the current directory.

We've used several different flags in the sample **tar** commands so far. Here's a list of the most common flags:

c   Create a new archive.

t   List the contents of an archive.

x   Extract the contents of an archive.

f   The archive file name is given on the command line (required whenever the **tar** output is going to a file).

M   The archive can span multiple floppies.

v   Print verbose output (list file names as they are processed).

u   Add files to the archive if they are newer than the copy in the **tar** file.

z   Compress or decompress files automatically.

The gzip and gunzip Commands

The **gzip** program compresses a single file. One important thing to remember about **gzip** is that, unlike **tar**, it replaces your original file with a compressed version. (The amount of compression varies with the type of data, but a typical text file will be reduced by 70 to 80 percent.) Say you enter this command:

```
gzip cheap.suit
```

You'll end up with a compressed file named **cheap.suit.gz**, and **cheap.suit** will be deleted.

To decompress the **cheap.suit.gz** file, enter this:

```
gunzip cheap.suit.gz
```

You'll get the original **cheap.suit** file back, and **cheap.suit.gz** will be deleted.

You can tell **gzip** to use different levels of compression with the *-n* flag, where *n* is a number from 1 to 9. The **-1** flag means "fast but less efficient" compression, and **-9** means "slow but most efficient" compression. Values of *n* between 1 and 9 will trade off speed and efficiency, and the default is **-6**. If you want to get the best possible compression and you don't mind waiting a little longer, use the **-9** flag, like this:

```
gzip -9 cheap.suit
```

One other useful option is the **-r** flag, which tells **gzip** and **gunzip** to recursively compress or decompress all files in the current directory and any subdirectories. (Even with the **-r** flag, **gzip** still compresses one file at a time.) Here are some examples:

`gzip -r somedir`	Zip all files in the somedir directory.
`gunzip -r somedir`	Unzip all files in the **somedir** directory.

Handling Compressed Archives

It's common to apply **gzip** to a tar file, which is why you see files with names like **something.tar.gz** on Linux systems. When you want to extract the contents of a gzipped tar file, you have several choices. The first is to use **gunzip** followed by **tar**, like this:

```
gunzip something.tar.gz
tar xvf something.tar
```

Or you could do it all in one command, like this:

```
gunzip -c something.tar.gz | tar xvf -
```

The **-c** flag tells **gunzip** to decompress the file, but instead of creating a **something.tar** file, it pipes the decompressed data directly to the **tar** command. The **tar** command on the right side of the pipeline looks a little strange, too—instead of a file name after the **xvf**, there's just a dash. The dash tells **tar** that the input is not an actual file on disk, but rather a stream of data from the pipeline. (Note that the **gunzip** input file is not deleted when you use the **-c** flag.)

Here's a third method of extracting the contents of a compressed tar file that's even easier. Remember the **z** flag with the **tar** command? You can use it to decompress and unbundle a tar file, like this:

```
tar xvzf something.tar.gz
```

The end result is exactly the same (the files that were in the compressed tar file are now in your current directory), but this is much easier than issuing multiple commands or writing a messy-looking **gunzip-tar** pipeline.

Note that this command will work on all Linux systems, but the **z** flag for **tar** is not always available on other flavors of Unix. (However, you can download and compile the source code for the GNU version of the **tar** command. See the note near the beginning of this chapter about getting the source code for the GNU utilities.)

THE COMPRESS, UNCOMPRESS, AND ZCAT COMMANDS

The **compress** and **uncompress** programs work just like **gzip** and **gunzip**, but they use an older and less efficient compression technique. If you're using Linux, you shouldn't have to bother with **compress** and **uncompress** at all. Even if you come across a file created with **compress** (something with a .Z suffix), you can decompress it with **gunzip**, because **gunzip** understands both formats.

Still, just for completeness, here's how to use the **compress** and **uncompress** programs:

`compress some.file`	Create compressed **some.file.Z**
`uncompress some.file`	Create decompressed **some.file**

The **zcat** program is another Linux antique. It does the same thing as **uncompress** with the **-c** flag (decompresses and writes output to the pipeline), so the following two commands would be equivalent:

```
uncompress -c something.tar.X | tar xvf -
zcat something.tar.X | tar xvf -
```

You should have to use these commands only if you're running some version of Unix besides Linux. (Even then, many Unix systems will have the GNU versions of **gzip, gunzip,** and **tar** available.)

THE ZMORE AND ZLESS COMMANDS

The **zmore** command is a handy utility that lets you view gzipped files one screen at a time (much like the **more** command) without first decompressing them. The **zmore** command pauses after each screenful, printing *--More--* at the bottom of the screen. You can press **ENTER** to display one more line, or press the spacebar to view the next screen of data.

The **zless** command works the same way, except the decompressed output is displayed by the **less** command for additional viewing flexibility. Keep in mind that **zmore** and **zless** do not modify the input file.

THE ZIP AND UNZIP COMMANDS

The **zip** and **unzip** programs work almost exactly like their cousins PKZIP and PKUNZIP in the DOS environment. You can squash a bunch of files together into a zip file like this:

```
zip squash.zip file1 file2 file3
```

Then you can extract the original files like this:

```
unzip squash.zip
```

Most of the flags are the same as for PKZIP and PKUNZIP, but there are a few differences, so you might like to view the help with **zip -h** or **unzip -h** if you need anything fancier than the basic commands shown here.

If you use the **-k** flag when you zip a file under Linux, you can apply PKUNZIP to it under DOS. This flag tells **zip** to translate the Unix file and directory names into something that fits the more restrictive DOS naming conventions.

For example, if you have Linux files named **another.longunix. filename** and **wontwork.withDOS,** the **-k** flag will cause these files to be stored in the zip file as **another.lon** and **wontwork.wit.** If you don't use the **-k** flag, the PKUNZIP command under DOS will give you an error message and refuse to create the files with the invalid names.

SHELL ARCHIVES

A shell archive is like a tar file, but it is used only for packaging source code and other plain-text files. It provides a convenient way to smash together all the source files for a project into one file that can be distributed by email. (The original files are not deleted.)

Shell archives (commonly called *shar*—for shell archive—files) get their name from the fact that they contain the Linux commands needed to extract the original files.

By convention, shell archives are named with a **.shar** extension. To create a shar file, use a command like this:

```
shar input_files > shar_file
```

So, to create a **panda.shar** file containing all the files from the **panda/source** directory, you'd issue a command like this (note the use of the asterisk as a wildcard):

```
shar panda/source/* > panda.shar
```

If you look inside a shar file, you'll see the original files sandwiched between the commands to extract them. But you don't have to execute those commands directly to unpack a shar file. Just enter this command to extract the files to the current directory:

```
sh panda.shar
```

The **sh** command will run the Linux commands embedded in the **panda.shar** file and re-create all the original files.

You might be wondering why you'd want to use shar files when tar files seem to serve the same purpose. The answer is that shar files are ready to send (because they're plain text), whereas a tar file must be encoded first. See the next section for more on encoding and decoding.

GRAPHICAL ARCHIVING AND COMPRESSION

If you find all those commands and flags for archiving and compressing a bit daunting, get a copy of gxTar–a GNOME front-end to common archive utilities under Linux (see Figure 11-1). The author of this program says his goal is to make it the WinZip of the Unix world. Currently, zip, gzip, tar, and a few other file formats are supported. You can create zip files and archives or add, delete, extract, and view files.

Dragging and dropping from the File Manager is also supported. All those nasty **tar, gzip, gunzip, zip,** and **unzip** commands happen behind the pretty point-and-click interface. Learn more about **gxTar** or download it from http://gxtar.netpedia.net/ on the Web.

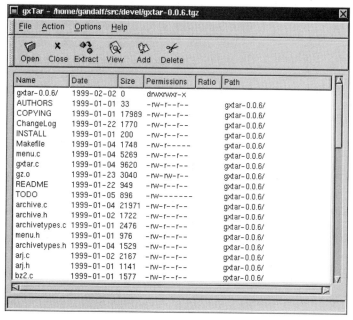

Figure 11-1: *The gxTar utility*

Decoder Rings Sold Here

When you encode a file, you translate it into a format that other types of computers can understand. For example, if you want to send an executable program, compressed files, word processor file, or any other binary data by email, you have to encode it in ASCII (plain text) format first, or it will most likely be unreadable on the receiving end.

Most modern email programs can send and receive binary files, encoding them as MIME attachments and decoding them when they're received. (Almost any Windows-based email program can handle attachments, as can Pine, Exmh, or Netscape Mail under Linux.) But if you're partial to a low-tech mailer like the Unix **mail** command, or if you know that the intended recipient cannot handle attachments, you'll have to uuencode your files before sending them or uudecode them after they arrive.

The uuencode and uudecode Commands

The **uuencode** program creates an encoded ASCII copy of a binary file, suitable for email transmission. The encoded file will be 35 percent larger than the original and will look something like this (with the word *begin*, a number, and the original file name on the first line, followed by a bunch of 61-character lines that all begin with "M"):

```
begin 644 panda.tar
M4$L#!`H`!@`.`/6H?18.$$ Z$F@P```@?```,`````5$$,2@@S,34N5%%XD=84g0I[
M!!LP89s!KL,2P,)!PL).PD.oD'%%@.(!1@.!%P%-4.B.E%PL*!@@*..P4.`4.
. . . . . . (and so on)
```

By convention, uuencoded files are named with a **.uue** extension. To create a uuencoded file under Linux, enter a command like this:

```
uuencode panda.tar panda.tar > panda.uue
```

The first **panda.tar** on the preceding line is the name that appears on the "begin" line of the output file; the second **panda.tar** is the name of the file you want to encode. (You might want to put a name other than the actual input file name on the "begin" line if you're sending the encoded file to a DOS system where file names are more restricted.)

To decode a uuencoded file, enter a command like this:

```
uudecode panda.uue
```

The uudecode program will look for the "begin" line and create a decoded file with the name and file permissions specified there. In the example here, the **panda.tar** file will be created in the current directory with permissions set to **644** (shorthand notation for **rw-r--r--**, which equates to the following: owner: read/write; group: read; others: read).

■ *NOTE: To calculate the numeric equivalent of a file permissions string, look at each triplet in the permissions. Read gets 4 points, write gets 2, and execute gets 1. See Chapter 5, "The Linux File System," for more on file permissions.*

Files that are created with the **tar**, **gzip**, **compress**, or **zip** command in Linux must be uuencoded before they can be sent by email.

HANDLING ENCODED FILES AND EMAIL

If you want to uuencode a file and email it in one step, try a command like this:

```
uuencode panda.tar | mail whoever@whatever.com
```

This tells **uuencode** to pipe the output directly to the mail program instead of creating a **.uue** file. If you want to take it one step further, you could even archive, encode, and mail in one command, like this:

```
tar cvf - panda | uuencode | mail whoever@whatever.com
```

That should all make sense if you read about pipelines in Chapter 4, "Living in a Shell," and understand that the dash in the **tar** command means send the file to a pipeline instead of creating a tar file on disk. Of course you could also do this:

```
tar cvf panda.tar panda
uuencode panda.tar > panda.uue
mail whoever@whatever.com < panda.uue
rm panda.uue
```

But that's a lot more work!

MAKING YOUR MAIL TOP SECRET

Internet email is about as secure as sending a postcard—any postal clerks along the delivery path can read your message if they wanted to since there's no envelope to protect it. So if you're concerned about your private email falling into the wrong hands, encryption is the solution.

Encryption will scramble your message so that only the holder of the secret decryption key will be able to read it. The de facto standard for encryption is the PGP (Pretty Good Privacy) program, written by Phil Zimmerman. Actually *pretty good* privacy is a pretty serious understatement. If you use a sufficiently long password key, the computing power required to crack the code that PGP uses becomes astronomically large.

ARE YOU A CRYPTO CRIMINAL?

PGP is such a good program that the United States government has classified it as a "munition" and made exporting it illegal, for reasons of national security. Apparently the feds are worried that the bad guys will be able to correspond in a way they can't decode. Although it is not illegal to send a message that has been encoded by PGP, you can't export (via email, FTP, or any other means) the PGP sofware from the United States, except to Canada (or from Canada, except to the United States), without a license from the federal government. The one strange exception to this rule is that printed books containing the PGP source code can be exported.

It is also illegal to use PGP in some countries (it's legal in the United States), so if you are an evil terrorist or are plotting the overthrow of your government, check with your local authorities first before using PGP. The Crypto Law Survey at http://cwis.kub.nl/~frw/people/koops /lawsurvy.htm summarizes the legalities of PGP around the world.

GETTING PGP

If you're interested in learning more about PGP, see the PGP FAQ at http://www.cam.ac.uk.pgp.net/pgpnet/pgp-faq/ on the Web.

To get a copy of the PGP software, visit http://web.mit.edu/
network/pgp-form.html to see the PGP Distribution Authorization
Form. If you are a citizen of the United States or Canada and promise
to use it for noncommercial purposes and never export it to any other
countries, you can download the Unix source code for PGP, which you
will have to compile yourself. If you plan to use PGP for commercial
use, you can purchase it from Network Associates, at
http://www.nai.com.

COMPRESSION, ENCODING, AND ENCRYPTION UNDER DOS

If you're working on a DOS system and you come across a tar file, a
gzip file, or a file that has been uuencoded, all is not lost. Fortunately,
you can find DOS tools for dealing with compressed and encoded files
at a variety of sites on the Internet, and most of them are free.

Visit http://www.shareware.com or http://www.download.com and
use the search engines there to find DOS or Windows versions of tar,
gzip, uuencode, and PGP. The Wincode and WinZip shareware programs are very popular, so you might want to try them first.

12

LINUX DOES DOS AND WINDOWS

Even though Linux is a very complete operating system, you will probably have occasion to access the programs and files you left behind in the DOS world. Fortunately, there are several ways to do so without shutting down Linux and booting up DOS.

This chapter will show you how to use the MTOOLS package to read and write DOS floppy disks under Linux, and how to mount your DOS hard drive partition to access a DOS file system while running Linux. You'll also learn about DOSemu, a DOS emulator that runs under Linux, as well as WINE, a Windows emulator that enables you to run Microsoft Windows applications in Linux's X Windows environment.

Accessing DOS Floppies with MTOOLS

Do you need to list the files on a DOS-formatted floppy disk while running Linux? Do you need to copy a file from a DOS disk to your Linux file system, or vice versa? You can use the MTOOLS commands to do these and lots of other DOS-like things with Linux.

The MTOOLS package is a set of Linux commands that mimic the DOS commands **DIR, COPY, TYPE, DEL, RENAME,** and a few others. They're called the MTOOLS because they all start with the letter *m*, and they work much like their DOS counterparts.

Here's a list of the MTOOLS commands and what they do:

matttrib	Modify the attributes of a file.
mcd	Change the current directory.
mcopy	Copy a file.
mdel	Delete a file.
mdir	List the files in the directory.
mformat	Format a disk.
mlabel	Change the disk label.
mmd	Make a new directory.
mrd	Remove a directory.
mren	Rename a file.
mtype	Display the contents of a file.

Okay, pop a DOS disk in the machine and let's try some examples. Here we see the **mdir** command in action, listing the files on a disk:

```
mdir A:

Volume in drive A has no label
Volume Serial Number is 1205-1049
Directory of A:\


COMMAND  COM       54,645 05-31-94   6:22a
FORMAT   COM       22,974 05-31-94   6:22a
SYS      COM        9,432 05-31-94   6:22a
MOUSE    COM       28,949 04-02-93   4:39p
EDIT     COM          413 05-31-94   6:22a
FDISK    EXE       29,336 01-01-97  12:39a
         6 file(s)       145,749 bytes
                       1,311,915 bytes free
```

Now let's copy a file from Linux to the disk, and vice versa:

```
mcopy A:pandavu.tgz /tmp
mcopy /tmp/kornmeal.txt A:
```

The **mcopy** command figures out in which direction to perform the file transfer by looking for the **A:** in either the source or the target file name. If you have two floppy drives, you can use **B:** when referring to the second floppy drive.

Here's an example showing the use of the **mdel** command to delete a file on the disk:

```
mdel mouse.com
```

Note that we didn't prefix the name of the file to be deleted with **A:** this time. All of the MTOOLS commands (except **mcopy**) assume that you're working with the A drive, so you can omit the **A:** if you like, but I recommend that you don't, just for safety's sake.

Accessing DOS Partitions with mount

Most people running Linux have a DOS partition on their hard drive, and if you followed the instructions in Chapter 1, "Installing Linux on Your PC," you should, too. You can read, write, and manipulate your DOS files just as if they were native Linux files by mounting the DOS partition.

When you mount the DOS partition, it becomes just another directory under the root of your Linux file system, and you can treat it like any other Linux directory. When you move a Linux file to the DOS partition (or vice versa), Linux figures out whether the file is plain text or binary data and performs any appropriate conversions behind the scenes. And it's pretty cool to use **find, grep,** and other Linux commands on your DOS files.

Before you perform the mount, you have to create a new directory in the root of your Linux file system. You can call this directory whatever you like, but I recommend **/dos** for simplicity. Create the directory with this command (you must be logged in as **root**):

```
mkdir /dos
```

Now we're ready to mount the DOS partition on top of the **/dos** directory. Here's the command to use:

```
mount -t msdos /dev/hda1 /dos
```

Translated into English, this tells Linux to mount the file system of type MSDOS (**-t msdos**) found on the first partition of the first hard drive (**/dev/hda1**) on top of the **/dos** directory. If your DOS partition uses the newer FAT32 file system, you may need to replace **-t msdos** with **-t vfat** in the **mount** command.

If you have a SCSI hard drive, you should use **/dev/sda1** instead of **/dev/hda1** in the preceding example. If you have a second hard drive on your system with a DOS partition, reference it as **/dev/hdb1**. (See Chapter 1, "Installing Linux on Your PC," for more information on hard drives, devices, and partitions.)

Okay, your DOS partition is mounted—now have a look around. If you issue the **ls /dos** command, you'll see the same list of files that would result from a **dir C:** command under DOS. You can use **cd** to see other directories under **/dos** and use any Linux command to slice and dice your DOS files.

It's great to have the ability to copy files back and forth between Linux and DOS, but you can also do some clever things if you think creatively. I find it particularly helpful to use the **ln** (link) command to share my Netscape bookmarks file between Linux and DOS, like this:

```
ln -s /dos/netscape/bookmark.htm $HOME/.netscape/bookmarks
```

By linking these files together, I need to manage just one bookmark file. Of course, this trick works only if both the DOS and Linux versions of a product use the same format for the files being shared.

If you want your DOS partition to mount each time you boot Linux, add the line shown here to the **/etc/fstab** file:

```
/dev/hda1   /dos   msdos   umask=022
```

When Linux boots up, it looks in the **/etc/fstab** file and mounts all the file systems specified there, so you won't have to issue the **mount** command manually to access your DOS partition. The line you just added to **/etc/fstab** has the same effect as the **mount** command shown earlier. The same caveat about FAT32 file systems applies here, so you may need to replace **msdos** with **vfat** in the previous example.

RUNNING DOS PROGRAMS WITH DOSEMU

DOSemu (DOS Emulator) is a program that lets you run many of your favorite DOS applications under Linux. The name is a little bit misleading—it doesn't actually emulate DOS; it boots DOS to a virtual machine using the special hardware features in Intel 80386 and higher CPUs.

A DOSemu session looks and acts like a real DOS session, with a few limitations on what can be done. Not all video and sound cards are supported under DOSemu, and some programs that require DPMI (DOS Protected-Mode Interface) will not run. The most notable example of this is Windows 3.1, although some people do report being able to run it under DOSemu.

Setting Up DOSemu

Setting up DOSemu is not hard, but it does require a few steps to get a fully functional DOS session. Unfortunately, the DOSemu package is not present on the CD in this book, so you'll have to download it from the DOSemu Web site — http://www.dosemu.org/. I recommend that you get the latest stable version (v0.98 at press time) and stay away from the developer versions, since they tend to be buggy.

After downloading the RPM file for DOSemu, issue a command like the one below while logged in as root. The filename may be slightly different, depending on the version you download. (See Chapter 14, "Updating Your Linux System," for more about the **rpm** command.

`rpm -i dosemu-0.98.6-1.i386.rpm`   Install DOSemu v0.98

Configuring DOSemu

The package is now installed, but we need to tweak the DOSemu configuration file before using it. Edit the **/etc/dosemu.conf** file and modify the **$_hdimage** entry so that it reads as follows:

`$_hdimage = "hdimage.test /dev/hda1"`

The **hdimage.test** file resides in your **/var/lib/dosemu** directory and is a *hard disk image* — a special Linux file that contains a complete DOS system. The line you just modifed tells DOSemu to treat the **hdimage.test** file as the C drive when DOSemu is started. This C drive is not your beloved DOS partition; it's a simulated bootable hard-disk partition containing the FreeDOS operating system – a freeware clone of MS-DOS. The **/dev/hda1** portion of the modified line tells DOSemu to treat your real DOS partition as the next drive letter, or the D drive. (You can boot DOSemu directly from your real DOS partition, but we'll address that later.)

Starting a DOSemu Session

Before starting a DOSemu session, which will be accessing **/dev/hda1** (your MS-DOS partition), it's very important to unmount the partition.

Otherwise, the DOS virtual machine and your Linux system might be trying to write to the disk simultaneously, with potentially disastrous results. To unmount the partition, issue this command:

```
umount /dev/hda1
```

Now we're ready to fire up DOSemu. Issue the command shown here from your Linux command prompt:

```
dos
```

In a few seconds, you should see a DOS session start, and the familiar C:> prompt will appear. Voila—you're running DOS under Linux! Issue the **dir** command and have a look at the results. Don't panic if the listing of files is unfamiliar. Remember—what you have here is a special C drive with the FreeDOS files that DOSemu will use to boot up (see Figure 12-1).

You can switch to your D drive (your DOS partition) by issuing the **D:** command and then change directories, view files, execute programs, and so on. Because we booted from the C drive with FreeDOS, the config.sys and autoexec.bat files from your DOS partition were not executed. This means that your normal DOS PATH variable will not be set, so you may have to use **cd** to get to the appropriate directory before running a program.

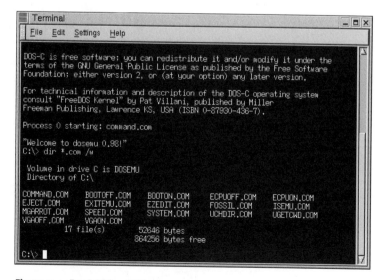

Figure 12-1: *FreeDOS in a DOSemu session*

Exiting from DOSemu

You can exit the DOSemu session by entering the following command at your C: prompt (note that it won't work if you are at the D: prompt):

```
exitemu
```

If that doesn't work, or if your DOSemu session is frozen, log in from another virtual console and then use the **ps** and **kill** commands to find and terminate the DOSemu task. (See Chapter 4, "Living in a Shell," for details on killing an active task.)

It's a good idea to copy the **exitemu.com** file from the C drive to the D drive so you can exit from DOSemu cleanly if you later decide to run DOSemu directly from your "real" DOS partition. To do so, enter this command from the C: prompt:

```
copy C:\exitemu D:\
```

Starting DOSemu with "Real" DOS

If any of your DOS programs don't run correctly as a result of finding themselves on a D drive instead of a C drive, you can start a DOSemu session by booting your "real" DOS partition. To do so, edit the **/etc/dosemu.conf** file and modify the **$_hdimage** entry so that it reads like this:

```
$_hdimage = "/dev/hda1"
```

This tells DOSemu to treat your DOS partition as the C drive and to boot the MS-DOS operating system instead of FreeDOS. Upon restarting DOSemu, MS-DOS will try to start Windows 95/98, if you have it installed. This will surely lock up your machine, because DOSemu does not support Microsoft Windows. To avoid this problem, press the **F8** key as soon as the message "Starting MS-DOS" appears and then select option 6, "Command Prompt Only," to boot MS-DOS without starting Windows.

Additional DOSemu Configuration

By default, DOSemu starts with text-only video support and no support for serial ports. So if you want to run any graphics programs or use the mouse or modem, exit DOSemu and continue.

To enable support for graphics or the mouse or modem, edit the **/etc/dosemu.conf** file as described here. I recommend that you configure only the features you really need. Take these steps one at a time and test each new feature separately by starting DOSemu. That way, if a problem arises, you'll know which feature caused it and you can go back to the **/etc/dosemu.conf** file and disable it or try an alternative.

Setting Up VGA Graphics

Look for the **$_graphics** and **$_videoportaccess** entries and change them to read as follows:

```
$_graphics = (1)
$_videoportaccess = (1)
```

Start DOSemu and test your graphics program. If it doesn't work, see the copious comments in the **/etc/dosemu.conf** file or at the DOSemu Web site for other things to try.

Setting Up Mouse Support

Look for the **$_com1, $mouse**, and **$mouse_dev** entries and change them as follows:

```
$_com1 = "/dev/mouse"
$_mouse = "microsoft"
$_mouse_dev = "/dev/mouse"
```

If your mouse is not on COM1, select the **$comX** entry corresponding to your mouse port. Set the **$_mouse** value according to the type of mouse you have. Most systems use a Microsoft mouse, but this value can be **microsoft, mousesystems, logitech, mmseries, mouseman, hitachi, busmouse,** or **ps2**. Start DOSemu and test your mouse application. Again, if you have problems getting the mouse to work, refer to the **/etc/dosemu.conf** file or the DOSemu Web site–http:// www.dosemu.org/.

Setting Up Modem Support

Look for the **$_com2** entry and change it to read as follows:

```
$_com2 = "/dev/modem"
```

If your modem is not on COM2, select the **$comX** entry corresponding to your modem port. Start DOSemu and test your modem application.

Running DOSemu under X Windows

You can run a DOSemu session under X Windows by issuing the **xdos** command from an xterm window. A new window titled DOS in a Box should appear on the screen. The xdos session should behave the same as any other DOSemu session, except that it doesn't support graphics.

Getting More Information on DOSemu

The volunteer developers of DOSemu are working hard to fix bugs and resolve existing compatibility problems. You can visit James Maclean's DOSemu home page at http://www.dosemu.org to get the latest news on DOSemu and download new versions as they are made available. If you are a programmer, you can find out how to contribute to the DOSemu development effort.

Running Windows Programs with Wine

Wine (Windows Emulator – or "Wine Is Not an Emulator") is a program that allows you to run some Windows 3.1 and Windows 95/98 applications under Linux. Wine works by intercepting the internal Windows program calls and translating them into equivalent X Windows functions.

Although work on Wine has come a long way, it is still considered to be alpha (experimental) code. Many people have reported varying degrees of success running some of the larger shareware and commercial programs under Wine, but some programs still run poorly or not at all.

While some time ago the Wine documentation flatly stated that 32-bit Windows 95/98 applications would *never* run under Wine, today many run quite well.

The newsgroup comp.emulators.ms-windows.wine is the best place to look for the latest news on Wine and occasionally has postings that tell of successes and failures in running various Microsoft Windows programs under Wine. The official WineHQ Web site maintains a searchable database of programs that have been tested under Wine. (See http://www.winehq.com)

How Do I Get a Taste of Wine?

The Wine package is not included on the CD that comes with this book because a new version of Wine is distributed about twice a month. If you want to try out Wine, you'll have to get the latest executable and configure the package on your Linux system. Look for the **RPM** file corresponding to the latest Wine release at the WineHQ Web site and download it to your system. For instance, the version released on May 23, 1999, was called **wine-990523-1.i386.rpm**.

How Do I Run Wine?

You'll need about 10MB of hard drive space to store Wine files, and it's recommended that you have at least 16MB of RAM and a 16MB swap partition to run Wine. You'll also need to have a mounted DOS partition with Microsoft Windows 3.1 or 95/98 installed on it.

To install Wine from the **RPM** file, issue a command like this, replacing the *xxxx* with the date stamp of the Wine file you just downloaded:

```
rpm -i wine-99xxxx-1.i386.rpm
```

When the installation is finished, you have just one more setup step to perform. Edit the **/usr/local/wine.conf** file and edit the **Path=** line in the **[Drive C]** section so that it reads **Path=/dos** (assuming that's the name you assigned to your mounted DOS partition); then save the file. If you have an older-style FAT file system on your DOS partition, use **msdos** instead of **win95** on the **Filesystem** line.

```
[Drive C]
Path=/dos
Type=hd
Label=MS-DOS
Filesystem=win95
```

To run a Microsoft Windows program under Wine, you must first enter X Windows with the **startx** command. From an xterm window, enter a command like this:

```
wine /path/program
```

For example, if you want to run the Microsoft Windows Solitaire program and you've mounted the DOS partition as **/dos,** then you would enter

```
wine /dos/windows/sol.exe
```

A new window for the Solitaire game should appear on the screen in a few seconds (see Figure 12-2). All of the applets that come with

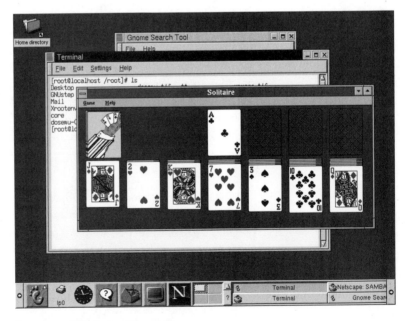

Figure 12-2: *Solitaire in a Wine window*

Microsoft Windows—such as File Manager, Clock, Calculator, Notepad, WordPad, and Paintbrush—will work fine, as will most of the games in the Microsoft Entertainment pack. However, larger and more complex programs such as Microsoft Word for Windows may run poorly, or sometimes not at all.

If you're intoxicated by the mere thought of learning more about Wine, the best source of up-to-date information is the comp. emulators.ms-windows.wine newsgroup. You can also find lots of information online at the WineHQ Web site.

Running VMware: Industrial-Strength Virtual Windows

VMware is a very cool software package that enables multiple operating systems and associated applications to run concurrently on a single machine, without disk partitioning or rebooting. In practical terms, that means you can boot up Windows 95/98 under Linux and run both at the same time!

This is not emulation – you actually boot Windows from your DOS partition and run the Windows desktop right along with your windowed Linux applications (see Figure 12-3). You can even cut and paste between Linux and Windows applications. Right now, I'm writing this with Windows 95 and Microsoft Word in a VMware window, while Netscape for Linux and a bunch of other Linux stuff is happily running on my X Windows desktop.

VMware works wonderfully and is an indispensable tool for anyone who wants to run Linux full-time but can't live without certain Windows software packages. The only drawback is that VMware isn't free. Students, hobbyists, and home users can buy the noncommercial version for $99, which includes all the powerful capabilities of the VMware commercial product but with minimal support. For more information, visit the VMware Web site at http://www.vmware.com/.

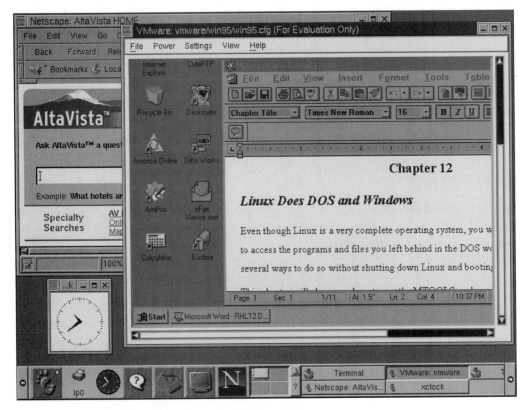

Figure 12-3: *Running Microsoft Windows on the X Windows desktop*

MORE LINUX COMPATIBILITY TOOLS

If you're a Macintosh user, you might want to check out the Executor 2 product from ARDI, which is a Macintosh emulator for Linux. Not only does it read and write Macintosh-format files on floppies and hard drives, but it also runs many Macintosh applications flawlessly.

And if you have multiple computers running a mixture of Windows and Linux, you should have Samba. Samba gives you an easy way to share disks and printers between the two systems, and best of all, it's free. You can learn more about Samba on the Web at http://www.samba.org/.

TWEAKING LINUX

nstalling a new operating system on your computer sets you apart from the great unwashed masses. Getting it to do what you want elevates you to near-guru status. This chapter will show you how to tweak the Red Hat startup process and configure all your Linux hardware and software settings to your liking. If you're the type of person who can't keep your hands off the **autoexec.bat** and **config.sys** files under DOS, or if you derive hours of pleasure fooling with the Windows Device Manager, you'll appreciate what follows.

We'll start by exploring the Setup utility, Linuxconf, the GNOME Control Center, and a few other customization tricks to help you gain the upper hand in controlling the way your Linux system operates.

USING THE SETUP UTILITY

The Setup utility is a simple menu that makes it easy to launch six different system configuration tools. You can use it to configure your keyboard, mouse, system services, sound card, time zone, and X Windows. You could try to remember the commands **kbdconfig, mouseconfig, ntsysv, sndconfig, timeconfig,** and **Xconfigurator** to perform these tasks, but it's easier to type **setup** at the command prompt and then use the arrow keys to select the tool you want to use (see Figure 13-1). Each of these tools should look familiar, because the

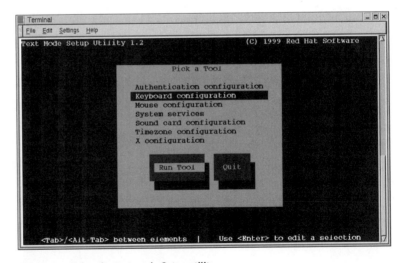

Figure 13-1: *Using the text mode Setup utility*

installation program used them, too. If you made a mistake during installation, or if you want to change the way any of these components is set up, Setup provides the solution. Or maybe you've put in a new mouse, sound card, or video adapter. If so, you will need to run the appropriate configuration utility so Linux will properly detect and interface with the device.

KEYBOARD CONFIGURATION

The Keyboard configurator (see Figure 13-2) isn't very exciting. Just tell Linux what type of keyboard you have and select **OK** to exit. If you live in the U.S.A. and speak English, you probably have a U.S.-style keyboard.

MOUSE CONFIGURATION

If your mouse isn't working properly, use the Mouse configurator (see Figure 13-3) to check things out. If you have a brand-name mouse that appears in the list, select it. Most PCs come with a cheap, no-name mouse, so it's likely that one of the "Generic" options will work. If you have a trackball instead of a mouse, or a laptop with a built-in pointing device (like the "fuzzy red button" on the IBM laptops), try configuring the device as a PS/2 mouse.

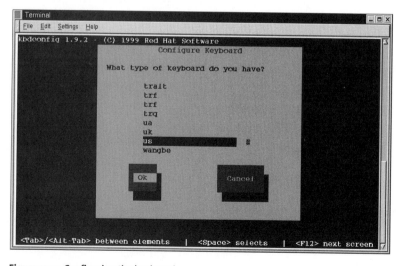

Figure 13-2: *Configuring the keyboard*

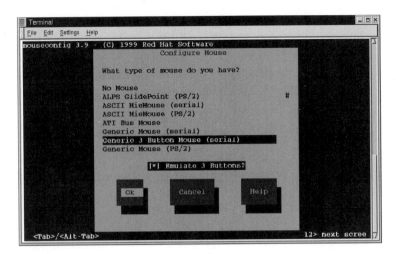

Figure 13-3: *Configuring the mouse*

If you have a two-button mouse, check the "Emulate 3 Buttons?" box, and you'll be able to simulate the middle button by pressing both buttons at once. Also check that your mouse is configured for the same serial port it used under DOS. If you think you did everything right and the mouse still doesn't work, sometimes whacking it on a hard surface while shouting, "You stupid mouse," works wonders.

At startup, Red Hat Linux loads a program called **gpm** that enables cut-and-paste operations at a text-mode command prompt. Hold down the left button and drag to mark the text; then press the middle button to paste the text at any text-mode prompt. In some cases, the gpm program interferes with X Windows, so if you get a "device busy" error message when starting X Windows, disable gpm with this command:

```
gpm -k
```

SYSTEM SERVICES CONFIGURATION

Use the System Services configurator (shown in Figure 13-4) to specify which services should be automatically started at boot time. Unless you're really sure you know what you're doing, you shouldn't mess with the defaults here. One possible exception is the **gpm** service, which provides support for the mouse and cut-and-paste operations in text-based applications.

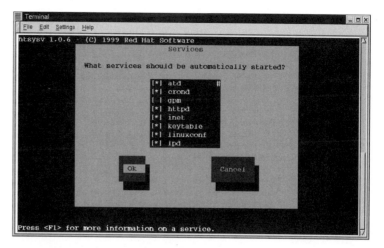

Figure 13-4: *The Systems Services configurator*

SOUND CARD CONFIGURATION

No sound? Try the Sound configurator (shown in Figure 13-5). Most sound cards are SoundBlaster compatible, so that's a good choice if you can't figure out which driver to use. The most common problem is an IRQ conflict, so try different IRQ numbers until you find one that

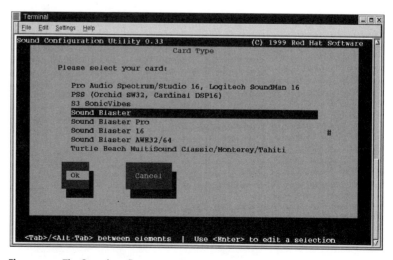

Figure 13-5: *The Sound configurator*

works. You'll know you got it right if you can hear the sound clip of Linus Torvalds saying, "My name is Leenus Tourrrvalds, and I pronounce Linux *lihnooks.*"

TIME ZONE CONFIGURATION

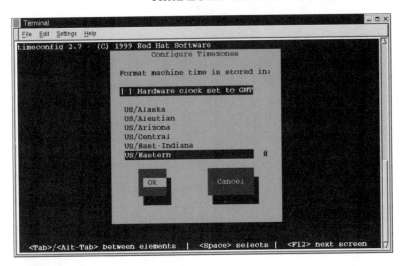

If you move your PC from one time zone to another, you should use the Timezone configurator (shown in Figure 13-6) to tell Linux about your new location.

Figure 13-6: *The Timezone configurator*

X WINDOWS CONFIGURATION

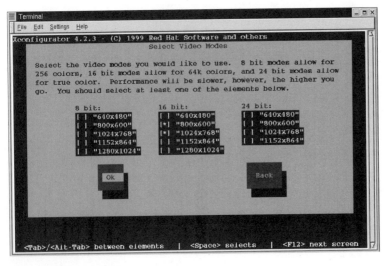

If you're having trouble getting X Windows working, or if you want to try a different screen resolution, run the X Configurator (shown in Figure 13-7) again. If you run into trouble, try using the configuration for a Generic Multisync monitor at 800x600 resolution.

Figure 13-7: *The X configurator*

RUNNING PROGRAMS AT STARTUP

If you're curious about exactly what happens when you boot Linux, here's the story. The Linux kernel starts a program called **init**, which is responsible for initializing all the hardware components and bringing up daemons for networking, email, the Web server, printing, and any other services you specify in the System Services configurator mentioned earlier in this chapter. There are a few places where you can hook into the startup process, if you need to run a program at startup to load a special device driver or perform some other custom initialization task.

THE RC.SERIAL SCRIPT

The init program runs a script called **/etc/rc.d/rc.serial** (if it exists), which is the place to put any serial port (mouse or modem) initialization commands. If your system is configured to autostart PPP services at boot time and you need to use the **setserial** command to get your modem working under Linux, you should run **setserial** in the **rc.serial** script. The **rc.serial** script is run early in the init process, so this ensures that your modem is properly initialized before the PPP daemon tries to dial up your ISP.

THE RC.LOCAL SCRIPT

The other hook into the startup process is the **/etc/rc.d/rc.local** script, which is run at the very end of the init process. By default, the **rc.local** script just prints a log-in banner with your kernel version and machine type, but you can add other commands if you need to initialize a device or print special instructions for the use of your system.

THE .BASHRC SCRIPT

Only the root user can modify the rc.serial and rc.local scripts, since they affect all users on the system. If you want to run some special startup commands that apply only to one user account, put them in **.bashrc**, the Bash shell user profile script, located in your home directory. This is the correct place to define personal aliases for commonly used commands, set environment variables, and so on. Here's a sample .bashrc script:

```
### Include the username and hostname in the shell prompt
set prompt=$user-`hostname`'% '
### Set the screen for 24 rows
stty rows 24

### Define p as a synonym for pico
alias p pico
### Delete any leftover coredump files
rm -f core
### Show how much disk space is in use
du -sk
```

If you want to run some startup commands that apply to all users of the Bash shell, put them in the **/etc/bashrc** file. This system-wide Bash profile runs just before the user-level Bash profile.

Using Linuxconf

Linuxconf is a handy utility that will help you to configure many different aspects of your Linux system. If you need to configure your Internet connection or Web server, add or delete users, change the root password, or perform almost any other system administration task, Linuxconf is the place to go.

You could do any of the things that Linuxconf does by entering commands at the shell prompt, but Linuxconf saves you the trouble of learning and remembering all those arcane system configuration commands. In this section, we'll highlight the Linuxconf features you will use most often.

After logging in as the root user, start Linuxconf by typing

```
linuxconf
```

at a shell prompt, and you'll see the initial Linuxconf menu, as shown in Figure 13-8. The left panel uses a tree-like interface (similar to that of the File Manager) from which you select a configuration task. When you make a selection, the configuration options appear in the right panel. Context-sensitive help is available for most screens, via the "Help" button.

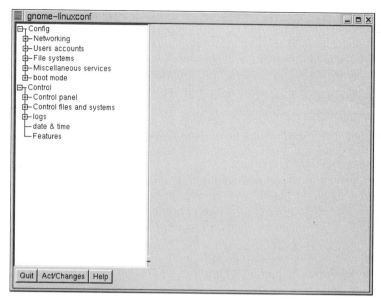

Figure 13-8: *The Linuxconf menu*

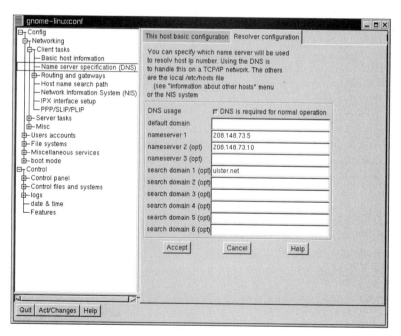

Figure 13-9: *Configuring name server settings*

SPECIFYING THE NAME SERVER

The illustration shown in Figure 13-9 shows the options for configuring the name server settings of your Internet (PPP) connection. Plug in the values provided by your ISP (not the sample values shown in the illustration) and choose "Accept."

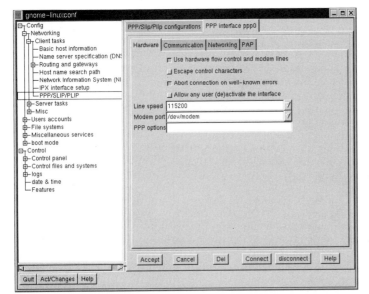

CONFIGURING PPP

If you need to modify your PPP setup, use the screen shown in Figure 13-10. Configuring a PPP connection is covered in more detail in Chapter 3, "Connecting to the Internet."

Figure 13-10: *Modifying your PPP setup*

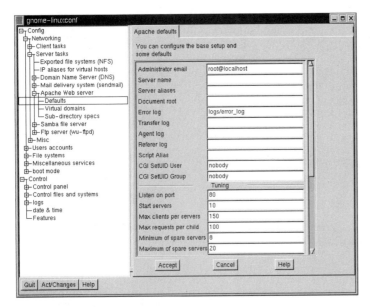

SETTING APACHE WEB SERVER OPTIONS

The Apache Web server comes preconfigured, so your Web site can be up and running as soon as you put your HTML files in the **/home/httpd/html** directory. If you want to tweak any of the Apache settings, use the screen shown in Figure 13-11.

Figure 13-11: *Tweaking Apache settings*

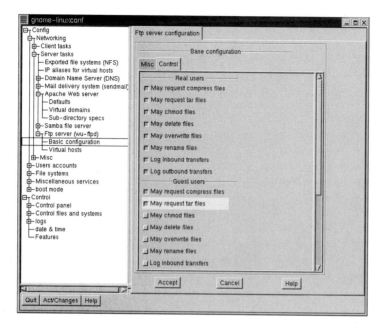

Figure 13-12: *Configuring FTP*

SETTING FTP SERVER OPTIONS

If you plan to allow Internet users to access files on your machine via FTP connections, use the screen shown in Figure 13-12 to configure the FTP server options.

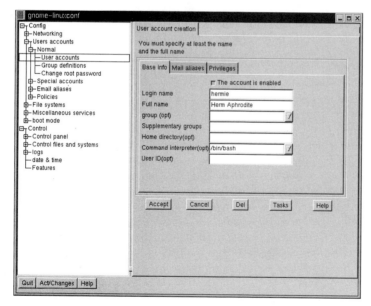

Figure 13-13: *Adding new users*

ADDING NEW USERS

Use the screen shown shown in Figure 13-13 to add new users to your system. Only the "Login name" field is mandatory, but it's a good idea to fill in the "Full name" field as well, so you can remember the real names of your users. If the new users want a command shell other than Bash, select it from the "Command interpreter" list. After you press the "Accept" button, you will be prompted to enter the initial password for the new account.

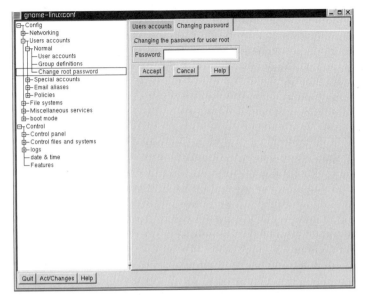

CHANGING THE ROOT PASSWORD

If you need to change the password for the root user, use the screen shown shown in Figure 13-14. Enter root's old password in the input box and press "Accept," and then you'll be prompted to enter and confirm the new password.

Figure 13-14: *Changing the password for the root user*

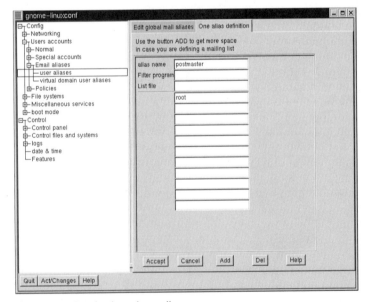

EMAIL ALIASES

If you'd like to route incoming mail for a certain user to an alternative inbox, use the screen shown in Figure 13-15. In the example shown, mail addressed to **postmaster** will be delivered to **root** instead. You can enter more than one address in the lower panel if you want mail rerouted to multiple users.

Figure 13-15: *Routing incoming mail*

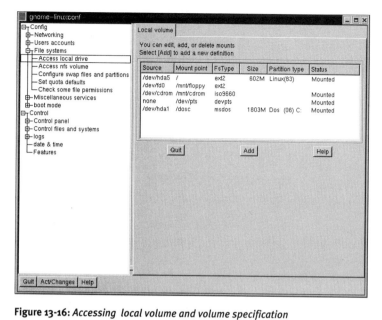

Figure 13-16: *Accessing local volume and volume specification*

SETTING UP LOCAL DRIVES

Use the screen shown in Figure 13-16 to modify, add, or delete drives or partition mounts. Double-click an item to modify the mount parameters.

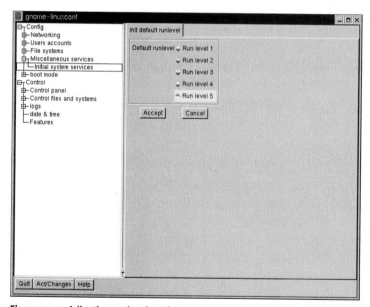

Figure 13-17: *Adjusting runlevel settings*

SETTING THE SYSTEM RUNLEVEL

The system runlevel settings control (see Figure 13-17) whether your system boots up in single-user mode (level 1), text mode (level 3), or graphical mode (level 5). Single-user mode boots with a minimal set of essential drivers and is typically used only in cases of emergency, similar to the Safe Mode of Windows 95/98. (Runlevels 2 and 4 are not used.)

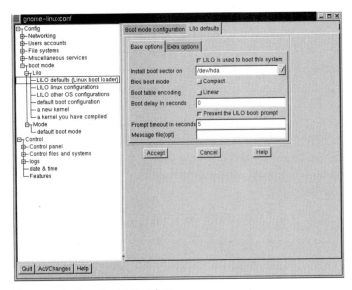

Figure 13-18: *Changing LILO settings*

Configuring LILO

If you want to change any of the LILO settings, use the screen shown in Figure 13-18. If your computer accesses a hard drive in LBA mode, make sure the "Use linear mode" box is checked. You can change the LILO boot prompt timeout from the default of five seconds. Setting the timeout to zero tells LILO to wait indefinitely for user input, instead of booting the default system after the time delay. The dialog box shown here shows how to select the operating system LILO starts by default if you have a nonzero timeout value.

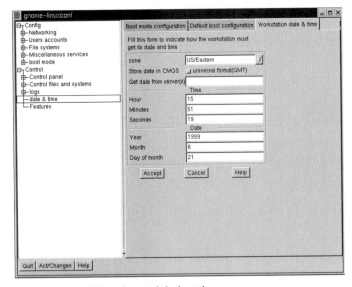

Figure 13-19: *Modifying date and clock settings*

Setting the System Clock

Use the screen shown in Figure 13-19 to modify the system date, clock, or time zone.

LEARNING MORE ABOUT LINUXCONF

The best place to learn more Linuxconf is the Linuxconf Project home page at http://www.solucorp.qc.ca/linuxconf/. This site is maintained by the developer of Linuxconf and includes detailed usage instructions along with information on the most recent release.

THE GNOME CONTROL CENTER

The GNOME Control Center is a graphical tool that helps you customize your GNOME desktop using a set of tools called *capplets*. Click on the taskbar button with the toolbox icon, and you'll launch the GNOME Control Center. Select an item from the menu on the left and double-click on it to modify that part of the system. Desktop capplets enable you to modify the appearance and behavior of the desktop's background, screensavers, themes, and Window Manager.

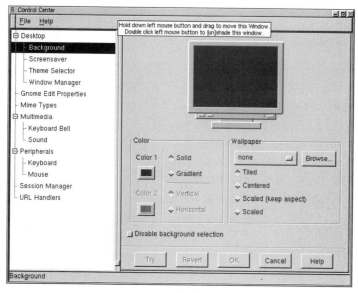

BACKGROUND SETTINGS
Use this selection to modify the desktop's background color or wallpaper (see Figure 13-20).

Figure 13-20: *Modifying background settings*

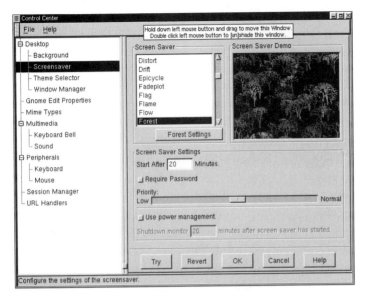

Figure 13-21: *Adjusting screensaver settings*

SCREENSAVER SETTINGS

Use this selection to choose a screensaver that will run after a specified period of idle time (see Figure 13-21). I think you'll find this set of screensavers much more interesting than the ones shipped with Microsoft Windows.

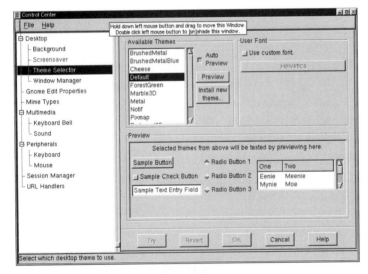

Figure 13-22: *Choosing your GNOME theme*

THEME SELECTOR

Use this selection to modify your GNOME theme settings (see Figure 13-22) and customize the look and feel of your desktop. For a look similar to Windows 95, try the Redmond95 theme.

Changing GNOME themes affects only applications that use the GTK libraries, such as GNOME, Linuxconf, and others written specifically for GNOME. You can find more themes on the Web at http://gtk.themes.org/. After downloading a new theme, press the button labeled "Install new theme." Find the new theme in the file browser, press **OK,** and the theme will appear in the Available Themes list.

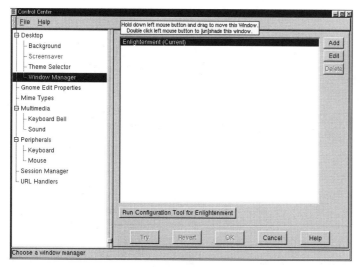

Figure 13-23: *Specifying a Window Manager*

WINDOW MANAGER

Use this selection to choose the Window Manager you want to use (see Figure 13-23). The default Window Manager is Enlightenment, and it may be the only choice on the list unless you download another Window Manager. See the section "Customizing Enlightenment" later in this chapter for more information on customizing the look and behavior of your desktop.

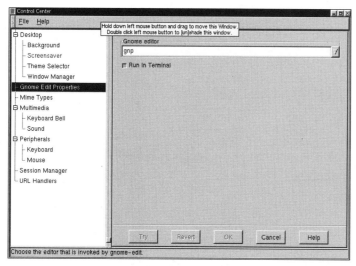

Figure 13-24: *Choosing a text editor*

GNOME EDIT PROPERTIES

Use the screen shown here to specify your favorite text editor (see Figure 13-24). This editor will be launched automatically when you double-click on text files in the File Manager, and at other times when the GNOME system requires you to use a text editor.

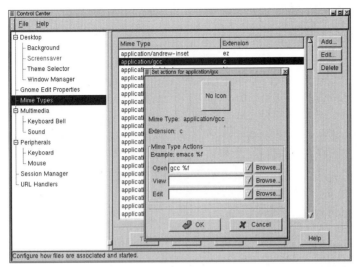

Figure 13-25: *Adding a new MIME type*

GNOME MIME TYPES

This screen (Figure 13-25) allows you to view the associations between file extensions and applications. The application will automatically start when you double-click on a file with the specified application. You can change the associations or add your own. This illustration shows a new MIME type is being added to associate the C compiler with files that have the **.c** extension.

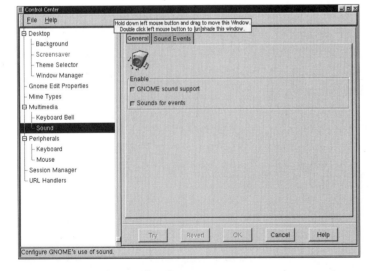

Figure 13-26: *Adjusting sound settings*

MULTIMEDIA CAPPLETS

Use the screen shown in Figure 13-26 to enable sound support in GNOME and associate sounds with various actions.

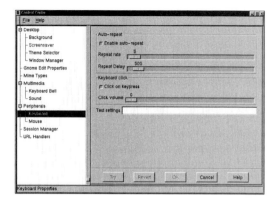
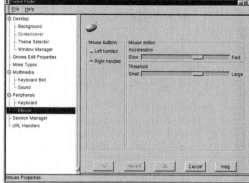

Figure 13-27: *Setting peripherals in the Control Center*

PERIPHERALS

Use these screens (Figure 13-27) to modify the keyboard repeat settings and click volume or the mouse behavior. If you're left-handed, you can use this dialog box to reverse the order of the mouse buttons.

SESSION MANAGER

Use this screen (Figure 13-28) to control the behavior of the GNOME log-out dialog box. By default, the screen prompts for log-out confirmation and asks if you want to save the desktop settings.

Figure 13-28: *Choosing logout options in the Session Manager*

CUSTOMIZING ENLIGHTENMENT

If you are using Enlightenment, the default Window Manager for GNOME, you can use a graphical configuration tool to control the behavior of your desktop, the number of desktops available, special effects, backgrounds, themes, and keyboard shortcuts. With a little fiddling, you can achieve a high degree of customization.

Launch the Enlightenment Configuration tool from the Window Manager capplet described earlier in this chapter and select one of the options to configure.

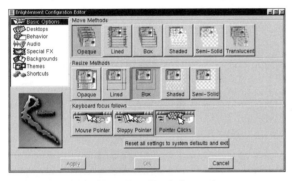

Figure 13-29: *Exploring options for window and cursor appearance*

BASIC OPTIONS

Allows you to customize the window move methods, resize methods, and keyboard focus rules. These options change the way windows and the mouse pointer appear while you're moving them around or resizing them. You'll probably like the defaults best, but it's fun to play with the various options, as shown in Figure 13-29.

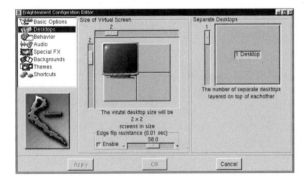

Figure 13-30: *Setting edge flip resistance too low might prove annoying*

DESKTOPS

Allows you to control the number of desktop areas on the virtual desktop. The default is four areas in a 2-x-2 grid, but you can configure the desktop any way you like. If edge flip resistance is enabled, you can switch to an adjoining desktop by moving the mouse pointer to the edge of the screen. My experience shows that an edge flip resistance of less than 50 (half a second) will be annoying, resulting in accidental desktop area switches when the mouse moves too close to the screen edge, as shown in Figure 13-30.

You can also define multiple desktops, each with its own set of desktop areas. Personally, I can't imagine juggling that many desktop areas, but you may find a practical use for this feature.

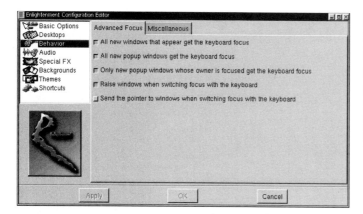

Figure 13-31: *Defining your keyboard-to-window relationship*

BEHAVIOR

Allows you to define how the keyboard focus changes when new windows appear, and whether or not to raise (bring to the front) windows when the focus is switched with **ALT-TAB** (see Figure 13-31).

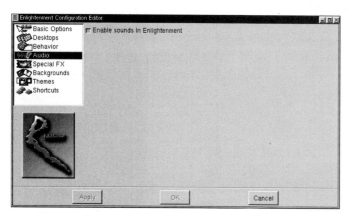

Figure 13-32: *Enabling sounds*

AUDIO

Allows you to enable or disable sounds in Enlightenment. Pundits seem to disagree on whether this actually affects your system—it may depend on your sound card. If your system sounds aren't working, try enabling sound here (see Figure 13-32).

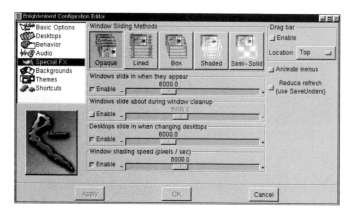

Figure 13-33: *Choosing window sliding options under Special FX*

SPECIAL EFFECTS

Use this option if you want to animate your windows or desktops as they slide on and off the screen (see Figure 13-33). This is a cool feature you'll probably like, and if you have sounds enabled also, you'll hear a nifty swooshing sound when the windows move.

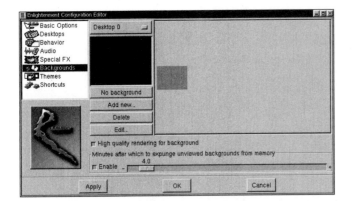

Figure 13-34: *Choosing background options for your desktop*

BACKGROUNDS

Allows you to set the background for the desktop (see Figure 13-34).

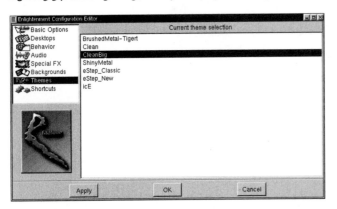

Figure 13-35: *Exploring different desktop themes*

THEMES

Allows you to select a new theme for your desktop (see Figure 13-35). You can also find more themes on the Web at http://e. themes.org/. If you're wondering how this option differs from the theme selector in the GNOME Control Center, you get extra credit for paying attention. The GNOME themes affect only the look of applications written specifically for GNOME, whereas Enlightenment themes affect the overall look of the desktop. The effect of using both theme selectors is cumulative.

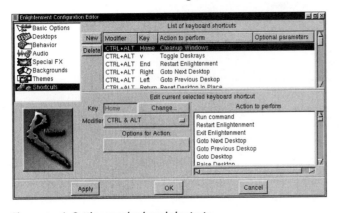

Figure 13-36: *Setting your keyboard shortcuts*

SHORTCUTS

Use this option to modify the keyboard shortcuts (see Figure 13-36). I found it very handy to redefine the ALT-F4 key as "Close Window," to match the behavior of Microsoft Windows.

For more information on the Enlightenment Window Manager, visit www.enlightenment.org.

14

UPDATING YOUR LINUX SYSTEM

nstalling, uninstalling, and upgrading the software packages on your computer is an important part of keeping up with the latest technology, improving your productivity, and efficiently managing your hard disk space. These skills are especially important when you run Linux since it is constantly evolving and improving. From time to time, you may want to upgrade certain components of your Linux system or install useful new packages as you learn about them.

Linux has an excellent utility called *RPM* (Red Hat Package Manager) that makes it painless to install, uninstall, and upgrade software packages. Software distributed in an RPM package comes as a compressed archive, with a special header file that gives information about the package, such as its name, description, version number, size, and author.

Although RPM was created by Red Hat Software, it is available for anyone to use and works on other Linux and Unix systems. The RPM package format has become widely used in recent years and is now the de facto standard for software distribution in the Linux arena.

RPM FEATURES

Here are some of the features that make RPM so useful and popular:

INTELLIGENT UPGRADES

RPM makes it possible to upgrade individual components of your system without completely reinstalling everything. For example, when a new version of the Red Hat Linux operating system is released, you don't have to reinstall the entire system as you do with most other operating systems. Since RPM maintains a database of all the software installed on your system, it can perform intelligent upgrades of your system, replacing old packages with updated versions and removing obsolete ones. Your configuration files are preserved in the process so you won't lose your customizations.

Package Querying

RPM has many powerful querying options so you can easily search to find out what software is installed on your system or what package a file belongs to or to get a list of files that belong to a certain package.

System Verification

If you think you may have accidentally deleted a file belonging to a certain package, you can use RPM to verify the package. If RPM finds anything amiss, you can reinstall the package without disturbing any configuration files that you have modified.

Why Use RPM?

Before RPM was developed, most Unix software packages were distributed as compressed tar files, and this arrangement is still fairly common. But if you install software that comes packaged this way, you run certain risks and lose some potential benefits:

- What if the new package overlays certain files that other packages depend upon, and the new version is not compatible with the old one? You could end up rendering one or more packages useless.

- What happens if you want to remove the package from your system? It can be a real nuisance to find all the files associated with a package and manually remove them without affecting other software that shares common files.

- What if the new version of PandaCalc replaces all your customization files with default versions? You'll have to do all that work again.

RPM solves all these problems—by warning you when new packages may affect existing ones, by providing an intelligent uninstall feature, and by preserving your customization files during upgrades. If you're thinking of downloading and installing some new software, always check to see if an RPM version is available first, and you'll save yourself some trouble later on.

In this chapter, you'll learn about the command-line interface to RPM and a graphical front-end called *GnoRPM*. They both get the job done, so it's up to you to decide which one to use.

RPM: THE COMMAND-LINE INTERFACE

It's easy to use RPM from the command line. Using the **rpm** command, you can install, uninstall, upgrade, query, or verify any package with a single command. This section contains an overview and examples of each type of RPM operation.

- ■ *NOTE: If you want to install, upgrade, or uninstall packages, you must be logged in as root. Any user can use the query and verify options.*

INSTALLING PACKAGES

Before we talk about how to install a new package with RPM, let's look at the file name of a typical RPM package. If the file is named **panda-2.0-1.i386.rpm**, then the package name is **panda**, the version number is **2.0**, the release number is **1**, and the format is **i386** (Intel compatible). The file name of an RPM package doesn't have to be in this format, but this is the convention that is commonly used.

To install the panda package, you enter the command

```
rpm -ivh panda-2.0-1.i386.rpm
panda                ###################################
```

In response, RPM prints the name of the package, followed by a bunch of pound signs as the package is installed, to let you know something is happening.

PACKAGE ALREADY INSTALLED?

If the package is already installed, RPM will quit and print an error message like this:

```
panda           package panda-2.0-1 is already installed
error: panda-2.0-1.i386.rpm cannot be installed
```

If you want to ignore the error and install the package anyway, add the **--replacepkgs** flag to the RPM command line, as in this example:

```
rpm -ivh --replacepkgs panda-2.0-1.i386.rpm
panda                ###################################
```

Conflicting Files?

If you're installing a package that contains a file that is part of a previously installed package, RPM will quit and print an error message like this:

```
rpm -ivh panda-2.0-1.i386.rpm
panda               /usr/bin/fluff conflicts with file from spiff-1.0-1
error: panda-2.0-1.i386.rpm cannot be installed
```

If you're sure that it's okay to replace the existing **/usr/bin/fluff** file with the copy in the panda package, you can tell RPM to ignore that error by adding the **--replacefiles** flag to the RPM command line, as in this example:

```
rpm -ivh --replacefiles panda-2.0-1.i386.rpm
panda               ####################################
```

Unresolved Dependencies?

If you try to install a package that requires some other packages to run properly, RPM will quit and print an error message like this:

```
rpm -ivh hotrod-1.0-1.i386.rpm
failed dependencies:
        gasoline is needed by hotrod-1.0-1
```

In this case, RPM is saying that the hotrod package requires that the gasoline package be installed first. If you think RPM is just trying to spoil your fun, you can add the **--nodeps** flag, as in the next example. RPM will skip the dependency checks and install the package anyway, but the hotrod package probably won't run correctly without gasoline.

```
rpm -ivh --nodeps panda-2.0-1.i386.rpm
panda               ####################################
```

Uninstalling Packages

If you're short on disk space, use RPM to uninstall one or more packages. Uninstalling is even easier than installing, because you need to know only the package name, not the name of the original package file. Here's how to remove the dogfood package:

```
rpm -e dogfood
```

RPM will tell you if the removal of the package will cause problems for other installed packages. If it will, you may see a message like this:

```
removing these packages would break dependencies:
        dogfood is needed by fido-1.0-1
```

If you're sure you know what you're doing, you can add the **--nodeps** flag, and RPM will skip the dependency checks and uninstall the package anyway.

UPGRADING AND FRESHENING PACKAGES

Upgrading a package is similar to installing one, but RPM automatically uninstalls existing versions of the package before installing the new one. If an old version of the package is not found, the upgrade option will still install it. (This is different than the freshen option, which will install *only* if an old version of the package is found.)

Note that RPM flags are case sensitive, so be sure to use a capital "U" when upgrading, as in this example:

```
rpm -Uvh panda-2.0-1.i386.rpm
panda                  ####################################
```

Since RPM performs intelligent upgrading of packages with configuration files, you may see a message like this:

```
saving /etc/panda.conf as /etc/panda.conf.rpmsave
```

RPM is saying that it saved a copy of your original configuration file and installed a new one. You should use **diff** or a visual inspection to find any differences between the two files to ensure that your customizations are applied to the new version.

HEY, THAT'S A DOWNGRADE!

If RPM thinks you are trying to upgrade to a package with an older version number, you will see an error message like this:

```
rpm -Uvh panda-2.0-1.i386.rpm
panda     package panda-3.0-1 (which is newer) is already installed
error: panda-2.0-1.i386.rpm cannot be installed
```

If you want RPM to ignore this condition, you can add the **--oldpackage** flag, as in the example here:

```
rpm -Uvh --oldpackage panda-2.0-1.i386.rpm
panda          ###################################
```

GETTING FRESH WITH LINUX

Freshening a package is the same as upgrading, but RPM will perform the upgrade only if an older version of the package is already installed. Note that RPM flags are case sensitive, so be sure to use a capital "F" when freshening, as in this example:

```
rpm -Fvh pinesol-3.2-1.i386.rpm
panda          ###################################
```

RPM's freshen option is especially handy if you've just downloaded a bunch of packages, and you want to upgrade only those packages that are already installed on your system. Use a command like this to tell RPM to look for all package files in the current directory and freshen only the previously installed packages:

```
rpm -Fvh *.rpm
```

QUERYING PACKAGES

RPM has a powerful query feature that allows you to find out what packages are installed on your system, the files associated with a package, or the package that owns a particular file. Use the **-q** flag to tell RPM to display the package name, version number, and release number of a package that's already installed, as in this example:

```
rpm -q panda
panda-2.0-1
```

Here are some other flags you can use to specify the packages you want to query:

FLAG	MEANING
-a	Queries all currently installed packages
-f *somefile*	Queries the package that owns the specified file
-p *packagefil*	Queries the specified package

And here are the flags you can use to control and format the information that your query returns:

FLAG	MEANING
-i	Displays detailed package information such as name, description, release, size, build date, install date, and vendor
-l	Displays all files associated with the package
-d	Displays documentation and help files associated with the package
-c	Displays configuration files associated with the package
-v	Outputs file listings in the format of the **ls -l** command

SOME QUERY EXAMPLES

You can combine the flags for querying in may useful ways. Here are some examples.

To find out which package owns a file, enter

```
rpm -qf /usr/bin/panda
panda-2.0-1
```

To find the documentation that came with a package, enter

```
rpm -qd hotrod
/usr/man/man1/hotrod.1
/usr/info/hotrod.info.gz
/usr/doc/hotrod-1.0-1/README
```

To learn about a package before installing it, enter

```
rpm -qip hotrod-1.0-1.i386.rpm
Name        : hotrod        Distribution: Red Hat Linux
Version     : 1.0                 Vendor: Faster Software
Release     : 1              Build Date: Sun Jul 04 14:35:27 1999
Install date: (none)        Build Host: dev.faster.com
Group       : Games         Source RPM: hotrod-1.0-1.src.rpm
Size        : 3141593
Summary     : simulated hotrod racing game for SVGA
Description :
An action game that pits you against other maniacal drivers
on the Los Angeles freeway.  Experience the thrill of road
rage as you attempt to get to work on time.
```

To see what files a package contains, enter

```
rpm -qlp hotrod-1.0-1.i386.rpm
/usr/man/man1/hotrod.1
/usr/info/hotrod.info.gz
/usr/doc/hotrod-1.0-1/README
/usr/lib/games/hotrodlib/cars.dat
/usr/lib/games/hotrodlib/drivers.dat
/usr/lib/games/hotrodlib/weapons.dat
/usr/lib/games/hotrodlib
/usr/games/hotrod
```

To find all installed packages that match a specific pattern, enter

```
rpm -qa | grep panda
panda-2.0-1
pandacalc-3.1-4
xpanda-1.2-3
```

Since the **-q** flag does accept a package name, you might wonder why we didn't use a command like this:

```
rpm -q panda*
```

This won't work because of the way the Bash shell treats wildcard characters, so we have to tell RPM to spit out all the installed package names and use **grep** to filter the list.

Finally, here's an advanced form of the query command that will tell you which packages are taking up the most room:

```
rpm -qa -queryformat='%{SIZE} %{NAME}' | sort -n
```

This command uses the **-queryformat** flag to specify that only the size and name information are to be printed for each package. The RPM output is piped to the sort command, which displays the package list sorted by size, from smallest to largest.

VERIFYING PACKAGES

RPM includes a verify feature to help you identify problems with your installed packages. If you've deleted some files by accident or you think a file may have been corrupted, you can use the verify feature to find and fix the problem. RPM will compare the size, checksum, permissions, type, owner, and group information from its database against the files installed on your system and report any differences. Remember that RPM flags are case sensitive, so be sure to use a capital "V" when verifying, as in the examples shown here.

To verify a specific package, enter

```
rpm -V panda
```

To verify the package that contains a specific file, enter

```
rpm -Vf /usr/games/hotrod
```

To verify an installed package against the RPM package file, enter

```
rpm -Vp hotrod-1.0-1.i386.rpm
```

To verify *all* installed packages, enter

```
rpm -Va
```

If RPM finds no problems, there will be no output. If any problems are found, RPM will display a file name preceded by a string of eight characters. Each column of this string specifies whether or not there was a problem with a particular attribute of the file. If a period (.) appears in a column, there was no problem. If any of the characters in the following table appears, a problem related to that attribute occurred.

COLUMN	CODE	EXPLANATION
1	5	MD5 checksum
2	S	File size
3	L	Symbolic link
4	T	File modification time
5	D	Device
6	U	User
7	G	Group
8	M	Mode (read, write, and execution permissions and file type)

Here's an example showing that the checksum, size, and permissions are messed up for one of the man files in the hotrod package:

```
5S.....M /usr/man/man1/hotrod.1
```

If you see any output, you can remove and then reinstall the package, or you can fix the problem some other way if you know what to do.

GnoRPM: The Graphical Interface

If you prefer a point-and-click interface, try the GnoRPM program—a graphical RPM front-end for the GNOME environment that lets you manage packages without having to learn the RPM commands. This section contains an overview and examples of GnoRPM in action. If you used the Glint application in previous versions of Red Hat Linux, you will quickly see that GnoRPM is faster, more powerful, and easier to use. One unique feature of GnoRPM is the Web Find option, which will search the Internet for new packages that may be of interest to you.

Starting GnoRPM

To start GnoRPM from a shell prompt running under GNOME, enter this command:

```
gnorpm
```

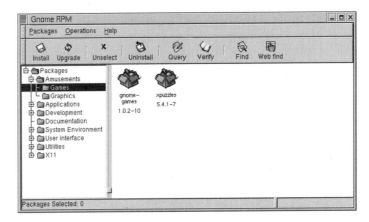

Figure 14-1: *Main window of the GnoRPM interface*

Let's take a quick tour of the GnoRPM interface, starting with the main window as shown in Figure 14-1. The Package panel on the left side of the window shows the packages installed on your system. You can navigate the tree-like structure by clicking on the plus (+) and minus (-) signs. Clicking on a folder icon will display the packages from that category in the Display panel, to the right of the Package panel. The toolbar provides buttons for the most common RPM operations, such as "Install," "Uninstall," "Query," and "Verify." Generally, you select one or more icons in the Display panel and then press one of the buttons on the toolbar to act on them.

INSTALLING PACKAGES

To install a new package, click the "Install" button on the toolbar, and an Install dialog box like the one shown in Figure 14-2 will appear.

Figure 14-2: *GnoRPM's Install dialog box*

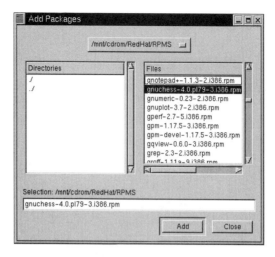

Figure 14-3: *Available packages on the Red Hat CD*

Click the "Add" button to select packages to install. Figure 14-3 shows the next dialog box, which lists all the available packages on the Red Hat CD. If you want to install packages located on your hard disk, click the button at the top of the screen, and you can navigate to the directory where you've stored the RPM files.

When you're done selecting packages, return to the Install dialog box and click the "Install" button to begin installing the packages. (See Figure 14-4, where I've selected a couple of new games to install.) If you want more information about any of the selected packages, you can click the "Query" button before performing the installation.

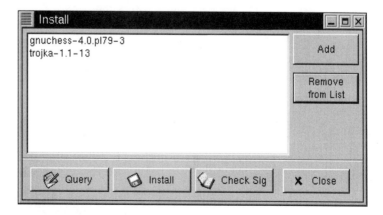

Figure 14-4: *Choose packages to install in GnoRPM*

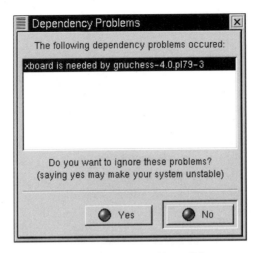

Figure 14-5: *The Dependency Problems dialog box asks for additional direction*

If the selected package requires some other package to operate correctly, GnoRPM will display a dialog box like the one shown in Figure 14-5. Normally, the correct response is to click "No" to cancel and then install the prerequisite package first. But in this case, I know that GNU Chess will operate in nongraphical mode without the xboard package, so I'm clicking "Yes" to ignore the warning and continue with the installation.

UNINSTALLING PACKAGES

To uninstall a package, navigate to the correct folder, select the icon for that package, and click the "Uninstall" button in the GnoRPM main window, as shown in Figure 14-6. GnoRPM will prompt you for confirmation (see Figure 14-7), and if any packages depend on the soon-to-be-removed package, a warning dialog box will appear.

QUERYING PACKAGES

To query a package, navigate to the correct folder, select the icon for that package, and click the "Query" button in the GnoRPM main window. A dialog box like the one shown in Figure 14-8 will display all available information and the associated files for the selected package. If you select multiple packages to query, you can find the query results for each one by clicking on the tabs near the top of the window.

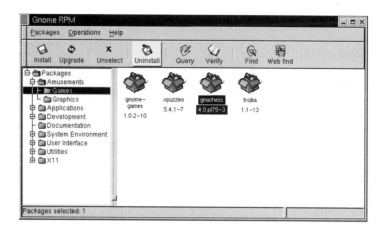

Figure 14-6: *Uninstall a package in GnoRPM*

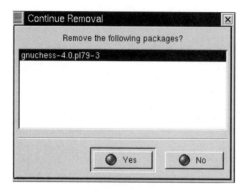

Figure 14-7: *Confirm package removal*

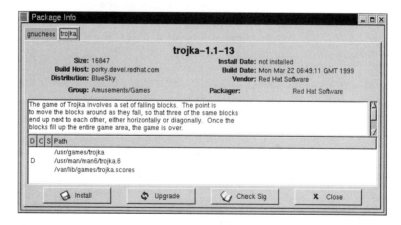

Figure 14-8: *Package information and associated files*

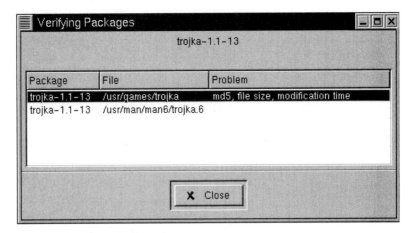

Figure 14-9: *Verify output for packages*

VERIFYING PACKAGES

To verify a package, navigate to the correct folder, select the icon for that package, and click the "Verify" button in the GnoRPM main window. A dialog box like the one shown in Figure 14-9 will display the verification output for the selected package.

FINDING PACKAGES

If you find it a bit frustrating to point and click your way through the folders to find a package, use the "Find" button in the GnoRPM main window. A dialog box like the one shown in Figure 14-10 will help you find a package, if you know the name of a file in it. You can use the "Query," "Uninstall," and "Verify" buttons in the Find dialog box to act on a package.

USING WEB FIND

The Web Find option (Figure 14-11) will search the Internet for new packages that may be of interest to you. By default, it will connect to the redhat.com site and display a list of packages. You can enter a search word at the top of the screen to narrow the list of packages. Select a package from the list on the left to view its details and then click the "Install" or "Upgrade" button if you want to download and install the package.

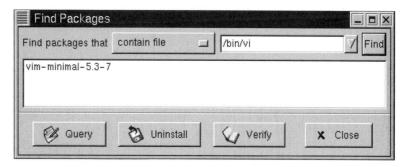

Figure 14-10: *Use Find to search for installed packages*

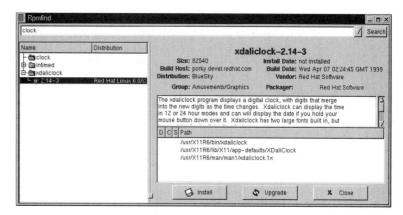

Figure 14-11: *Use Web Find to search for packages online*

LEARNING MORE ABOUT RPM

For more information on RPM, check out the man page (use the **man rpm** command), use the built-in help (use the **rpm --help** command), visit the RPM Web site at http://www.rpm.org/, or subscribe to the RPM mailing list. To subscribe, send email to **rpm-list-request@redhat.com** with the word **subscribe** in the subject line, or check the archives at http://www.redhat.com/support/mailing-lists/.

15

LEARNING MORE ABOUT LINUX

This book is not intended to be the final word on Linux. Rather, it's meant to provide enough Linux knowledge to get you up and running without being too terribly overwhelming or geeky. By now, you've learned how to install Linux and use it productively. You know what shells are, and how to move around in the Linux file system. You can use a text editor or one of many Linux commands to manipulate the contents of a file.

Running your favorite DOS and Windows programs under X Windows is no problem, and hey—you're a programmer now! You can even connect your Linux system to the Internet, explore the online world, and operate your own Web site.

But still, there's a lot more to learn about Linux. And since Linux is constantly under development by a small army of volunteers all around the world, you should be aware of how to get the latest information. This chapter will tell you how to find Linux software, Web sites, FTP sites, bulletin board systems, Usenet newsgroups, mailing lists, news, and search engines.

FINDING SOFTWARE FOR LINUX

If you're looking for a program for a specific task, check out one of these resources:

Freshmeat.net on the Web at http://www.freshmeat.net offers a list of new Linux software packages that's updated daily. There's a well-organized applications index, and a search engine to help you filter through over 4,000 packages.

The Linux Software Map (LSM) at http://www.boutell.com/lsm. The LSM is a searchable database of over 2,500 noncommercial software packages available for Linux. You can search by keyword or title, or just browse through all the titles to see what's available. Whether you're looking for a new game or a GIF manipulator for Linux, this is a good place to start. If you want software written specifically for the GNOME GUI, visit the **GNOME Software Map** at http://www.gnome.org/.

The **Commercial-HOWTO** file in the **doc/HOWTO** directory on the CD-ROM is a good place to look next. This file contains information on commercial software packages that you can buy for Linux. The categories covered include databases, CAD, application development, finance, mathematics, networking, and text processing. Pricing and contact information is supplied.

LINUX FTP SITES

You can find the source code for Linux distributions and applications at many FTP sites. Here are some of the best places to find Linux files via FTP. Try to use a site that's geographically close to get faster downloads.

USA DOWNLOAD SITES

ftp.redhat.com	/pub/linux	North Carolina, USA
tsx-11.mit.edu	/pub/linux	Massachusetts, USA
ftp.cdrom.com	/pub/linux	California, USA
metalab.unc.edu	/pub/Linux	North Carolina, USA
wuarchive.wustl.edu	/systems/linux	Missouri, USA

INTERNATIONAL DOWNLOAD SITES

ftp.dstc.edu.au	/pub/linux	Australia
swdsrv.edvz.univie.ac.at	/unix/systems/linux	Austria
ftp.funet.fi	/pub/Linux	Finland
ftp.ibp.fr	/pub/linux	France
ftp.cs.tu-berlin.de	/pub/linux	Germany
ftp.sun.ac.za	/pub/linux	South Africa
nic.switch.ch	/mirror/linux	Switzerland
ftp.luth.se	/pub/linux	Sweden
nwg.nectec.or.th	/pub/mirrors/linux	Thailand
ftp.mcc.ac.uk	/pub/linux	United Kingdom
sunsite.doc.ic.ac.uk	/packages/linux	United Kingdom

Linux-Specific Search Engines

Several search engines are available to help you find Linux-related information. Here's a list of some Web-based search tools you might find useful.

SearchLinux.com   (http://www.searchlinux.com) is a comprehensive Linux search engine.

Linux Hardware Net   (http://www.linuxhardware.net/) searches the Linux hardware database.includes compatibility information on hundreds of devices, along with user comments and ratings.

LDP Search   (http://metalab.unc.edu/mdw/search.html) searches the Linux Documentation Project files.

Linux man pages   (http://www.ctyme.com/linuxdoc.htm) performs an online search of Linux man pages.

LSM search   (http://www.boutell.com/lsm) searches the Linux Software Map.

InterBoard   (http://www.theforge.com:8090/) is a discussion board with a searchable question-and-answer area for both newbies and pros.

Linux Support and News on the Web

There are many excellent sites on the Web where you can get information on Linux. One of the best is the **Linux Documentation Project** (LDP) (http://metalab.unc.edu/LDP/), which is an effort to develop reliable and freely available documents for the Linux operating system.

You can find several introductory and tutorial documents, as well as a complete and current set of Linux **HOWTO** files. If you're interested in learning about Linux versions for Atari, Amiga, Macintosh, or DEC Alpha systems, or Linux information in languages other than English, this is the place to look. The LDP also has dozens of pointers to other Web sites with Linux information.

The **Red Hat Knowledge Base** (http://www.redhat.com/knowledge-base) is a good place to go if you have problems before, during, or after installation. Check the searchable list of Red Hat Linux Frequently Asked Questions to see if your problem has already been solved.

The **Red Hat Hardware Compatibility List** (http://support.redhat.com/hardware) is a list of hardware that has been verified to be compatible with Red Hat Linux.

The Red Hat Errata/Update Pages (http://support.redhat.com/) errata are a very important resource. Check in often to get the latest security patches and bug fixes.

Linux Administrator's Security Guide (https://www.seifried.org/lasg/) is a great place to learn about Linux security (and security holes).

Linux Programming (http://www.linuxprogramming.com) is a site dedicated to Linux programming resources.

LinuxHQ (http://www.linuxhq.com) organizes and catalogs many of the Linux kernel patches in one central location. Also, this site maintains an active archive of the linux-kernel mailing list and other useful Linux information.

Links to Linux Users Groups (http://www.linux.org/users) is a list of Linux user groups, sorted by location. Find out if there are any Linux fanatics in your neighborhood!

The **Linux Journal** is also an important resource. This printed publication's mission is to serve the Linux community and to promote the use of Linux worldwide. It helps both in getting started and in staying on the cutting edge. For subscription information, see http://linuxjournal.com/.

Linux Online (http://www.linux.org) is designed to act as a central clearinghouse for information and promotion of Linux and as a comprehensive resource for potential and current users of the Linux operating system.

Linux.com's mission is to enrich the Linux community by providing a centralized place for individuals of all experience levels to learn (and teach) the power and virtues of the Linux operating system. Nicely situated at http://www.linux.com, this site is operated by VA Linux Systems, a hardware vendor offering preconfigured Linux systems.

Linux Today (http://www.linuxtoday.com) is a resource for business professionals interested in maintaining a high level of awareness of the news pertaining to Linux and the Open Source communities.

SlashDot (http://slashdot.org) is a "news for nerds" site run by a bunch of geeky twentysomething Linux aficionados. The site features technology news, lively user forums, and book reviews.

Linux Weekly News (http://lwn.net) brings you the latest news from the Linux world. It's a good place for Linux users to stay current with developments related to the Linux kernel, new distributions, and the open source movement.

LINUX NEWSGROUPS

Usenet is another great place to ask questions and share Linux information. Here's a listing of Usenet newsgroups where Linux is spoken.

comp.os.linux.advocacy   Benefits of Linux compared to other operating systems.

comp.os.linux.announce   Announcements important to the Linux community (moderated).

comp.os.linux.answers   FAQs, HOWTOs, READMEs, and so on, about Linux (moderated).

comp.os.linux.development.apps   Writing Linux applications, porting to Linux.

comp.os.linux.development.system   Linux kernels, device drivers, modules.

comp.os.linux.hardware   Hardware compatibility with the Linux operating system.

comp.os.linux.m68k   Linux operating system on 680X0 Amiga, Atari, VME.

comp.os.linux.misc   Linux-specific topics not covered by other groups.

comp.os.linux.networking   Networking and communications under Linux.

comp.os.linux.setup   Linux installation and system administration.

comp.os.linux.x   Linux X Window servers, clients, libraries, and fonts.

LINUX MAILING LISTS

If you don't have Usenet access, mailing lists are a good alternative to the newsgroups. To get a long list of Linux-related mailing lists, visit http://www.liszt.com and search for **linux**, or send email to **listzer@bluemarble.net** with **search linux** in the message body.

Another good resource is the set of support mailing lists operated by Red Hat Software. To subscribe to any of these lists, send email with **subscribe** in the Subject line to <***list-name***>-**request@redhat.com,** where <*list-name*> is one of the following:

applixware-list	Discussion of the ApplixWare suite
cde-list	Discussion of the CDE desktop
gnome-announce	Announcements from GNOME developers
linux-alert	Linux news flashes
linux-security	Discussion of Linux security
redhat-announce-list	Announcements from Red Hat developers
redhat-install-list	Discussion of Linux installation
redhat-list	Discussion of Red Hat Linux (general)
redhat-ppp-list	Discussion of Linux PPP connections
rpm-list	Discussion of RPM
sound-list	Discussion of sound cards and drivers

If you have general Linux questions, start with the **redhat-list** mailing list. It's a fairly high-volume site, but lots of very knowledgeable people hang out there, and most questions do get answered by one of the readers. You can also search the archives of **redhat-list** to see if your questions have already been answered there. To search, visit http://www.redhat.com/support/mailing-lists/.

Also, there are several dozen Linux mailing lists hosted by the Majordomo server at Rutgers University. For information, send email to **majordomo@vger.rutgers.edu** with lists in the message body.

Linux Bulletin Board Systems

If you don't have convenient access to the Internet, many BBSs around the world have Linux file libraries. Here's a list with some of the best Linux BBSs. All phone numbers are specified for dialing in the country where the system is located.

LOCATION	NAME	PHONE NUMBER
Buenos Aires, ARGENTINA	Boixos Nois	730 02946
Hamadtown, BAHRAIN	Jalal	442566
Liege, BELGIUM	Bad Wa ZOO BBS	4-3445020
Sao Paulo, BRAZIL	Wintech BBS	5238883
Sechelt, CANADA	Warlord	604-740-9567
Oshawa, CANADA	Bgouin	905-720-3645
Beijing, CHINA	Guojy	68417802
Cali, COLOMBIA	Guzapata	4337051
Cali, COLOMBIA	William Ayala	4938507
Cairo, EGYPT	Ayman	23532607
Valbonne, FRANCE	Digital Info Exch.	49312-2155
Roissy, FRANCE	RamLine BBS	60642415
Siegen, GERMANY	Asgard	271-890-92-78
Berlin, GERMANY	InterWorld	30-251-37-71
JAPAN	Miko	030-965-6854
Damansara, MALAYSIA	Version 64	03-7167673
Mexico City, MEXICO	Shadow	56781384
Hoofddorp, NETHERLANDS	Columbus	23-547-0578
Mty, NETHERLANDS	Francisco	8-3805582
A Courunna, SPAIN	FiC BBS	981-167162
Keelung, TAIWAN	James Kan	886224690159
SWITZERLAND	STB-iNSoMNiA	71-2601571
Cardiff, UNITED KINGDOM	Dream Machine II	1222-689812
Chugiak, Alaska, USA	Adam	907-688-3288
Fort Lauderdale, Florida, USA	Infinite Darkness	954-797-0666
Riverdale, Georgia, USA	Information Overload	770-477-1549
Fresno, California, USA	Smith & Company	805-995-2679
Baton Rouge, Louisiana, USA	Gildbert	504-753-5372
Las Vegas, Nevada, USA	The Board	702-221-0083
Austin, Texas, USA	Solar Soyuz Zaibatsu	512-451-6009
Houston, Texas, USA	Chase	713-869-4554

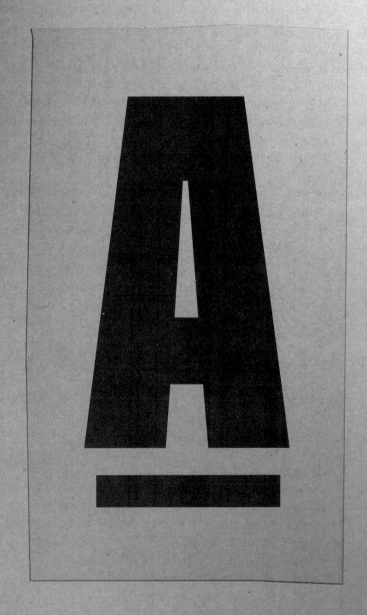

WHAT'S ON THE CD-ROM?

he CD that comes with this book is the Red Hat Linux Publisher's Edition, which contains over 600 software packages. This differs from other Red Hat CDs in that source code is provided for all packages, and a few less popular packages have been removed. (Visit the Updates Web site at http://www.nostarch.com/rhl_updates.htm for more info.) Use this appendix as a handy guide for finding a tool to suit the task at hand.

You may not have all of these packages installed on your Linux system. To install packages from the CD-ROM or remove packages from your hard disk, use the **gnorpm** command under X Windows. It's a very friendly point-and-click application that guides you through the process.

AMUSEMENTS

This section lists the games and graphics packages that make Linux fun. Install them all, and you'll have your choice of over forty things to do when vi, grep, and awk just don't seem to give you the thrill they once did.

GAMES

This section lists packages that are associated with Linux games.

CXHEXTRIS (VERSION 1.0, 39K) CXHextris is a color version of the popular xhextris game, which is a Tetris-like game for X Windows.

FORTUNE-MOD (VERSION 1.0, 2,342K) Fortune-mod contains the ever-popular fortune program, which doles out a bit of random wisdom when you log in.

GNOME-GAMES (VERSION 1.0.2, 3,356K) This package installs some GNOME games on your system, such as solitaire and Tetris.

GNUCHESS (VERSION 4.0.PL79, 1,428K) The gnuchess package contains the text-based GNU chess program. To use the graphical X Windows version of GNU chess, install the xboard package, too.

KDEGAMES (VERSION 1.1, 5,289K) This package contains games for the K Desktop Environment. Included are kabalone, kasteroids, kblackbox, kmahjongg, kmines, konquest, kpat, kpoker, kreversi, ksame, kshisen, ksokoban, ksmiletris, ksnake, and ksirtet.

TROJKA (VERSION 1.1, 16K) The game of Trojka involves a set of falling blocks. (This package does not require X Windows.)

XBILL (VERSION 2.0, 183K) Seek out and destroy all forms of Bill before he can install rival operating systems on your network—funny, but bloody.

XBOARD (VERSION 4.0.0, 601K) This X Windows graphical chessboard can be used with GNU chess and other chess programs.

XBOING (VERSION 2.4, 1,043K) Xboing is an X Windows–based game similar to the Breakout arcade game.

XGAMMON (VERSION 0.98, 3,282K) Xgammon is an X Windows–based backgammon game.

XJEWEL (VERSION 1.6, 52K) Xjewel is an X Windows game much like Sega's Columns or Tetris.

XPAT2 (VERSION 1.04, 456K) Xpat2 is a generic patience or solitaire game for X Windows.

XPILOT (VERSION 3.6.2, 1,617K) Xpilot is an X Windows–based multi-player game of aerial combat.

XPUZZLES (VERSION 5.4.1, 469K) This package contains a set of geometric puzzles and toys for X Windows: Rubik's Cube and various other geometric cube puzzles.

XTROJKA (VERSION 1.2.3, 216K) The xtrojka game is an X Windows game of falling blocks, like Xjewel or Tetris.

GRAPHICS

This section lists packages that provide graphics that are fun to look at.

MXP (VERSION 1.0, 55K) The mxp (Mandelbrot explorer) program is an X Windows application for computing and exploring Mandelbrot sets.

XBANNER (VERSION 1.31, 505K) XBanner displays text, patterns, and images in the root window, so users can customize the XDM-style log-in screen and the normal X Windows background.

XDALICLOCK (VERSION 2.14, 80K) This package displays a digital clock, with digits that melt into the new digits as the time changes.

XEARTH (VERSION 1.0, 192K) Xearth is an X Windows–based graphic that shows a globe of the Earth, correctly shaded for the current position of the sun.

XFISHTANK (VERSION 2.0, 388K) Xfishtank displays an animated aquarium background on your screen.

XLOADIMAGE (VERSION 4.1, 255K) The xloadimage utility displays images in an X Windows window or loads images into the root window.

XLOCKMORE (VERSION 4.13, 759K) This package locks an X session and runs a screensaver until you type in your password.

XMORPH (VERSION 1996.07.12, 127K) This package is a digital image warping (or morphing) program.

XSCREENSAVER (VERSION 3.08, 3,172K) This package provides a variety of interesting screensavers for X Windows.

XWPICK (VERSION 2.20, 50K) This package helps you take screen shots of X Windows screens.

APPLICATIONS

This section lists the packages that contain various archiving, communications, database, editor, emulation, engineering, file management, Internet, multimedia, productivity, publishing, system management, and text processing applications for Red Hat Linux.

ARCHIVING

This section lists packages that are associated with the efficient storage or copying of files.

CPIO (VERSION 2.4.2, 70K) GNU cpio copies files into or out of a cpio or tar archive.

DUMP (VERSION 0.4B4, 153K) The dump package has utilities for backing up file systems and restoring file systems after backup.

LHA (VERSION 1.00, 56K) LHA is an archiving and compression utility that can be used to extract DOS files from LHA archives.

NCOMPRESS (VERSION 4.2.4, 31K) This package contains the old compress and uncompress utilities, which are used with Unix .Z file extensions.

RMT (VERSION 0.4B4, 12K) The rmt utility provides remote access to tape devices.

SHARUTILS (VERSION 4.2, 221K) This package contains the GNU shar utilities, for encoding and decoding shell archives (shar files).

TAPER (VERSION 6.9, 847K) Taper is a backup and restoration program with a user-friendly interface.

TAR (VERSION 1.12, 474K) This package saves many files together in an archive (tar file, tarball) or restores individual files from an archive.

UNARJ (VERSION 2.41A, 26K) The UNARJ program is used to uncompress .arj-format archives.

UNZIP (VERSION 5.31, 370K) This utility lists, tests, or extracts files from a zip archive. It is compatible with PKUNZIP for DOS.

ZIP (VERSION 2.1, 217K) This compression and file-packaging utility is compatible with PKZIP for DOS.

COMMUNICATIONS

This section lists packages that are associated with communications.

DIP (VERSION 3.3.70, 88K) This modem dialer handles both incoming and outgoing SLIP/PPP dial-up connections.

EFAX (VERSION 0.8A, 205K) This package sends and receives faxes using any Class 1, 2, or 2.0 fax/modem.

GETTY_PS (VERSION 2.0.7J, 127K) This package contains the getty and uugetty programs for the log-in process on a Linux system.

KPILOT (VERSION 3.1B8, 876K) This package synchronizes your PalmPilot with your desktop.

LRZSZ (VERSION 0.12.20, 391K) The lrz and lsz programs implement the zmodem upload/download protocol used by Minicom and other communications programs.

MGETTY-SENDFAX (VERSION 1.1.14, 272K) The mgetty and sendfax programs allow you to send faxes through a Class 2 modem.

MGETTY-VIEWFAX (VERSION 1.1.14, 94K) Viewfax displays the fax files received using mgetty. It requires X Windows.

MGETTY-VOICE (VERSION 1.1.14, 651K) This package contains the vgetty system, which lets your modem act as an answering machine.

MINICOM (VERSION 1.82, 302K) This simple text-based modem and terminal emulation program is similar to MS-DOS Telix.

PILOT-LINK (VERSION 0.9.0, 2,222K) This package allows you to upload and download files between Linux and the US Robotics Pilot.

SLIPLOGIN (VERSION 2.1.1, 54K) This package enables dial-in SLIP connections; it is probably obsolete.

UUCP (VERSION 1.06.1, 2,079K) The uucp command copies files between systems.

DATABASES

This section lists packages that are associated with databases.

POSTGRESQL **(VERSION 6.4.2, 6,918K)** This package enables you to create and maintain SQL databases.

POSTGRESQL-CLIENTS **(VERSION 6.4.2, 917K)** This package contains programs you'll need to access a PostgreSQL database management server.

EDITORS

This section lists packages that are associated with the editing of text files.

GXEDIT **(VERSION 1.23, 570K)** This graphical text editor features a toolbar, network bar, and spell checker.

EMACS **(VERSION 20.3, 17,340K)** Emacs is a powerful and customizable text editor.

EMACS-X11 **(VERSION 20.3, 5,782K)** This package is Emacs for X Windows. You'll also need to install the emacs package to run Emacs.

EMACS-EL **(VERSION 20.3, 21,631K)** This package contains the source code for many of the elisp programs included with the main Emacs text editor package.

EMACS-LEIM **(VERSION 20.3, 4,216K)** This package contains the Emacs Lisp code for input methods for various international character scripts.

EMACS-NOX **(VERSION 20.3, 2,434K)** This is the Emacs text editor without support for X Windows.

GEDIT **(VERSION 0.5.1, 340K)** This small but powerful text editor is designed expressly for GNOME.

GNOTEPAD+ **(VERSION 1.1.3, 189K)** This text editor makes Notepad for Windows look bad.

JED **(VERSION 0.98.7, 140K)** This package is yet another text editor. Programmers may like the syntax highlighting.

JED-XJED **(VERSION 0.98.7, 166K)** This package contains Jed for X Windows.

JOE **(VERSION 2.8, 282K)** Hey, I'm a text editor, too! This package is appropriate for novices.

VIM-X11 **(VERSION 5.3, 1,395K)** This package contains X Windows support for VIM (Visual Editor Improved), an updated and improved version of the vi editor. Help stamp out vi before it's too late.

VIM-COMMON (VERSION 5.3, 4,355K) This package contains files required to run any version of the VIM editor.

VIM-ENHANCED (VERSION 5.3, 1,297K) This package contains VIM with support for the Python and Perl script interpreters.

VIM-MINIMAL (VERSION 5.3, 445K) VIM is an updated and improved version of the vi editor. Use this bare-bones version when only the root partition is available.

EMULATORS

This section lists packages associated with the emulation of other operating systems.

DOSEMU (VERSION 0.99.10, 1,812K) This DOS emulator for Linux runs some DOS programs in a virtual machine.

DOSEMU-FREEDOS (VERSION 0.99.10, 8,194K) This freeware MS-DOS clone is for use with DOSemu.

XDOSEMU (VERSION 0.99.10, 26K) This package contains X Windows support for DOSemu.

ENGINEERING

This section lists packages that are associated with engineering and mathematics.

BC (VERSION 1.05A, 128K) This package includes bc and dc, which implement a text-mode calculator.

GNUPLOT (VERSION 3.7, 918K) This command-line interactive plotting program is for scientific data representation.

UNITS (VERSION 1.0, 25K) This package converts an amount from one unit to another. How many tablespoons are there in a cup?

XLISPSTAT (VERSION 3.52.9, 2,871K) This package contains XLISP-PLUS, an implementation of the Lisp programming language for X Windows with statistical capabilities.

FILE MANAGEMENT

This section lists packages that are associated with file manipulation.

BZIP2 (VERSION 0.9.0B, 233K) This package is yet another freeware file compression utility.

FILE (VERSION 3.26, 206K) This package identifies a file according to the type of data it contains.

FILEUTILS (VERSION 4.0, 1,283K) This package includes many frequently used file-management utilities, such as chgrp, chown, chmod, cp, dd, df, du, dircolors, ln, ls, mkdir, mv, and touch.

FINDUTILS (VERSION 4.1, 118K) This package contains programs that will help you locate files on your system.

GIT (VERSION 4.3.17, 715K) GIT (GNU Interactive Tools) provides a file system browser, an ASCII and hex file viewer, a process viewer and killer, and other related utilities.

GZIP (VERSION 1.2.4, 242K) This package contains the popular GNU gzip data compression program.

SLOCATE (VERSION 1.4, 19K) This package searches through a database to quickly find files anywhere on your system.

STAT (VERSION 1.5, 6K) The stat utility prints information about a specified file, including size, permissions, link count, and inode.

TREE (VERSION 1.2, 19K) This package recursively displays the contents of directories in a tree-like format, similar to the DOS tree utility.

INTERNET

This section lists packages that are associated with the Internet.

ELM (VERSION 2.5.0, 616K) This text-based email client was the basis for the more modern Pine program.

EXMH (VERSION 2.0.2, 1,814K) This is an email client for X Windows.

FACES (VERSION 1.6.1, 144K) This program visually monitors a list of incoming mail messages, a list of jobs in a print queue, or a list of system users. It also lets you include or view face images in the exmh email program.

FACES-XFACE (VERSION 1.6.1, 21K) This package enables the exmh email program to display the face image included in a message.

FETCHMAIL (VERSION 4.7.0, 538K) This utility retrieves mail over SLIP or PPP connections.

FETCHMAILCONF (VERSION 4.7.0, 55K) This package contains a utility for configuring your fetchmail preferences file.

FINGER (VERSION 0.10, 32K) This utility displays information about system users.

FTP (VERSION 0.10, 89K) This package contains a command-line file-transfer client.

FWHOIS (VERSION 1.00, 8K) This package is a variant of the whois program, which queries Internet whois databases to find information about domain names and network administrators.

GFTP (VERSION 1.13, 553K) This package is an FTP client for X Windows.

IRCII (VERSION 4.4, 997K) This package contains a popular Internet Relay Chat (IRC) client.

KDENETWORK (VERSION 1.1, 7,317K) This package contains network applications for the K Desktop Environment, including karchie, kbiff, kfinger, kmail, kppp, krn, ktalkd, and ksirc.

KPPPLOAD (VERSION 1.04, 88K) This package monitors the load on your PPP connection. It looks a lot like xload.

LYNX (VERSION 2.8.1, 2,011K) Lynx is a text-based Web browser.

MAILX (VERSION 8.1.1, 89K) This package includes a text-based mail program; it is used to send quick email messages.

METAMAIL (VERSION 2.7, 341K) This package contains a helper application for handling multimedia email; it is used by email clients.

MUTT (VERSION 0.95.4US, 1,369K) This package is yet another text-based email client.

NC (VERSION 1.10, 105K) This package contains a utility for reading and writing data across network connections, using the TCP or UDP protocol.

NCFTP (VERSION 3.0BETA18, 725K) This package contains a text-based FTP client.

NETSCAPE-COMMON (VERSION 4.51, 7,128K) This package contains the files that are shared between the Netscape Navigator Web browser and the Netscape Communicator suite. It is required by the netscape-navigator and netscape-communicator programs.

NETSCAPE-COMMUNICATOR (VERSION 4.51, 13,522K) This is the Web browser, newsreader, FTP, and email client thingie that dims the lights when you start it.

NETSCAPE-NAVIGATOR (VERSION 4.51, 7,242K) This package contains just the Netscape Navigator browser.

PINE (VERSION 4.10, 3,427K) This popular, easy-to-use, full-featured email client includes a simple text editor called Pico. What more could you want?

RSH (VERSION 0.10, 127K) This package contains a set of programs that enable users to run commands on remote machines, log in to other machines, and copy files between machines (rsh, rlogin, and rcp).

RSYNC (VERSION 2.3.0, 223K) This package brings remote and host files into sync over a network.

SLRN (VERSION 0.9.5.4, 425K) SLRN is a powerful, easy-to-use, threaded Internet newsreader. You gotta have threads.

SLRN-PULL (VERSION 0.9.5.4, 66K) This package helps you set up of a local news spool for offline news reading.

TALK (VERSION 0.10, 33K) This text-based utility allows you to chat with other users.

TCPDUMP (VERSION 3.4, 214K) This command-line tool lets you monitor network traffic.

TELNET (VERSION 0.10, 180K) This text-based tool lets you log in to remote systems over the Internet.

TIN (VERSION 1.4_990216, 1,193K) This package is a basic, easy-to-use Internet newsreader.

TRACEROUTE (VERSION 1.4A5, 27K) This package displays the route used by IP packets on their way to a specified network host.

TRN (VERSION 3.6, 446K) This package is yet another text-based Usenet newsreader.

URLVIEW (VERSION 0.7, 37K) This package extracts URLs from a given text file and presents a menu of URLs for you to view.

WGET (VERSION 1.5.3, 335K) This file retrieval utility can use either the HTTP or FTP protocol; it is useful for mirroring Web sites or FTP directories.

XCHAT (VERSION 0.9.4, 205K) This package is an IRC client for X Windows.

XMAILBOX (VERSION 2.5, 33K) This X Windows program notifies you when mail arrives.

XRN (VERSION 9.01, 253K) This package is a simple Usenet newsreader for X Windows.

YTALK (VERSION 3.1, 68K) This package is a chat program for multiple users; it is an enhanced version of talk.

MULTIMEDIA

This section lists packages that are associated with multimedia.

IMAGEMAGICK (VERSION 4.2.2, 3,150K) This package is an image display, conversion, and manipulation tool for X Windows.

AKTION (VERSION 0.3.3, 314K) This package contains a movie player for the K Desktop Environment. It requires xanim.

AUMIX (VERSION 1.18.2, 65K) This package lets you control a sound card mixer; the input levels from the CD, microphone, and on-board synthesizers; and the output volume.

AWESFX (VERSION 0.4.3A, 299K) This package contains the necessary utilities for the AWE32 sound driver.

CDP (VERSION 0.33, 39K) This package plays audio CDs in your computer's CD-ROM drive.

DESKTOP-BACKGROUNDS (VERSION 1.0.0, 5,451K) This package contains images to spruce up your GNOME desktop background.

EE (VERSION 0.3.8, 450K) This package contains the Electric Eyes image viewer and manipulator for the GNOME desktop environment.

GIFTRANS (VERSON 1.12.2, 22K) This package converts a GIF87 file to GIF89 format, to create transparent GIF files.

GIMP (VERSION 1.0.4, 8,060K) This image manipulation program is suitable for photo retouching, image composition, and image authoring. It is touted as "PhotoShop for Linux."

GIMP-DATA-EXTRAS (VERSION 1.0.0, 7,825K) This package contains patterns, gradients, and other goodies for GIMP.

GNOME-AUDIO (VERSION 1.0.0, 828K) This package contains sound files for the GNOME desktop environment.

GNOME-MEDIA (VERSION 1.0.1, 291K) This package contains a set of applications and desktop tools to be used in conjunction with GNOME for X Windows.

KDEGRAPHICS (VERSION 1.1, 2,685K) This package contains graphics applications for the K Desktop Environment, including kfax, kfract, kghostview, kiconedit, kpaint, ksnapshot, and kview.

KDEMULTIMEDIA (VERSION 1.1, 2,277K) This package contains multimedia applications for the K Desktop Environment, including kmedia, kmidi, kmix, and kcsd.

LIBGR-PROGS (VERSION 2.0.13, 1,580K) This package contains a set of scripts for manipulating the graphics files in formats that are supported by the libgr library.

LIBUNGIF-PROGS (VERSION 4.1.0, 336K) This package contains various programs for manipulating GIF-format image files.

MIKMOD (VERSION 3.1.5, 784K) This package contains a MOD music file player for Unix-like systems.

MPG123 (VERSION 0.59Q, 207K) This package contains a fast, free, and portable MPEG audio player for Unix; it supports MP3.

MULTIMEDIA (VERSION 2.1, 344K) This package contains several X Windows utilities for handling multimedia files: xplaycd, xmixer, and xgetfile.

PLAYMIDI (VERSION 2.4, 133K) This package plays MIDI (Musical Instrument Digital Interface) sound files through a sound-card synthesizer.

PLAYMIDI-X11 (VERSION 2.4, 39K) This package contains Playmidi for X Windows.

RHSOUND (VERSION 1.8, 11K) This package contains a script that can save and restore the mixer settings and volume level of the standard kernel sound drivers.

SNDCONFIG (VERSION 0.31, 221K) This text-based tool sets up the configuration files you'll need to use a sound card with a Red Hat Linux system.

SOX (VERSION 12.15, 233K) This package contains a sound file format converter for Linux, Unix, and DOS PCs.

TRANSFIG (VERSION 3.2.1, 292K) This package translates FIG or PIC files into a specified LaTeX graphics language (for example, PostScript).

X11AMP (VERSION 0.9_ALPHA3, 1,341K) This package contains an MP3 player with a nice interface borrowed from WinAMP.

XANIM (VERSION 27070, 847K) This package contains an animation, video, and audio viewer for X Windows.

XFIG (VERSION 3.2.2, 2,545K) This package contains an X Windows tool for creating basic vector graphics, including bezier curves, lines, and rulers.

XPAINT (VERSION 2.4.9, 448K) This X Windows color image editing program supports most standard paint program options and some advanced image manipulation. It's Paintbrush on steroids.

ZGV (VERSION 3.0, 175K) This image viewer can display graphics in GIF, JPEG/JFIF, PNG, PBM/PGM/PPM, BMP, TGA, PCX, and MRF formats on VGA and SVGA monitors.

Productivity

This section lists packages that are associated with increased productivity—you on steroids.

GNOME-PIM (VERSION 1.0.3, 673K) The GNOME Personal Information Manager consists of gnomecal (personal calendar and to-do list) and gnomecard (card file manager).

GNUMERIC (VERSION 0.21, 5,008K) This package is the GNOME spreadsheet program—industrial-strength number crunching.

ICAL (VERSION 2.2, 790K) Ical is an X Windows–based calendar program.

KORGANIZER (VERSION 1.1, 1,220K) KOrganizer is a complete calendar and scheduling program for the K Desktop Environment.

Publishing

This section lists packages that are associated with publishing.

ENSCRIPT (VERSION 1.6.1, 1,515K) Enscript is a print filter that takes ASCII input and formats it as PostScript output.

GHOSTSCRIPT (VERSION 5.10, 3,330K) GhostScript is used to display PostScript files and to print PostScript files to non-PostScript printers.

GHOSTSCRIPT-FONTS (VERSION 5.10, 1,490K) This package contains fonts used by the GhostScript interpreter.

GROFF (VERSION 1.11A, 2,842K) This document formatting system allows you to specify the font, type size, boldfacing, italics, the number and size of columns on a page, and more.

GROFF-GXDITVIEW (VERSION 1.11A, 73K) Gxditview displays the groff text processor's output on an X Windows display.

GV (VERSION 3.5.8, 424K) Gv provides a user interface for the GhostScript PostScript interpreter.

LOUT (VERSION 3.08, 3,452K) Lout is a high-level language for document formatting.

LOUT-DOC (VERSION 3.08, 2,069K) This package provides documentation for the Lout document-formatting language.

MPAGE (VERSION 2.4, 90K) This package takes plain text files or PostScript documents as input, reduces the size of the text, and prints the files on a PostScript printer with several pages on each sheet of paper.

PRINTTOOL (VERSION 3.40, 113K) The printtool package is a printer configuration tool with a graphical user interface.

RHS-PRINTFILTERS (VERSION 1.51, 101K) The rhs-printfilters package contains a set of print filters that are meant to be used primarily with Red Hat printtool.

SGML-TOOLS (VERSION 1.0.9, 1,877K) This text-formatting package is based on SGML (Standard Generalized Markup Language).

TETEX (VERSION 0.9, 39,613K) This package contains an implementation of TeX for Linux or Unix systems.

TETEX-AFM (VERSION 0.9, 3,030K) This package contains the afm2tfm program, which converts PostScript font metric (AFM) files to TFM format for use with Tex.

TETEX-DOC (VERSION 0.9, 29,426K) This package provides documentation for the TeX text-formatting system.

TETEX-DVILJ (VERSION 0.9, 351K) Dvilj and dvilj's siblings (included in this package) convert TeX text-formatting system output .dvi files to HP PCL (HP Printer Control Language) commands.

TETEX-DVIPS (VERSION 0.9, 856K) Dvips converts .dvi files produced by the TeX text-formatting system (or by another processor such as GFtoDVI) to PostScript format.

TETEX-LATEX (VERSION 0.9, 7,898K) LaTeX is a front end for the TeX text-formatting system.

TETEX-XDVI (VERSION 0.9, 1,030K) Xdvi allows you to preview the TeX text-formatting system's output .dvi files in X Windows.

TEXINFO (VERSION 3.12F, 799K) Texinfo is a documentation system that can produce both online information and printed output from a single source file. It is useful if you are going to write documentation for the GNU Project.

XPDF (VERSION 0.80, 1,351K) Xpdf is an X Windows–based viewer for Adobe Acrobat Portable Document Format (PDF) files.

SYSTEM MANAGEMENT

This section lists packages that are associated with system-level operations.

SVGATEXTMODE (VERSION 1.8, 852K) SVGATextMode is a utility for reprogramming (S)VGA hardware, which can improve the appearance of text consoles.

ARPWATCH (VERSION 2.1A4, 104K) The arpwatch package contains network monitoring tools arpwatch and arpsnmp.

BIND-UTILS (VERSION 8.2, 1,320K) This package contains a collection of utilities for querying DNS (Domain Name Service) name servers to find information about Internet hosts.

COMANCHE (VERSION 990330, 372K) Comanche (Configuration Manager for Apache) is a front end for the Apache Web server, the most popular Web server used on the Internet.

CONSOLE-TOOLS (VERSION 19990302, 1,393K) This package contains utilities for loading console fonts and keyboard maps. It also includes a number of different fonts and keyboard maps.

CONTROL-PANEL (VERSION 3.11, 186K) The Red Hat control panel is a configuration program launcher for X Windows.

DIALOG (VERSION 0.6, 88K) This utility allows you to display dialog boxes (containing questions or messages) in text-mode interfaces.

EXT2ED (VERSION 0.1, 288K) This program provides a text and window interface for examining and editing an ext2 file system.

FBSET (VERSION 2.0.19990118, 34K) This utility lets you query and change video modes of fbcon consoles.

GNOME-LINUXCONF (VERSION 0.21, 320K) This package contains GNOME's front end for the Linuxconf system configuration utility.

GNOME-UTILS (VERSION 1.0.1, 774K) This package contains GNOME utilities, such as the calendar and calculator.

GNORPM (VERSION 0.7, 374K) GNOME RPM is a graphical front end for RPM, similar to Glint. It is useful for installing and uninstalling software packages.

GTOP (VERSION 1.0.1, 267K) This package contains the GNOME system monitor gtop, which shows memory graphs and processes.

HDPARM (VERSION 3.3, 37K) This package is a useful system utility for setting (E)IDE hard-drive parameters.

IPXUTILS (VERSION 1.0, 53K) This package includes utilities (ipx_configure, ipx_internal_net, ipx_interface, and ipx_route) necessary for configuring and debugging IPX interfaces (Novell's NetWare) and networks under Linux.

ISICOM (VERSION 1.0, 38K) This package contains binary images and a loader for Multitech IntelligentSerialInternal (ISI) data files.

KDEADMIN (VERSION 1.1, 1,378K) This package contains system administration tools for the K Desktop Environment. Included with this package are kdat (tape backup), ksysv (sysV init editor), and kuser (user administration tool).

KDEUTILS (VERSION 1.1, 2,977K) This package contains utilities for the K Desktop Environment. It includes ark (tar/gzip archive manager), kab (address book), karm (personal time tracker), kcalc (scientific calculator), kedit (simple text editor), kfloppy (floppy formatting tool), khexedit (hex editor), kjots (note taker), klipper (clipboard tool), kljettool (HP printer configuration tool), klpq (print queue manager), and knotes (Post-it notes for the desktop).

KERNELCFG (VERSION 0.5, 58K) This package contains an X Windows–based graphical user interface tool for configuring the kernel daemon (kerneld).

KNFSD-CLIENTS (VERSION 1.2, 10K) This package contains the showmount program, which queries the mount daemon on a remote host for information about the NFS (Network File System) server on the remote host.

LINUXCONF (VERSION 1.14R2, 11,322K) This package contains a Linux system configuration tool to manage your system's operations, including networking, user accounts, file systems, and boot parameters.

MACUTILS (VERSION 2.0B3, 218K) The macutils package includes a set of utilities for manipulating files that are commonly used by Macintosh machines. Macutils includes utilities such as binhex, hexbin, and macunpack.

MKDOSFS-YGG (VERSION 0.3B, 17K) The mkdosfs program is used to create an MS-DOS FAT file system on a Linux system device, usually a disk partition.

MKISOFS (VERSION 1.12B5, 153K) This premastering program generates the ISO9660 file system for writing CD-ROMs.

MKXAUTH (VERSION 1.7, 15K) This package contains a utility to create and maintain X authentication databases (.Xauthority files).

MODEMTOOL (VERSION 1.21, 15K) This package contains a simple graphical configuration tool for selecting the serial port to which your modem is connected.

MT-ST (VERSION 0.5B, 67K) This package contains the mt and st tape drive management programs (for magnetic tape drives and SCSI tape devices), which can control file rewinding, ejecting, skipping, and more.

MTOOLS (VERSION 3.9.1, 486K) This collection of utilities allows you to read, write, and move around MS-DOS file system files.

NCPFS (VERSION 2.2.0.12, 553K) Ncpfs is a file system that understands the Novell NetWare NCP protocol.

NETCFG (VERSION 2.20, 165K) This Red Hat Linux tool provides a graphical user interface for setting up and configuring networking for your machine.

OPEN (VERSION 1.4, 13K) This package starts a specified command on the first available virtual console or on a virtual console that you specify.

PCIUTILS (VERSION 1.99.4, 120K) This package contains various utilities for inspecting and setting devices connected to the PCI bus.

PROCINFO (VERSION 16, 54K) This package gets system data from the /proc directory (the kernel file system) and formats and displays it.

PROCPS (VERSION 2.0.2, 298K) This set of system utilities provides system information. Procps includes ps, free, skill, snice, tload, top, uptime, vmstat, w, and watch.

PROCPS-X11 (VERSION 2.0.2, 0K) The procps-X11 package contains the XConsole shell script, a backward compatibility wrapper for the xconsole program.

PSACCT (VERSION 6.3, 87K) This package contains several utilities for monitoring process activities, including ac, lastcomm, accton, and sa.

PSMISC (VERSION 18, 46K) This package contains utilities for managing processes on your system: pstree, killall, and fuser.

RDATE (VERSION 0.960923, 5K) This package retrieves the date and time from another machine on your network using the protocol described in RFC 868.

RDIST (VERSION 6.1.5, 141K) This package maintains identical copies of files on multiple hosts. If possible, rdist will preserve the owner, group, mode, and mtime of files, and it can update programs that are executing.

RHMASK (VERSION 1.0, 8K) This package creates mask files from original and updated files.

RHS-HWDIAG (VERSION 0.35, 75K) This package contains the Red Hat Hardware Discovery Tools. These tools probe the serial and parallel ports on your system and are useful for finding and reporting hardware errors to Red Hat support if you're having problems.

SCREEN (VERSION 3.7.6, 368K) The screen utility allows you to have multiple log-ins on just one terminal. It is useful for users who telnet to another machine.

SETCONSOLE (VERSION 1.0, 3K) This basic system utility lets you set up the /etc/inittab, /dev/systty, and /dev/console files to handle a new console.

SETSERIAL (VERSION 2.15, 37K) This basic system utility lets you display or set serial port information, such as I/O port and IRQ numbers.

SETUPTOOL (VERSION 1.2, 17K) This user-friendly text mode menu utility allows you to access all of the text-mode configuration programs included in the Red Hat Linux operating system.

STATSERIAL (VERSION 1.1, 289K) This package displays a table of the signals on a standard 9-pin or 25-pin serial port and indicates the status of the handshaking lines.

SWATCH (VERSION 2.2, 129K) This package monitors system log files, filters out unwanted data, and takes specified actions (for instance, sending email or executing a script) based on what it finds in the log files.

SYMLINKS (VERSION 1.2, 212K) Symlinks checks for symlink problems, including dangling symlinks, which point to nonexistent files.

TIME (VERSION 1.7, 18K) The GNU time utility runs another program, collects information about the resources used by that program while it is running, and displays the results.

TIMECONFIG (VERSION 2.6, 107K) This package contains two utilities: timeconfig and setclock.

TIMETOOL (VERSION 2.5, 22K) This package provides a graphical user interface for setting the current date and time on your system.

TKSYSV (VERSION 1.0, 35K) Tksysv is an X Windows–based graphical interface for editing the services provided by different run levels.

TUNELP (VERSION 1.3, 9K) This package sets various parameters for lp devices (/dev/lpo, /dev/lp1, /dev/lp2)—for instance, the interrupt usage and polling rate.

UCD-SNMP-UTILS (VERSION 3.6.1, 253K) This package contains various utilities for use with the UCD-SNMP network management project.

USERMODE (VERSION 1.6, 94K) This package contains several graphical tools for users: userinfo, usermount, and userpasswd.

USERNET (VERSION 1.0.9, 24K) This package provides a graphical interface for manipulating network interfaces (bringing them up or down and viewing their status).

VLOCK (VERSION 1.3, 9K) The vlock program locks one or more sessions on the console.

WHICH (VERSION 1.0, 7K) This package shows the full path name of a specified program, if the specified program is in your PATH variable.

XCPUSTATE (VERSION 2.5, 33K) This X Windows–based monitor shows the amount of time that the CPU is spending in different states.

XOSVIEW (VERSION 1.7.1, 109K) This package displays a set of bar graphs that show the current system state, including the memory use, CPU use, and system load.

XSYSINFO (VERSION 1.6, 22K) This package contains a graphic kernel monitoring tool for X Windows.

XTOOLWAIT (VERSION 1.2, 10K) Xtoolwait is a utility that starts an X client in the background, waits for a window to appear on the root window, and then exits.

TEXT PROCESSING

This section lists packages that are associated with the manipulation of text.

DIFFUTILS (VERSION 2.7, 152K) This package includes four text file comparison utilities: diff, cmp, diff3, and sdiff.

ED (VERSION 0.2, 102K) Ed is a line-oriented text editor, used to create, display, and modify text files (both interactively and via shell scripts). Hint: Don't click here.

GAWK (VERSION 3.0.3, 2,303K) This package contains the GNU version of awk, a text processing utility.

GREP (VERSION 2.3, 287K) This package contains GNU versions of commonly used grep utilities. Grep searches one or more input files for lines that match a specified pattern and then prints the matching lines.

INDENT (VERSION 1.9.1, 81K) This package contains a GNU program for beautifying C code so that it is easier to read.

ISPELL (VERSION 3.1.20, 4,049K) This package contains the GNU interactive spelling checker. Ispell will check a text file for spelling and typographical errors.

LESS (VERSION 332, 142K) This text file browser resembles more, but has more capabilities. Less allows you to move backward in a file as well as forward.

M4 (VERSION 1.4, 120K) This package is a GNU implementation of the traditional Unix macro processor.

MAWK (VERSION 1.2.2, 131K) This package contains a version of the awk programming language.

RGREP (VERSION 0.98.7, 17K) The rgrep utility can recursively descend through directories as it greps for the specified pattern.

SED (VERSION 3.02, 68K) The Sed (Stream Editor) editor is a stream or batch (noninteractive) editor that performs an operation or set of operations on the text and outputs the modified text.

TEXTUTILS (VERSION 1.22, 694K) This package contains a set of GNU utilities for modifying the contents of files, including programs for splitting, joining, comparing, and modifying files.

DEVELOPMENT

This section lists packages that are used when developing new software for Red Hat Linux. It contains debugging and development tools, programming languages, application-specific subroutine libraries, and code samples that programmers can use to simplify and expedite the software development process.

DEBUGGERS

Here are some debugging tools that programmers can use to find and squash those nasty software bugs.

GDB (VERSION 4.17.0.11, 1,171K) Gdb is a full-featured, command-driven debugger that allows you to trace the execution of programs and examine their internal state at any time.

LSLK (VERSION 1.19, 35K) Lslk attempts to list all of the locks on the executing system's local files.

LSOF (VERSION 4.40, 547K) This package lists information about files that are open by the processes running on a Unix system.

LTRACE (VERSION 0.3.6, 75K) This debugging program runs a specified command until the command exits.

STRACE (VERSION 3.1, 123K) This package intercepts and records the system calls issued and received by a running process.

XXGDB (VERSION 1.12, 103K) This package contains an X Windows graphical interface for the GNU gdb debugger.

DEVELOPMENT TOOLS

This section lists development tools that ease the process of developing software for specific applications or environments.

ELECTRICFENCE (VERSION 2.0.5, 44K) ElectricFence is a tool that can be used for C programming and debugging.

AUTOCONF (VERSION 2.13, 580K) This package contains a tool for configuring source code and makefiles.

AUTOMAKE (VERSION 1.4, 867K) This package contains an experimental makefile generator.

BIN86 (VERSION 0.4, 73K) This package provides an assembler and linker for real-mode 80x86 instructions.

BINUTILS (VERSION 2.9.1.0.22B, 5,165K) This package contains a collection of binary utilities, including ar (for creating, modifying, and extracting from archives), nm (for listing symbols from object files), objcopy (for copying and translating object files), objdump (for displaying information from object files), ranlib (for generating an index of the contents of an archive), size (for listing the section sizes of an object or archive file), strings (for listing printable strings from files), strip (for discarding symbols), and c++filt (a filter for demangling encoded C++ symbols).

BISON (VERSION 1.27, 153K) This package contains a general-purpose parser generator that converts a grammar description for an LALR context-free grammar into a C program to parse that grammar.

BLT (VERSION 2.4G, 4,007K) This package contains an extension to the Tk toolkit. BLT's most useful feature is the provision of more widgets for Tk.

BYACC (VERSION 1.9, 54K) Byacc (Berkeley Yacc) is a public-domain LALR parser generator that is used by many programs during their build processes.

CDECL (VERSION 2.5, 80K) This package includes the cdecl and c++decl utilities, which are used to translate English to C or C++ function declarations, and vice versa.

CPROTO (VERSION 4.6, 85K) This package generates function prototypes and variable declarations from C source code.

CTAGS (VERSION 3.2, 146K) This package generates an index (or tag) file of C language objects found in C source and header files.

CVS (VERSION 1.10.5, 3,088K) Concurrent Version System (CVS) is a version-control system that can record the history of your files (usually, but not always, source code).

DIFFSTAT (VERSION 1.25, 11K) This package compares files line by line. Diffstat reads the output of the diff command and displays a histogram of the insertions, deletions, and modifications in each file.

FLEX (VERSION 2.5.4A, 302K) The flex program generates scanners, which can recognize lexical patterns in text.

GETTEXT (VERSION 0.10.35, 889K) This package provides a set of tools and documentation for producing multilingual messages in programs.

GPERF (VERSION 2.7, 122K) This package contains a perfect hash function generator written in C++.

LIBTOOL (VERSION 1.2F, 973K) This package contains GNU libtool, a set of shell scripts that automatically configure Unix and Unix-like architectures to generically build shared libraries.

MAKE (VERSION 3.77, 265K) This package contains a GNU tool for controlling the generation of executables and other nonsource files for a program from the program's source files.

PATCH (VERSION 2.5, 99K) The patch program applies a set of updates to a file.

PMAKE (VERSION 2.1.33, 1,031K) Pmake is a GNU tool that allows users to build and install programs without any significant knowledge of the build process.

PMAKE-CUSTOMS (VERSION 2.1.33, 982K) Customs is a remote-execution facility for PMake.

RCS (VERSION 5.7, 536K) The Revision Control System (RCS) is a system for managing multiple versions of files.

PROGRAMMING LANGUAGES

This section lists the many programming languages and compilers included in the Red Hat distribution.

CPP (VERSION 1.1.2, 135K) The C preprocessor is a macro processor that is used automatically by the C compiler to transform your program before actual compilation.

EGCS (VERSION 1.1.2, 3,525K) EGCS is a free software project that intends to further the development of GNU compilers using an open development environment.

EGCS-C++ (VERSION 1.1.2, 5,912K) This package adds C++ support to the GNU C compiler.

EGCS-G77 (VERSION 1.1.2, 4,631K) The egcs-g77 package adds Fortran 77 support to the GNU gcc compiler.

EGCS-OBJC (VERSION 1.1.2, 1,969K) Egcs-objc provides Objective C support for the GNU C compiler (gcc).

EXPECT (VERSION 5.28, 748K) This package contains a Tcl extension for automating interactive applications such as telnet, ftp, passwd, fsck, rlogin, and tip.

GNOME-OBJC (VERSION 1.0.1, 497K) This package contains basic libraries you must have to use GNOME programs that are built with Objective C.

GUAVAC (VERSION 1.2, 2,157K) This package includes a stand-alone compiler and disassembler for the Java programming language.

GUILE (VERSION 1.3, 1,029K) GUILE (GNU's Ubiquitous Intelligent Language for Extension) is a library implementation of the Scheme programming language, written in C.

ITCL (VERSION 3.0.1, 4,251K) This package contains an object-oriented extension of the Tcl language, created to support more structured programming in Tcl.

KAFFE (VERSION 1.0.B3, 1,671K) This package contains a free virtual machine designed to execute Java bytecode.

P2C-DEVEL (VERSION 1.22, 26K) This package contains the files necessary for development of the p2c Pascal to C translation system.

PERL (VERSION 5.00502, 15,224K) Perl is a high-level programming language with roots in C, sed, awk, and shell scripting. It is useful for writing system administration utilities and for Web programming.

PERL-MD5 (VERSION 1.7, 30K) This package provides the RSA Data Security MD5 module for the Perl programming language.

PYGNOME (VERSION 1.0.1, 1,650K) This package contains an extension module for Python that gives you access to the base GNOME libraries.

PYGTK (VERSION 0.5.12, 2,259K) This package contains an extension module for Python that gives you access to the GTK+ widget set.

PYTHON (VERSION 1.5.1, 5,829K) Python is an interpreted, interactive, object-oriented programming language often compared to Tcl, Perl, Scheme, or Java.

TCL (VERSION 8.0.4, 5,516K) Tcl is a simple scripting language designed to be used with Tk, a widget set, which is provided in the tk package.

TCLX (VERSION 8.0.4, 1,964K) This package contains a set of extensions that make it easier to use the Tcl scripting language for common Unix or Linux programming tasks.

TIX (VERSION 4.1.0.6, 2,732K) This package contains an add-on for the Tk widget set; it is an extensive set of over forty widgets.

TK (VERSION 8.0.4, 5,289K) Tk is a X Windows widget set designed to work closely with the Tcl scripting language. It allows you to write simple programs with full-featured GUIs that can also be run on Windows and Macintosh platforms.

TKINTER (VERSION 1.5.1, 643K) This package contains a graphical user interface for the Python scripting language.

UMB-SCHEME (VERSION 3.2, 1,211K) This package contains a public-domain implementation of the Scheme programming language, a dialect of the Lisp programming language.

SOFTWARE LIBRARIES

This section lists application-specific subroutine libraries and code samples that ease the process of developing software for specific applications or environments.

IMAGEMAGICK-DEVEL (VERSION 4.2.2, 1,594K) This addition to ImageMagick includes static libraries and header files necessary to develop applications.

ORBIT-DEVEL (VERSION 0.4.2, 1,471K) This package contains a high-performance CORBA ORB (object request broker) with support for the C language.

XFREE86-DEVEL (VERSION 3.3.3.1, 7,875K) This package includes the libraries, header files, and documentation you'll need to develop programs that run in X clients.

XAW3D-DEVEL (VERSION 1.3, 657K) This package contains an enhanced version of the MIT Athena widget set for X Windows. Xaw3d adds a three-dimensional look to those applications with minimal or no source-code changes.

APACHE-DEVEL (VERSION 1.3.6, 269K) This package contains the source code for the Apache 1.3.1 Web server and the APXS executable code you'll need to build Dynamic Shared Objects (DSOs) for Apache.

AUDIOFILE-DEVEL (VERSION 0.1.6, 100K) This package contains libraries, include files, and other resources you can use to develop audiofile applications.

BIND-DEVEL (VERSION 8.2, 1,294K) This package contains all the include files and the library required for DNS (Domain Name Service) development for bind versions 8.x.x.

CONTROL-CENTER-DEVEL (VERSION 1.0.5, 38K) This package helps you create the "capplets" used in the Control Center.

E2FSPROGS-DEVEL (VERSION 1.14, 260K) This package contains the libraries and header files needed to develop ext2 file-system-specific programs.

ESOUND-DEVEL (VERSION 0.2.9, 45K) This package contains libraries, include files, and other resources you can use to develop Esound applications.

FACES-DEVEL (VERSION 1.6.1, 22K) This package contains the faces program development environment (that is, the static libraries and header files).

FNLIB-DEVEL (VERSION 0.4, 34K) This package contains headers, static libraries, and documentation for Fnlib.

FREETYPE-DEVEL (VERSION 1.2, 511K) This package provides support for the development and compilation of applications that rely on the FreeType library.

GD-DEVEL (VERSION 1.3, 7K) This package contains development libraries and header files for gd, the .gif graphics library.

GDBM-DEVEL (VERSION 1.7.3, 72K) This package contains development libraries and header files for gdbm, the GNU database system.

GEDIT-DEVEL (VERSION 0.5.1, 8K) This package allows you to develop plug-ins that work within gEdit. Plug-ins can create new documents and manipulate documents in arbitrary ways.

GIMP-DEVEL (VERSION 1.0.4, 258K) This package contains static libraries and header files for writing GIMP plug-ins and extensions.

GLIB-DEVEL (VERSION 1.2.1, 309K) This package contains static libraries and header files for the support library for the GIMP's X libraries, which are available as public libraries. GLIB includes generally useful data structures.

GLIBC-DEVEL (VERSION 2.1.1, 32,857K) This package contains standard header files and object files for developing programs that use the standard C libraries (which nearly all programs do).

GLIBC-PROFILE (VERSION 2.1.1, 30,448K) When programs are being profiled using gprof, they must use these libraries instead of the standard C libraries for gprof to enable correct profiling.

GMP-DEVEL (VERSION 2.0.2, 319K) This package contains the static libraries, header files, and documentation for using the GNU MP arbitrary precision library in applications.

GNOME-CORE-DEVEL (VERSION 1.0.4, 122K) This package contains panel libraries and header files for creating GNOME panels.

GNOME-GAMES-DEVEL (VERSION 1.0.2, 42K) This package installs the libraries and files needed to develop some GNOME games.

GNOME-LIBS-DEVEL (VERSION 1.0.5, 7,329K) This package contains the libraries and include files that you will need to develop GNOME applications.

GNOME-OBJC-DEVEL (VERSION 1.0.1, 694K) This package contains libraries, include files, and other files you can use to develop Objective C GNOME applications.

GNOME-PIM-DEVEL (VERSION 1.0.3, 38K) This package contains files needed to develop applications that interact with gnome-pim applications via CORBA.

GPM-DEVEL (VERSION 1.17.5, 27K) This package contains the libraries and header files needed for the development of mouse-driven programs.

GTK+-DEVEL (VERSION 1.2.1, 2,461K) This package contains the static libraries and header files needed for the development of GTK+ (GIMP Toolkit) applications.

GUILE-DEVEL (VERSION 1.3, 963K) This package includes the libraries, header files, and so on that you'll need to develop applications that are linked to the GUILE extensibility library.

IMLIB-DEVEL (VERSION 1.9.4, 547K) This package contains the header files, static libraries, and documentation needed for developing Imlib applications. Imlib is an image-loading and rendering library for X11R6.

INN-DEVEL (VERSION 2.2, 1,737K) This package contains the INN (InterNetNews) library, required by several programs that interface with INN (for example, newsgate and tin).

LIBGHTTP-DEVEL (VERSION 1.0.2, 42K) This package contains libraries and includes files you can use for libghttp development.

LIBGR-DEVEL (VERSION 2.0.13, 320K) This package contains the header files, static libraries, and so on for developing programs that can handle the various graphics file formats supported by the libgr library.

LIBJPEG-DEVEL (VERSION 6B, 233K) This package includes the header files and static libraries necessary for developing programs that can manipulate JPEG files using the libjpeg library.

LIBPCAP (VERSION 0.4, 121K) Libpcap provides a portable framework for low-level network monitoring.

LIBPNG-DEVEL (VERSION 1.0.3, 485K) This package contains the header files and static libraries necessary for developing programs using the PNG (Portable Network Graphics) library.

LIBTERMCAP-DEVEL (VERSION 2.0.8, 12K) This package includes the libraries and header files necessary for developing programs that can access the termcap database.

LIBTIFF-DEVEL (VERSION 3.4, 1,614K) This package contains the header files and static libraries for developing programs that can manipulate TIFF format image files using the libtiff library.

LIBUNGIF-DEVEL (VERSION 4.1.0, 271K) This package contains the static libraries, header files, and documentation necessary for the development of programs that will use the libungif library to load and save GIF format image files.

LIBXML-DEVEL (VERSION 1.0.0, 127K) This package contains the libraries, include files, and other files you can use to develop libxml applications.

LINUXCONF-DEVEL (VERSION 1.14R2, 3,742K) This package contains the components necessary for developing Linuxconf modules.

NCURSES-DEVEL (VERSION 4.2, 7,149K) This package contains the header files and libraries for developing applications that use the ncurses screen-handling and optimization package.

NEWT-DEVEL (VERSION 0.40, 120K) This package contains the header files and libraries necessary for developing applications that use newt.

PILOT-LINK-DEVEL (VERSION 0.9.0, 1,635K) This package contains the development headers that are used to build the pilot-link package.

POPT (VERSION 1.2.3, 54K) Popt is a C library for parsing command-line parameters.

POSTGRESQL-DEVEL (VERSION 6.4.2, 662K) This package contains the header files and libraries needed to compile applications that directly interact with a PostgreSQL server.

PYTHON-DEVEL (VERSION 1.5.1, 3,499K) This package contains the header files and libraries needed to extend the Python programming language's interpreter with dynamically loaded extensions.

QT-DEVEL (VERSION 1.44, 9,809K) This package contains the files necessary to develop applications using Qt: header files, the Qt meta object compiler, man pages, HTML documentation, and example programs.

READLINE-DEVEL (VERSION 2.2.1, 261K) The readline library reads a line from the terminal and returns it.

RPM-DEVEL (VERSION 2.93, 338K) This package contains the RPM C library and header files. These development files simplify the process of writing programs that manipulate RPM packages and databases.

SLANG-DEVEL (VERSION 1.2.2, 1,192K) This package contains the S-Lang extension language static libraries and header files needed to develop S-Lang-based applications.

SOX-DEVEL (VERSION 12.15, 855K) This package contains the library needed for compiling applications that use the SoX sound file format converter.

SVGALIB-DEVEL (VERSION 1.3.1, 505K) This package contains the libraries and header files needed to build programs that use the SVGAlib low-level graphics library.

UCD-SNMP-DEVEL (VERSION 3.6.1, 275K) This package contains development libraries and header files for use with the UCD-SNMP project's network management tools.

W3C-LIBWWW-DEVEL (VERSION 5.2.6, 1,512K) This package contains static libraries and header files for programs that use w3c-libwww.

X11AMP-DEVEL (VERSION 0.9_ALPHA3, 13K) This package contains static libraries and header files for building x11amp plug-ins.

XPM-DEVEL (VERSION 3.4J, 221K) This package contains the development libraries and header files necessary for developing applications that use the XPM library.

ZLIB-DEVEL (VERSION 1.1.3, 165K) This package contains the header files and libraries needed to develop programs that use the zlib compression and decompression library.

SYSTEM SOFTWARE

This section lists the packages that make up the Linux kernel source code.

KERNEL-HEADERS (VERSION 2.2.5, 2,692K) This package includes the C header files for the Linux kernel. The header files define structures and constants that are needed for building most standard programs.

KERNEL-SOURCE (VERSION 2.2.5, 46,139K) This package contains the source-code files for the Linux kernel—the very definition of *open source*.

DOCUMENTATION

This section lists packages that contain the documentation for Linux in general and Red Hat Linux in particular. These include FAQs, HOWTOs, man pages, and HTML-formatted help files. Almost all of these help files can be found on the Internet, but having them directly accessible on your Linux system can save you the time and trouble of searching for and downloading them.

BASH2-DOC (VERSION 2.03, 2,275K) This is a separate documentation package for the GNU Bourne Again shell.

FAQ (VERSION 5.2, 891K) The faq package includes the text of the Frequently Asked Questions (FAQ) for Linux.

GIMP-MANUAL (VERSION 1.0.0, 17,979K) This package contains the GIMP (GNU Image Manipulation Program) User Manual in HTML format.

GNOME-USERS-GUIDE (VERSION 1.0.5, 3,564K) This package installs the users' guide for the GNOME Desktop Environment on your computer.

HELPTOOL (VERSION 2.4, 23K) The helptool provides a unified graphical user interface for searching through many of the help sources available, including man pages and GNU texinfo documents.

HOWTO (VERSION 6.0, 11,103K) Linux HOWTOs are detailed documents that describe specific aspects of the configuration and use of Linux. There are translations of the HOWTO documents in various languages, but note that not all of the HOWTOs have been translated into all languages. If you need a complete set of HOWTOs, you'll need to install the English version (the howto package).

HOWTO-CHINESE (VERSION 6.0, 13,445K)

HOWTO-CROATIAN (VERSION 6.0, 1,897K)

HOWTO-FRENCH (VERSION 6.0, 29,195K)

HOWTO-GERMAN (VERSION 6.0, 22,361K)

HOWTO-GREEK (VERSION 6.0, 7,712K)

HOWTO-HTML (VERSION 6.0, 12,824K)

HOWTO-INDONESIAN (VERSION 6.0, 8,491K)

HOWTO-ITALIAN (VERSION 6.0, 21,596K)

HOWTO-JAPANESE (VERSION 6.0, 11,888K)

HOWTO-KOREAN (VERSION 6.0, 19,242K)

HOWTO-POLISH (VERSION 6.0, 9,474K)

HOWTO-SERBIAN (VERSION 6.0, 37K)

HOWTO-SLOVENIAN (VERSION 6.0, 3,791K)

HOWTO-SPANISH (VERSION 6.0, 7,739K)

HOWTO-SWEDISH (VERSION 6.0, 4,009K)

HOWTO-TURKISH (VERSION 6.0, 816K)

HOWTO-SGML (VERSION 6.0, 9,767K) The howto-sgml package contains the Linux HOWTO documents in SGML format.

INDEXHTML (VERSION 5.8, 6K) The indexhtml package contains the HTML page and graphics for a welcome page shown by your Web browser, which you'll see after you've successfully installed Red Hat Linux.

INSTALL-GUIDE (VERSION 3.2, 1,373K) The install-guide package contains the Linux Documentation Project (LDP) Getting Started Guide (a generic installation manual and an entry-level guide to Linux) in HTML format.

KERNEL-DOC (VERSION 2.2.5, 2,306K) This package contains documentation files from the kernel source.

LPG (VERSION 0.4, 1,739K) The lpg package includes a generic guide for programming on Linux systems, in HTML format.

MAN-PAGES (VERSION 1.23, 1,795K) This package contains a large collection of man pages (reference material) from the Linux Documentation Project (LDP).

NAG (VERSION 1.0, 1,217K) This package contains the Linux Documentation Project's Network Administrators' Guide.

PYTHON-DOCS (VERSION 1.5.1, 2,611K) This package contains documentation for the Python programming language and interpreter.

SAG (VERSION 0.6, 644K) This package contains the Linux Documentation Project's System Administrators' Guide, in HTML format.

SENDMAIL-DOC (VERSION 8.9.3, 1,360K) The sendmail-doc package contains documentation for the Sendmail Mail Transport Agent (MTA) program, including release notes, the sendmail FAQ, and a few papers written about sendmail.

SPECSPO (VERSION 6.0, 850K) The specspo package contains the portable object catalogs used to internationalize Red Hat packages.

System Environment

This section lists packages that make up the Red Hat Linux base and system environment.

Base

This section lists packages pertaining to the base (core) of Linux.

MAKEDEV (VERSION 2.4, 25K) MAKEDEV is a script that helps you create and maintain the files in your /dev directory.

SysVinit (VERSION 2.74, 151K) This package contains a group of processes that control the very basic functions of your system. SysVinit is the first program started by the Linux kernel when the system boots.

ADJTIMEX (VERSION 1.3, 23K) Adjtimex is a kernel clock management program that the superuser can use to correct any drift in the system clock.

AUTHCONFIG (VERSION 1.7, 27K) Authconfig is a terminal mode program for setting up Network Information Service (NIS) and shadow (more secure) passwords on your system.

BASESYSTEM (VERSION 6.0, 0K) Basesystem defines the components of a basic Red Hat Linux system (for example, the package installation order used during bootstrapping). Basesystem should be the first package installed on a system, and it should never be removed.

CHKCONFIG (VERSION 1.0.4, 69K) Chkconfig is a basic system utility that updates and queries run-level information for system services.

CHKFONTPATH (VERSION 1.3, 18K) This is a simple terminal mode program for adding, removing, and listing the directories contained in the X font server's path.

CRONTABS (VERSION 1.7, 4K) Crontab is the program used to install, uninstall, or list the tables used to drive the cron daemon, which checks the crontab files to see when particular commands are scheduled to be executed.

DEV (VERSION 2.7.3, 7K) The Red Hat Linux operating system uses file-system entries in the /dev directory to represent devices (CD-ROMs, floppy drives, and so on) attached to the machine.

E2FSPROGS (VERSION 1.14, 1,134K) This package contains a number of utilities for creating, checking, modifying, and correcting any inconsistencies in ext2 file systems.

EJECT (VERSION 2.0.2, 46K) The eject program allows the user to eject removable media (typically CDs, floppy disks, or Iomega Jaz or Zip disks) using software control.

ETCSKEL (VERSION 1.6, 2K) Part of the basic Red Hat system, etcskel provides the /etc/skel directory's files (.Xdefaults, .bash_logout, .bash_profile, and .bashrc), which are placed in every new user's home directory when new accounts are created.

FILESYSTEM (VERSION 1.3.4, 80K) One of the basic packages that is installed on a Red Hat Linux system, filesystem contains the basic directory layout for a Linux operating system, including the correct permissions for the directories.

GENROMFS (VERSION 0.3, 12K) Genromfs is a tool for creating romfs file systems, which are lightweight, read-only file systems supported by the Linux kernel.

INFO (VERSION 3.12F, 245K) The info package provides a stand-alone text-based browser program for viewing texinfo files.

INITSCRIPTS (VERSION 3.98, 148K) This package contains the basic system scripts used to boot your Red Hat system, change run levels, and shut down the system cleanly.

IPCHAINS (VERSION 1.3.8, 316K) Linux IP Firewalling Chains is an update to the normal Linux Firewalling code, for 2.0 and 2.1 kernels. It lets you use firewalls, IP masquerading, and so on.

ISAPNPTOOLS (VERSION 1.18, 237K) The isapnptools package contains utilities for configuring ISA Plug-and-Play (PnP) cards and boards that comply with the PnP ISA Specification version 1.0a.

KBDCONFIG (VERSION 1.9, 40K) This package contains a terminal mode program for setting the keyboard map for your system. Keyboard maps are necessary to use any keyboard other than the U.S. default keyboard.

LD.SO (VERSION 1.9.5, 247K) This package contains the shared library configuration tool, ldconfig, which is required by many packages. It also includes the shared library loader and dynamic loader for Linux libc 5.

LDCONFIG (VERSION 1.9.5, 223K) Ldconfig is a basic system program that determines run-time link bindings between ld.so and shared libraries.

LILO (VERSION 0.21, 1,095K) LILO (Linux Loader) is a boot manager that allows you to select the operating system that starts at boot time.

LOGROTATE (VERSION 3.1, 52K) The logrotate utility is designed to simplify the administration of log files on a system that generates a lot of log files.

LOSETUP (VERSION 2.9, 8K) Losetup is used to associate loop devices with regular files or block devices, to detach loop devices, and to query the status of a loop device.

MAILCAP (VERSION 2.0.1, 34K) Mailcap associates a particular type of file with a particular program that a mail agent or other program can call to handle the file.

MAN (VERSION 1.5F, 217K) The man package includes three tools for finding information and documentation about your Linux system: man, apropos, and whatis.

MGETTY (VERSION 1.1.14, 845K) This package contains a "smart" getty that allows log-ins over a serial line (that is, through a modem). If you're using a Class 2 or 2.0 modem, mgetty can receive faxes.

MINGETTY (VERSION 0.9.4, 32K) The mingetty program is a lightweight getty program for use only on virtual consoles.

MKBOOTDISK (VERSION 1.1, 5K) The mkbootdisk program creates a stand-alone boot floppy disk for booting the running system.

MKINITRD (VERSION 2.0, 7K) Mkinitrd creates file system images for use as initial ramdisk (initrd) images.

MKKICKSTART (VERSION 1.1, 4K) The mkkickstart program writes a kick-start file that can later be used during a CD-ROM or NFS installation to automatically build that machine's configuration of Red Hat Linux on one or more other machines.

MKTEMP (VERSION 1.5, 8K) The mktemp utility takes a given file-name template and overwrites a portion of it to create a unique file name.

MOUNT (VERSION 2.9, 115K) The mount package contains the mount, umount, swapon, and swapoff programs.

MOUSECONFIG (VERSION 3.7, 136K) Mouseconfig is a text-based mouse configuration tool.

NET-TOOLS (VERSION 1.51, 395K) The net-tools package contains the basic tools needed for setting up networking: arp, rarp, ifconfig, netstat, ethers, and route.

NTSYSV (VERSION 1.0.4, 23K) Ntsysv updates and queries run-level information for system services.

PAM (VERSION 0.66, 1,850K) PAM (Pluggable Authentication Modules) is a system security tool that allows system administrators to set authentication policy without having to recompile programs that perform authentication.

PASSWD (VERSION 0.50, 28K) The passwd package contains a system utility (passwd) that sets and changes passwords using PAM (Pluggable Authentication Modules).

PWDB (VERSION 0.56, 417K) The pwdb package contains libpwdb, the password database library, which implements a generic user-information database.

QUOTA (VERSION 1.66, 79K) The quota package contains system administration tools for monitoring and limiting users' and groups' disk use, per file system.

RAIDTOOLS (VERSION 0.90, 151K) This package includes the tools you need to set up and maintain a software RAID device under Linux.

ROOTFILES (VERSION 5.2, 1K) The rootfiles package contains basic required files that are placed in the root user's account.

RPM (VERSION 2.93, 1,599K) The Red Hat Package Manager (RPM) is a powerful command-line-driven package management system capable of installing, uninstalling, verifying, querying, and updating software packages.

SETUP (VERSION 2.0.1, 15K) The setup package contains a set of very important system configuration and setup files, such as passwd, group, and profile.

SHADOW-UTILS (VERSION 980403, 604K) The shadow-utils package includes the necessary programs for converting Unix password files to the shadow password format, plus programs for managing user and group accounts.

SHAPECFG **(VERSION 2.0.36, 6K)** The Shapecfg program configures and adjusts the standards for bandwidth consumption.

TERMCAP **(VERSION 9.12.6, 424K)** The termcap package provides the /etc/termcap file, a database that defines the capabilities of various terminals and terminal emulators.

TMPWATCH **(VERSION 1.5.1, 9K)** The tmpwatch utility recursively searches through specified directories and removes files that have not been accessed for a specified period of time.

UTEMPTER **(VERSION 0.3, 21K)** Utempter is a utility that allows programs to log information to a privileged file (/var/run/utmp) without compromising system security.

UTIL-LINUX **(VERSION 2.9o, 960K)** The util-linux package contains a large variety of low-level system utilities, such as the fdisk configuration tool and login program that are necessary for a Linux system to function.

VIXIE-CRON **(VERSION 3.0.1, 57K)** The vixie-cron package contains the Vixie version of cron, a standard Unix daemon that runs specified programs at scheduled times.

YP-TOOLS **(VERSION 2.1, 161K)** The Network Information Service (NIS) is a system that provides network information (log-in names, passwords, home directories, group information) to all of the machines on a network.

DAEMONS

This section lists packages associated with the daemons (background processes) that run under Red Hat Linux.

ORBIT **(VERSION 0.4.2, 1,273K)** ORBit is a high-performance CORBA ORB (object request broker). It allows programs to send requests and receive replies from other programs, regardless of the locations of the two programs.

XFREE86-XFS **(VERSION 3.3.3.1, 505K)** This is a font server for XFree86.

AM-UTILS **(VERSION 6.0, 1,954K)** Am-utils includes an updated version of Amd, the popular BSD automounter.

ANONFTP **(VERSION 2.8, 1,540K)** The anonftp package contains the files you need to allow anonymous FTP access to your machine.

APACHE **(VERSION 1.3.6, 2,111K)** Apache is a powerful, full-featured, efficient, and freely available Web server.

APMD (VERSION 3.0BETA5, 70K) Advanced Power Management daemon and utilities watch your notebook's battery and warn all users when the battery is low.

AT (VERSION 3.1.7, 64K) At and batch read commands from standard input or from a specified file and allow you to run a command at a particular time or when the system load drops to a particular level.

AUTOFS (VERSION 3.1.3, 126K) Autofs controls the operation of the automount daemons, which automatically mount file systems when you use them and unmount them after a period of inactivity.

BDFLUSH (VERSION 1.5, 10K) The bdflush process starts the kernel daemon that flushes dirty buffers back to disk (that is, writes all unwritten data to disk).

BIND (VERSION 8.2, 4,370K) Bind includes the named name server, which resolves host names to IP addresses (and vice versa) and a resolver library.

BOOTPARAMD (VERSION 0.10, 18K) This package contains bootparamd, a server process that provides the information diskless clients need to successfully boot.

CACHING-NAMESERVER (VERSION 6.0, 3K) This package includes the configuration files that make bind, the DNS name server, act as a simple caching name server.

CLEANFEED (VERSION 0.95.7B, 107K) Cleanfeed is an automatic spam filter for Usenet news servers and routers (INN, Cyclone, Typhoon, Breeze, and NNTPRelay).

COMSAT (VERSION 0.10, 17K) The biff client and comsat server provide an antiquated method of asynchronous mail notification.

DHCP (VERSION 2.0B1PL6, 257K) DHCP (Dynamic Host Configuration Protocol) is a protocol that allows individual devices on an IP network to get their own network configuration information (IP addresses, subnet-masks, broadcast addresses, and so on) from a DHCP server.

ESOUND (VERSION 0.2.9, 178K) The Enlightened Sound Daemon is a server process that allows multiple applications to share a single sound card.

GATED (VERSION 3.5.10, 2,434K) This modular software program consists of core services, a routing database, and protocol modules that support multiple routing protocols.

GPM (Version 1.17.5, 258K) Gpm provides mouse support to text-based Linux applications such as Emacs and the Midnight Commander. Gpm also enables text-based (console) cut-and-paste operations.

IMAP (Version 4.5, 1,485K) The imap package provides server daemons for both the IMAP (Internet Message Access Protocol) and POP (Post-Office Protocol) mail access protocols.

INEWS (Version 2.2, 74K) The inews program is used by some news programs (for example, inn and trn) to post Usenet news articles to local news servers.

INN (Version 2.2, 6,246K) INN (InterNetNews) is a complete system for serving Usenet news and private news feeds.

INTIMED (Version 1.10, 210K) The intimed package contains a server (in.timed) that keeps networked machines' clocks correctly synchronized to the server's time.

KNFSD (Version 1.2, 163K) This package contains the new kernel NFS server and related tools. It provides a much higher level of performance than the traditional Linux NFS server.

LPR (Version 0.35, 180K) The lpr package provides the basic system utility for managing printing services. Lpr manages print queues, sends print jobs to local and remote printers, and accepts print jobs from remote clients.

MARS-NWE (Version 0.99PL15, 657K) The mars_nwe (Martin Stover's NetWare Emulator) package enables Linux to provide both file and print services for NetWare clients.

MCSERV (Version 4.5.29, 122K) Mcserv provides remote clients running Midnight Commander with access to the host's file systems.

MOD_PERL (Version 1.18, 1,261K) Mod_perl incorporates a Perl interpreter into the Apache Web server, so that the Apache Web server can directly execute Perl code.

MOD_PHP (Version 2.0.1, 676K) PHP version 2 is an HTML-embedded scripting language that attempts to make it easy for developers to write dynamically generated Web pages.

MOD_PHP3 (Version 3.0.7, 3,892K) PHP version 3 is an HTML-embedded scripting language that attempts to make it easy for developers to write dynamically generated Web pages.

NETKIT-BASE (VERSION 0.10, 61K) The netkit-base package contains the basic networking tools ping and inetd.

PIDENTD (VERSION 2.8.5, 129K) The pidentd package contains identd, which look up specific TCP/IP connections and returns either the user name or other information about the process that owns the connection.

PORTMAP (VERSION 4.0, 49K) The portmapper program is a security tool that prevents the theft of NIS (YP), NFS, and other sensitive information.

PPP (VERSION 2.3.7, 301K) This package contains the PPP (Point-to-Point Protocol) daemon and documentation for PPP serial dial-up support.

PROCMAIL (VERSION 3.13, 207K) The procmail program is used by Red Hat Linux for all local mail delivery and can be used for automatic filtering, presorting, and other mail-handling jobs.

PUMP (VERSION 0.4, 30K) Pump is a combined BOOTP and DHCP client daemon that allows your machine to retrieve configuration information from a server.

ROUTED (VERSION 0.10, 39K) The routed routing daemon handles incoming RIP traffic and broadcasts outgoing RIP traffic over network traffic routes, to maintain current routing tables.

RUSERS (VERSION 0.10, 36K) The rusers program allows users to find out who is logged in to various machines on the local network.

RWALL (VERSION 0.10, 18K) The rwall command sends a message to all of the users logged in to a specified host.

RWHO (VERSION 0.10, 25K) The rwho command displays output similar to the output of the who command (it shows who is logged in) for all machines on the local network running the rwho daemon.

SAMBA (VERSION 2.0.3, 6,498K) Samba provides an SMB server, which can be used to provide file and print sharing services to users on Microsoft Windows, OS/2, and other Linux machines.

SENDMAIL (VERSION 8.9.3, 526K) The sendmail program is a very widely used mail transport agent, which sends mail from one machine to another.

SENDMAIL-CF (VERSION 8.9.3, 503K) This package includes the configuration files you need to generate the sendmail.cf file distributed with the sendmail package.

SQUID (VERSION 2.2.DEVEL3, 1,861K) Squid is a high-performance proxy caching server for Web clients, supporting FTP, gopher, and HTTP data objects.

SYSKLOGD (VERSION 1.3.31, 112K) This package contains two system utilities (syslogd and klogd) that provide support for system logging.

TCP_WRAPPERS (VERSION 7.6, 270K) This package provides small dae-mon programs that can monitor and filter incoming requests for systat, finger, ftp, telnet, rlogin, rsh, exec, tftp, talk, and other network services.

TFTP (VERSION 0.10, 34K) The Trivial File Transfer Protocol (TFTP) is nor-mally used only for booting diskless workstations.

TIMED (VERSION 0.10, 74K) Timed synchronizes its host machine's time with the time on other local network machines.

UCD-SNMP (VERSION 3.6.1, 1,504K) SNMP (Simple Network Manage-ment Protocol) is a protocol used for network management.

WU-FTPD (VERSION 2.4.2B18, 398K) This package contains the wu-ftpd FTP (File Transfer Protocol) server daemon. The FTP protocol is a method of transferring files between machines on a network and over the Internet.

XNTP3 (VERSION 5.93, 968K) The Network Time Protocol (NTP) is used to synchronize a computer's time with another reference time source.

KERNEL

This section lists packages that are related to the Linux kernel on which Red Hat Linux is based.

KERNEL (VERSION 2.2.5, 9,812K) The kernel package contains the Linux kernel (vmlinuz), the core of your Red Hat Linux operating system. The kernel handles the basic functions of the operating system: memory allo-cation, process allocation, device input and output, and so on.

KERNEL-BOOT (VERSION 2.2.5, 5,881K) This package includes a trimmed-down version of the Linux 2.2.5 kernel. This kernel is used on the installa-tion boot disks only and should not be used for an installed system.

KERNEL-PCMCIA-CS (VERSION 2.2.5, 561K) This package contains a set of loadable kernel modules that implement an application program inter-face, a set of client drivers for specific cards, and a card manager daemon that can respond to card insertion and removal events by loading and unloading drivers on demand.

KERNEL-SMP (VERSION 2.2.5, 9,494K) This package includes an SMP ver-sion of the Linux 2.2.5 kernel. It is required only on machines with two or more CPUs, although it should work fine on single-CPU boxes.

MODUTILS (VERSION 2.1.121, 841K) This package includes the kerneld program for the automatic loading of modules under 2.0 kernels and unloading of modules under 2.0 and 2.2 kernels, as well as other module-management programs.

LIBRARIES

This section lists the packages associated with the run-time libraries that are required to run programs under Red Hat Linux.

XFREE86-LIBS (VERSION 3.3.3.1, 2,060K) This package contains the shared libraries that most X programs need to run properly.

XAW3D (VERSION 1.3, 292K) This package contains an enhanced version of the MIT Athena widget set for X Windows. Xaw3d adds a three-dimensional look to applications.

AUDIOFILE (VERSION 0.1.6, 183K) This package contains a library for handling various audio file formats. It is used by the esound daemon.

CRACKLIB (VERSION 2.7, 75K) CrackLib tests passwords to determine whether they match certain security-oriented characteristics.

CRACKLIB-DICTS (VERSION 2.7, 235K) The cracklib-dicts package includes the CrackLib dictionaries.

FNLIB (VERSION 0.4, 352K) Fnlib is a library that provides full, scaleable, 24-bit color font-rendering abilities for X Windows.

FREETYPE (VERSION 1.2, 937K) The FreeType engine is a free and portable TrueType font-rendering engine.

GD (VERSION 1.3, 314K) Gd is a graphics library for drawing .gif files. Gd allows your code to quickly draw images (lines, arcs, text, multiple colors, cutting and pasting from other images, flood fills) and write the result as a .gif file.

GDBM (VERSION 1.7.3, 28K) Gdbm is a GNU database-indexing library, including routines that use extensible hashing. It is useful for developers who write C applications and need access to a simple and efficient database.

GIMP-LIBGIMP (VERSION 1.0.4, 173K) This package contains libraries used to communicate between the GIMP and other programs that may function as GIMP plug-ins.

GLIB (VERSION 1.2.1, 317K) Glib is a handy library of utility functions. This C library is designed to solve some portability problems and provide other useful functionality that most programs require.

GLIBC **(VERSION 2.1.1, 25,792K)** This package contains the standard libraries that are required by most programs on the system.

GMP **(VERSION 2.0.2, 117K)** The gmp package contains GNU MP, a library of functions for arbitrary precision arithmetic, signed integers operations, rational numbers, and floating-point numbers.

GNOME-AUDIO-EXTRA **(VERSION 1.0.0, 2,659K)** This package contains extra sound files useful for customizing the sounds that the GNOME desktop environment makes.

GNOME-LIBS **(VERSION 1.0.5, 2,210K)** This package includes run-time libraries that are needed by GNOME.

GSL **(VERSION 0.3F, 868K)** The gsl package includes the GNU Scientific Library, a collection of routines for numerical analysis, written in C.

GTK+ **(VERSION 1.2.1, 1,981K)** The gtk+ package contains the GIMP Toolkit (GTK+), a library for creating graphical user interfaces for X Windows.

GTK+10 **(VERSION 1.0.6, 1,139K)** This package contains the X libraries originally written for the GIMP, which are now used by several other programs as well.

GTK-ENGINES **(VERSION 0.5, 2,387K)** This package contains the graphical engines for the various GTK+ toolkit themes. Included themes are Notif, Redmond95, Pixmap, and Metal.

IMLIB **(VERSION 1.9.4, 423K)** Imlib is a display-depth-independent image loading and rendering library.

IMLIB-CFGEDITOR **(VERSION 1.9.4, 333K)** This package contains the imlib_config program, which you can use to configure the Imlib image loading and rendering library.

KDELIBS **(VERSION 1.1, 5,771K)** This package contains libraries for the K Desktop Environment.

KDESUPPORT **(VERSION 1.1, 2,138K)** This package contains support libraries for the K Desktop Environment.

LIBC **(VERSION 5.3.12, 5,259K)** This package includes the libc5 libraries and other libraries based on libc5. With these libraries installed, old applications that need them will be able to run on your glibc (libc version 6) system.

LIBELF **(VERSION 0.6.4, 76K)** The libelf package contains a library for accessing the internals of ELF object files.

LIBGHTTP (VERSION 1.0.2, 85K) This package contains a library for issuing HTTP 1.1 requests.

LIBGR (VERSION 2.0.13, 235K) The libgr package contains a library of functions that support programs for handling various graphics file formats.

LIBGTOP (VERSION 1.0.1, 431K) This package contains a library that fetches information about the running system, such as CPU and memory use and active processes.

LIBGTOP-EXAMPLES (VERSION 1.0.1, 937K) This package contains examples for LibGTop, a library that retrieves information about your system, such as CPU and memory use.

LIBJPEG (VERSION 6B, 239K) This package contains a library of functions for manipulating JPEG images.

LIBJPEG6A (VERSION 6A, 137K) This package contains a library of functions that manipulate JPEG images, along with simple clients for manipulating JPEG images.

LIBPNG (VERSION 1.0.3, 270K) The libpng package contains a library of functions for creating and manipulating PNG (Portable Network Graphics) image format files.

LIBSTDC++ (VERSION 2.9.0, 3,421K) This package includes the shared libraries necessary for running C++ applications, along with additional GNU tools.

LIBTERMCAP (VERSION 2.0.8, 58K) The libtermcap package contains a basic system library needed to access the termcap database.

LIBTIFF (VERSION 3.4, 568K) The libtiff package contains a library of functions for manipulating TIFF (Tagged Image File Format) image format files.

LIBUNGIF (VERSION 4.1.0, 80K) The libungif package contains a shared library of functions for loading and saving GIF format image files.

LIBXML (VERSION 1.0.0, 154K) This library allows you to manipulate XML files.

NCURSES (VERSION 4.2, 2,627K) The ncurses library routines provide a terminal-independent method of updating character (text-mode) screens with reasonable optimization.

NEWT (VERSION 0.40, 128K) Newt is a programming library for color text-mode, widget-based user interfaces and can be used to add stacked windows, check boxes, radio buttons, scrollbars, and so on to text-mode user interfaces.

P2C (VERSION 1.22, 723K) P2c is a system for translating Pascal programs into the C language. P2c accepts input source files in certain Pascal dialects.

PYTHONLIB (VERSION 1.22, 236K) The pythonlib package contains Python code used by a variety of Red Hat Linux programs.

QT (VERSION 1.44, 2,093K) Qt is a GUI software toolkit that simplifies the task of writing and maintaining GUI (graphical user interface) applications for X Windows.

READLINE (VERSION 2.2.1, 262K) The readline library reads a line from the terminal and returns it, allowing the user to edit the line with standard Emacs editing keys.

SLANG (VERSION 1.2.2, 250K) S-Lang is an interpreted language and a programming library.

SVGALIB (VERSION 1.3.1, 489K) The svgalib package provides the SVGAlib low-level graphics library for Linux.

W3C-LIBWWW (VERSION 5.2.6, 2,097K) Libwww is a general-purpose Web API written in C for Unix and Windows (Win32).

WORDS (VERSION 2, 411K) The words file is a dictionary of English words for the /usr/dict directory. Programs such as ispell use this database of words to check spelling.

XPM (VERSION 3.4J, 60K) The xpm package contains the XPM pixmap library for X Windows.

ZLIB (VERSION 1.1.3, 61K) The zlib compression library provides in-memory compression and decompression functions, including integrity checks of the uncompressed data.

SHELLS

This section lists packages that are associated with the shells that provide the command-line user interface on Red Hat Linux systems.

ASH (VERSION 0.2, 361K) The ash shell is a clone of Berkeley's Bourne shell. Ash supports all of the standard sh shell commands but is smaller than bash and uses less memory.

BASH2 (VERSION 2.03, 1,168K) Bash is a GNU project sh-compatible shell or command language interpreter. Bash (Bourne Again shell) incorporates useful features from the Korn shell (ksh) and the C shell (csh).

MC (VERSION 4.5.29, 2,449K) Midnight Commander is a visual shell much like a file manager, with many more features. It is in text mode, but it also includes mouse support if you are running GPM.

PDKSH (VERSION 5.2.13, 402K) PD-ksh is a clone of the Korn shell (ksh).

SASH (VERSION 2.1, 402K) Sash is a simple, stand-alone shell that includes simplified versions of built-in commands such as ls, dd, and gzip. Sash is statically linked so that it can work without shared libraries and is particularly useful for recovering from certain types of system failures.

SH-UTILS (VERSION 1.16, 355K) The GNU shell utilities are a set of useful system utilities that are often used in shell scripts. The sh-utils package includes basename, chroot, date, dirname, echo, expr, logname, nohup, printf, pwd, sleep, su, tee, test, uname, who, and whoami.

TCSH (VERSION 6.08.00, 488K) Tcsh is an enhanced but completely compatible version of csh, the C shell.

ZSH (VERSION 3.0.5, 956K) The zsh shell is a command interpreter that can be used as an interactive log-in shell and as a shell script command processor.

USER INTERFACE

This section lists the packages that are associated with the graphical user interface on Red Hat Linux. These include X Windows, GNOME, desktops, themes, hardware support files, and utilities.

DESKTOPS

This section lists packages that are associated with the desktop environments available on Red Hat Linux.

AFTERSTEP (VERSION 1.7.75, 3,870K) AfterStep was originally designed to emulate some of the look and feel of the NeXTSTEP user interface, but it has many additional features.

AFTERSTEP-APPS (VERSION 990329, 1,119K) This package contains a set of applets that can be used in the Wharf module for AfterStep or Window Maker.

ANOTHERLEVEL (VERSION 0.8, 302K) AnotherLevel is a custom configuration of the popular fvwm2 window manager.

WINDOWMAKER (VERSION 0.51.2, 3,933K) Window Maker is an X11 window manager that emulates the look and feel of the NeXTSTEP graphical user interface and is part of the official GNU project, which means that Window Maker can interoperate with other GNU projects, such as GNOME.

CONTROL-CENTER (VERSION 1.0.5, 981K) Control-center is a configuration tool for easily setting up your GNOME environment.

ENLIGHTENMENT (VERSION 0.15.5, 3,703K) Enlightenment is a window manager for X Windows that is designed to be powerful, extensible, and configurable. Enlightenment provides an appealing graphical shell from which to work and is the default window manager for the GNOME environment shipped with Red Hat version 6.

ENLIGHTENMENT-CONF (VERSION 0.15, 386K) This package contains a configuration tool for easily setting up Enlightenment.

FVWM2 (VERSION 2.2, 1,730K) This package contains a window manager for X Windows, designed to minimize memory consumption, to provide window frames with a 3D look, and to provide a simple virtual desktop.

FVWM2-ICONS (VERSION 2.2, 408K) The fvwm2-icons package contains icons, bitmaps, and pixmaps used by the FVWM and FVWM2 X Windows window managers.

GMC (VERSION 4.5.29, 7,078K) This package contains the GNOME version of Midnight Commander; it is a graphical file manager, with drag-and-drop support. It does not yet support all the features of the text-based version of Midnight Commander.

GNOME-CORE (VERSION 1.0.4, 3,253K) This package includes the basic programs and libraries that are needed to install GNOME.

KDEBASE (VERSION 1.1, 11,806K) This package contains the core applications for the K Desktop Environment.

SWITCHDESK (VERSION 1.5, 90K) The Desktop Switcher is a tool that enables users to easily switch between various desktop environments that they have installed.

SWITCHDESK-GNOME (VERSION 1.5, 10K) This package provides the desktop switching tool with a GNOME look and feel.

SWITCHDESK-KDE (VERSION 1.5, 22K) This package provides the desktop switching tool with a KDE look and feel.

WMAKERCONF (VERSION 1.7, 569K) Wmakerconf is a GTK+ graphical user interface configuration tool for the Window Maker window manager.

WMCONFIG (VERSION 0.9.3, 53K) The wmconfig program is a helper program that provides output for use in configuring window managers.

XFM (VERSION 1.3.2, 706K) Xfm is a file manager for X Windows. It is not as nice as GNU Midnight Commander, though.

X HARDWARE SUPPORT

This section lists packages that are associated with hardware support for specific video cards under Red Hat Linux.

XFREE86-3DLABS (VERSION 3.3.3.1, 2,211K) This package provides X server support for cards built around 3D Labs GLINT and Permedia chipsets, including GLINT 500TX with IBM RGB526 RAMDAC, GLINT MX with IBM RGB526 and IBM RGB640 RAMDAC, Permedia with IBM RGB526 RAMDAC, and Permedia 2 (classic, 2a, 2v).

XFREE86-8514 (VERSION 3.3.3.1, 1,743K) This package supports older IBM 8514 cards or 8514 compatibles from companies such as ATI.

XFREE86-AGX (VERSION 3.3.3.1, 1,925K) This package provides X server support for AGX-based cards, such as Boca Vortex, Orchid Celsius, Spider Black Widow, and Hercules Graphite.

XFREE86-FBDEV (VERSION 3.3.3.1, 2,001K) This package provides X server support for the generic frame buffer device used on Amiga, Atari, and Macintosh/m68k machines

XFREE86-I128 (VERSION 3.3.3.1, 2,182K) This package provides X server support for #9 Imagine 128 and similar video boards.

XFREE86-MACH32 (VERSION 3.3.3.1, 1,886K) This package provides X server support for video cards built around ATI's Mach32 chip, including the ATI Graphics Ultra Pro and Ultra Plus.

XFREE86-MACH64 (VERSION 3.3.3.1, 2,008K) This package provides X server support for cards based on ATI's Mach64 chip, such as the Graphics Xpression, GUP Turbo, and WinTurbo cards.

XFREE86-MACH8 (VERSION 3.3.3.1, 1,755K) This package provides X server support for video cards built around ATI's Mach8 chip, including the ATI 8514 Ultra and Graphics Ultra.

XFREE86-MONO (VERSION 3.3.3.1, 2,052K) This package provides generic monochrome (two-color) X server support for VGA cards. XFree86-

Mono will work for nearly all VGA-compatible cards, but it supports only a monochrome display.

XFREE86-P9000 (VERSION 3.3.3.1, 1,945K) This package provides X server support for video cards built around the Weitek P9000 chip, such as most Diamond Viper cards and the Orchid P9000 card.

XFREE86-S3 (VERSION 3.3.3.1, 2,431K) This package provides X server support for video cards based on S3 chips, including most #9 cards, many Diamond Stealth cards, Orchid Farenheits, Mirco Crystal 8S, most STB cards, and some motherboards with built-in graphics accelerators (such as the IBM ValuePoint line).

XFREE86-S3V (VERSION 3.3.3.1, 2,160K) This package provides X server support for video cards based on the S3 ViRGE chipset.

XFREE86-SVGA (VERSION 3.3.3.1, 3,097K) This package provides X server support for most simple framebuffer SVGA devices, including cards built from ET4000 chips, Cirrus Logic chips, Chips and Technologies laptop chips, Trident 8900 and 9000 chips, and Matrox chips. It also works for many other chips and cards, so try this server if you are having problems.

XFREE86-VGA16 (VERSION 3.3.3.1, 1,944K) This package provides generic 16-color X server support for VGA boards. XFree86-VGA16 will work on nearly all VGA-style graphics boards, but it supports only low-resolution, 16-color displays.

XFREE86-W32 (VERSION 3.3.3.1, 1,793K) This package provides X server support for cards built around ET4000/W32 chips, including Genoa 8900 Phantom 32i, Hercules Dynamite, LeadTek WinFast S200, Sigma Concorde, STB LightSpeed, TechWorks Thunderbolt, and ViewTop PCI.

XFREE86-XF86SETUP (VERSION 3.3.3.1, 596K) This package contains a graphical user interface configuration tool for setting up and configuring XFree86 servers. Note that Xconfigurator is the preferred X Windows configuration tool for Red Hat.

XFREE86-XNEST (VERSION 3.3.3.1, 2,242K) This package contains a nested X server that runs as a client of your real X server (perhaps for testing purposes).

XFREE86-XVFB (VERSION 3.3.3.1, 2,707K) X Virtual Frame Buffer is an X Windows system server that is capable of running on machines with no display hardware and no physical input devices. If you need to test your X server or your X clients, you may want to install Xvfb for that purpose.

XCONFIGURATOR (VERSION 4.1.3, 433K) Xconfigurator is a full-screen, menu-driven program that walks you through the X server setup.

X Windows

This section lists packages associated with the X Windows graphical user interface.

X11R6-contrib (Version 3.3.2, 474K) This package contains many useful programs from the X Windows, version 11, release 6, contrib tape. The programs, contributed by various users, include listres, xbiff, xedit, xeyes, xcalc, xload, and xman, among others.

XFree86-100dpi-fonts (Version 3.3.3.1, 1,228K) This package contains a set of 100-dpi fonts, useful if you have a high-res monitor capable of 100 dpi.

XFree86 (Version 3.3.3.1, 14,458K) XFree86 is the version of X that runs on Linux, as well as other platforms.

XFree86-75dpi-fonts (Version 3.3.3.1, 1,060K) This package contains the 75-dpi fonts used on most X Windows systems.

XFree86-ISO8859-2 (Version 1.0, 77K) This package contains a full set of Central European fonts, in compliance with the ISO 8859-2 standard.

XFree86-ISO8859-2-100dpi-fonts (Version 1.0, 1,003K) This package supports the special characters used by Central European languages at 100-dpi resolution.

XFree86-ISO8859-2-75dpi-fonts (Version 1.0, 877K) This package supports the special characters used by Central European languages at 75-dpi resolution.

XFree86-ISO8859-2-Type1-fonts (Version 1.0, 1,905K) This package contains Central European Type 1 fonts for X Windows.

XFree86-ISO8859-9-100dpi-fonts (Version 2.1.2, 1,142K) This package contains Turkish-language fonts in 100-dpi resolution and in accordance with the ISO8859-9 standard for X Windows.

XFree86-ISO8859-9 (Version 2.1.2, 85K) This package contains Turkish-language (ISO8859-9) terminal fonts, modmaps for the Q and F styles of Turkish keyboard mappings, and a simple utility for changing the modmap.

XFree86-ISO8859-9-75dpi-fonts (Version 2.1.2, 1,032K) This package contains Turkish-language (ISO8859-9) fonts in 75-dpi resolution for X Windows.

XFREE86-CYRILLIC-FONTS (VERSION 3.3.3.1, 301K) This package contains the Cyrillic fonts included with XFree86 3.3.2 and higher. Those who use a language requiring the Cyrillic character set should install this package.

GDM (VERSION 1.0.0, 246K) GNOME Display Manager allows you to log in to your system with X Windows running. It is highly configurable, allowing you to run several different X sessions at once on your local machine, and can manage log-in connections from remote machines as well.

GQVIEW (VERSION 0.6.0, 186K) GQview is a browser for graphics files. It offers single-click viewing of your graphics files and includes thumbnail view, zoom, and filtering features.

KTERM (VERSION 6.2.0, 154K) The kterm package provides a terminal emulator for the Japanese kanji character set.

RXVT (VERSION 2.6.PRE2, 490K) Rxvt is a color VT102 terminal emulator for X Windows.

URW-FONTS (VERSION 1.1, 2,160K) This package contains free versions of the 35 standard PostScript fonts. With X, LaTeX, or GhostScript, these fonts are a must.

X3270 (VERSION 3.1.1.6, 561K) The x3270 program opens a window in X Windows that emulates the actual look of an IBM 3278/3279 terminal, commonly used with mainframe applications. x3270 also allows you to telnet to an IBM host from the x3270 window.

XINITRC (VERSION 2.1, 8K) The xinitrc package contains the xinitrc file, a script that is used to configure your X Windows session or to start a window manager. It must be installed if you use X Windows.

THE GNU GENERAL PUBLIC LICENSE

Linux is not shareware, freeware, or public-domain software. It is licensed and distributed under the terms of the GNU General Public License (sometimes called the copyleft or GPL) and is copyrighted by Linus Torvalds and others who have contributed to its development.

The GPL is a document that was created by the Free Software Foundation (FSF) (the group responsible for the GNU project) as a means of allowing people to create "free software." In the context of the GPL, *free* refers to freedom, and not price.

The FSF believes that traditional copyrights and patents stifle innovation and slow the advance of software technology. FSF created the GPL as a way to give people the freedom to run, copy, distribute, study, change, and improve software without fear of being sued. You can even sell software covered under GPL at a profit, but you must provide the source code for your derivative product and a copy of the GPL when you redistribute it.

The Linux kernel and many of the utilities that collectively make up the Linux operating system are covered under the GPL. This means that all the Linux source code is available for you to study, improve, give away, or sell, so long as you abide by the terms of the GPL, which follows.

GNU GENERAL PUBLIC LICENSE
Version 2, June 1991
Copyright © 1989, 1991 Free Software Foundation, Inc.
675 Mass Ave., Cambridge, MA 02139, USA

Everyone is permitted to copy and distribute verbatim copies of this license document, but changing it is not allowed.

PREAMBLE

The licenses for most software are designed to take away your freedom to share and change it. By contrast, the GNU General Public License is intended to guarantee your freedom to share and change free software—to make sure the software is free for all its users. This General Public License applies to most of the Free Software Foundation's software and to any other program whose authors commit to using it. (Some other Free Software Foundation software is covered by the GNU Library General Public License instead.)

You can apply it to your programs, too.

When we speak of free software, we are referring to freedom, not price. Our General Public Licenses are designed to make sure that you have the freedom to distribute copies of free software (and charge for this service if you wish), that you receive source code or can get it if you want it, that you can change the software or use pieces of it in new free programs, and that you know you can do these things.

To protect your rights, we need to make restrictions that forbid anyone to deny you these rights or to ask you to surrender the rights.

These restrictions translate to certain responsibilities for you if you distribute copies of the software, or if you modify it.

For example, if you distribute copies of such a program, whether gratis or for a fee, you must give the recipients all the rights that you have. You must make sure that they, too, receive or can get the source code. And you must show them these terms so they know their rights.

We protect your rights with two steps: (1) copyright the software, and (2) offer you this license which gives you legal permission to copy, distribute, and/or modify the software.

Also, for each author's protection and ours, we want to make certain that everyone understands that there is no warranty for this free software. If the software is modified by someone else and passed on, we want its recipients to know that what they have is not the original, so that any problems introduced by others will not reflect on the original authors' reputations.

Finally, any free program is threatened constantly by software patents. We wish to avoid the danger that redistributors of a free program will individually obtain patent licenses, in effect making the program proprietary. To prevent this, we have made it clear that any patent must be licensed for everyone's free use or not licensed at all.

The precise terms and conditions for copying, distribution, and modification follow.

GNU General Public License — Terms and Conditions for Copying, Distribution, and Modification

0. This License applies to any program or other work which contains a notice placed by the copyright holder saying it may be distributed under the terms of this General Public License. The "Program," below, refers to any such program or work, and a "work based on the Program" means either the Program or any derivative work under copyright law: that is to say, a work containing the Program or a portion of it, either verbatim or with modifications and/or translated into another language. (Hereinafter, translation is included without limitation in the term "modification.") Each licensee is addressed as "you."

   Activities other than copying, distribution, and modification are not covered by this License; they are outside its scope. The act of running the Program is not restricted, and the output from the Program is covered only if its contents constitute a work based on the Program (independent of having been made by running the Program). Whether that is true depends on what the Program does.

1. You may copy and distribute verbatim copies of the Program's source code as you receive it, in any medium, provided that you conspicuously and appropriately publish on each copy an appropriate copyright notice and disclaimer of warranty; keep intact all the notices that refer to this License and to the absence of any warranty; and give any other recipients of the Program a copy of this License along with the Program.

   You may charge a fee for the physical act of transferring a copy, and you may at your option offer warranty protection in exchange for a fee.

2. You may modify your copy or copies of the Program or any portion of it, thus forming a work based on the Program, and copy and distribute such modifications or work under the terms of

Section 1 above, provided that you also meet all of these conditions:

a) You must cause the modified files to carry prominent notices stating that you changed the files and the date of any change.

b) You must cause any work that you distribute or publish, that in whole or in part contains or is derived from the Program or any part thereof, to be licensed as a whole at no charge to all third parties under the terms of this License.

c) If the modified program normally reads commands interactively when run, you must cause it, when started running for such interactive use in the most ordinary way, to print or display an announcement including an appropriate copyright notice and a notice that there is no warranty (or else, saying that you provide a warranty) and that users may redistribute the program under these conditions, and telling the user how to view a copy of this License. (Exception: If the Program itself is interactive but does not normally print such an announcement, your work based on the Program is not required to print an announcement.)

These requirements apply to the modified work as a whole. If identifiable sections of that work are not derived from the Program, and can be reasonably considered independent and separate works in themselves, then this License, and its terms, do not apply to those sections when you distribute them as separate works. But when you distribute the same sections as part of a whole which is a work based on the Program, the distribution of the whole must be on the terms of this License, whose permissions for other licensees extend to the entire whole, and thus to each and every part regardless of who wrote it.

Thus, it is not the intent of this section to claim rights or contest your rights to work written entirely by you; rather, the intent is to exercise the right to control the distribution of derivative or collective works based on the Program.

In addition, mere aggregation of another work not based on the Program with the Program (or with a work based on the Program) on a volume of a storage or distribution medium does not bring the other work under the scope of this License.

3. You may copy and distribute the Program (or a work based on it, under Section 2) in object code or executable form under the terms of Sections 1 and 2 above provided that you also do one of the following:

   a) Accompany it with the complete corresponding machine-readable source code, which must be distributed under the terms of Sections 1 and 2 above on a medium customarily used for software interchange; or,

   b) Accompany it with a written offer, valid for at least three years, to give any third party, for a charge no more than your cost of physically performing source distribution, a complete machine-readable copy of the corresponding source code, to be distributed under the terms of Sections 1 and 2 above on a medium customarily used for software interchange; or,

   c) Accompany it with the information you received as to the offer to distribute corresponding source code. (This alternative is allowed only for noncommercial distribution and only if you received the program in object code or executable form with such an offer, in accord with Subsection b above.)

The source code for a work means the preferred form of the work for making modifications to it. For an executable work, complete source code means all the source code for all modules it contains, plus any associated interface definition files, plus the scripts used to control compilation and installation of the executable. However, as a special exception, the source code distributed need not include anything that is normally distributed (in either source or binary form) with the major components (compiler, kernel, and so on) of the operating system on which the executable runs, unless that component itself accompanies the executable.

If distribution of executable or object code is made by offering access to copy from a designated place, then offering equivalent access to copy the source code from the same place counts as distribution of the source code, even though third parties are not compelled to copy the source along with the object code.

4. You may not copy, modify, sublicense, or distribute the Program except as expressly provided under this License. Any attempt otherwise to copy, modify, sublicense, or distribute the Program is void, and will automatically terminate your rights under this License. However, parties who have received copies, or rights, from you under this License will not have their licenses terminated so long as such parties remain in full compliance.

5. You are not required to accept this License, since you have not signed it. However, nothing else grants you permission to modify or distribute the Program or its derivative works. These actions are prohibited by law if you do not accept this License. Therefore, by modifying or distributing the Program (or any work based on the Program), you indicate your acceptance of this License to do so, and all its terms and conditions for copying, distributing, or modifying the Program or works based on it.

6. Each time you redistribute the Program (or any work based on the Program), the recipient automatically receives a license from the original licensor to copy, distribute, or modify the Program subject to these terms and conditions. You may not impose any further restrictions on the recipients' exercise of the rights granted herein. You are not responsible for enforcing compliance by third parties to this License.

7. If, as a consequence of a court judgment or allegation of patent infringement or for any other reason (not limited to patent issues), conditions are imposed on you (whether by court order, agreement, or otherwise) that contradict the conditions of this License, they do not excuse you from the conditions of this License. If you cannot distribute so as to satisfy simultaneously your obligations under this License and any other pertinent obligations, then as a consequence you may not distribute the Program at all. For example, if a patent license would not permit royalty-free redistribution of the Program by all those who receive copies directly or indirectly

through you, then the only way you could satisfy both it and this License would be to refrain entirely from distribution of the Program.

If any portion of this section is held invalid or unenforceable under any particular circumstance, the balance of the section is intended to apply and the section as a whole is intended to apply in other circumstances.

It is not the purpose of this section to induce you to infringe any patents or other property right claims or to contest validity of any such claims; this section has the sole purpose of protecting the integrity of the free software distribution system, which is implemented by public license practices. Many people have made generous contributions to the wide range of software distributed through that system in reliance on consistent application of that system; it is up to the author/donor to decide if he or she is willing to distribute software through any other system and a licensee cannot impose that choice.

This section is intended to make thoroughly clear what is believed to be a consequence of the rest of this License.

8. If the distribution and/or use of the Program is restricted in certain countries either by patents or by copyrighted interfaces, the original copyright holder who places the Program under this License may add an explicit geographical distribution limitation excluding those countries, so that distribution is permitted only in or among countries not thus excluded. In such case, this License incorporates the limitation as if written in the body of this License.

9. The Free Software Foundation may publish revised and/or new versions of the General Public License from time to time. Such new versions will be similar in spirit to the present version, but may differ in detail to address new problems or concerns.

Each version is given a distinguishing version number. If the Program specifies a version number of this License which applies to it and "any later version," you have the option of following the terms and conditions either of that version or of any later version published by the Free Software Foundation. If the

Program does not specify a version number of this License, you may choose any version ever published by the Free Software Foundation.

10. If you wish to incorporate parts of the Program into other free programs whose distribution conditions are different, write to the author to ask for permission. For software which is copyrighted by the Free Software Foundation, write to the Free Software Foundation; we sometimes make exceptions for this. Our decision will be guided by the two goals of preserving the free status of all derivatives of our free software and of promoting the sharing and reuse of software generally.

NO WARRANTY

11. BECAUSE THE PROGRAM IS LICENSED FREE OF CHARGE, THERE IS NO WARRANTY FOR THE PROGRAM, TO THE EXTENT PERMITTED BY APPLICABLE LAW. EXCEPT WHEN OTHERWISE STATED IN WRITING THE COPYRIGHT HOLDERS AND/OR OTHER PARTIES PROVIDE THE PROGRAM "AS IS" WITHOUT WARRANTY OF ANY KIND, EITHER EXPRESSED OR IMPLIED, INCLUDING, BUT NOT LIMITED TO, THE IMPLIED WARRANTIES OF MERCHANTABILITY AND FITNESS FOR A PARTICULAR PURPOSE. THE ENTIRE RISK AS TO THE QUALITY AND PERFORMANCE OF THE PROGRAM IS WITH YOU. SHOULD THE PROGRAM PROVE DEFECTIVE, YOU ASSUME THE COST OF ALL NECESSARY SERVICING, REPAIR, OR CORRECTION.

12. IN NO EVENT UNLESS REQUIRED BY APPLICABLE LAW OR AGREED TO IN WRITING WILL ANY COPYRIGHT HOLDER, OR ANY OTHER PARTY WHO MAY MODIFY AND/OR REDISTRIBUTE THE PROGRAM AS PERMITTED ABOVE, BE LIABLE TO YOU FOR DAMAGES, INCLUDING ANY GENERAL, SPECIAL, INCIDENTAL, OR CONSEQUENTIAL DAMAGES ARISING OUT OF THE USE OR INABILITY TO USE THE PROGRAM (INCLUDING BUT NOT LIMITED TO LOSS OF DATA OR DATA BEING RENDERED INACCURATE OR LOSSES SUSTAINED BY YOU OR THIRD PARTIES OR A FAILURE OF THE PROGRAM TO OPERATE WITH ANY OTHER PROGRAMS), EVEN IF SUCH HOLDER OR OTHER PARTY HAS BEEN ADVISED OF THE POSSIBILITY OF SUCH DAMAGES.

END OF TERMS AND CONDITIONS

Appendix: How to Apply These Terms to Your New Programs

If you develop a new program, and you want it to be of the greatest possible use to the public, the best way to achieve this is to make it free software which everyone can redistribute and change under these terms.

To do so, attach the following notices to the program. It is safest to attach them to the start of each source file to most effectively convey the exclusion of warranty; and each file should have at least the "copyright" line and a pointer to where the full notice is found.

<one line to give the program's name and a brief idea of what it does>
Copyright © 19yy <name of author>
This program is free software; you can redistribute it and/or modify it under the terms of the GNU General Public License as published by the Free Software Foundation; either version 2 of the License, or (at your option) any later version.

This program is distributed in the hope that it will be useful, but WITHOUT ANY WARRANTY; without even the implied warranty of MERCHANTABILITY or FITNESS FOR A PARTICULAR PURPOSE. See the GNU General Public License for more details.

You should have received a copy of the GNU General Public License along with this program; if not, write to the Free Software Foundation, Inc., 675 Massachusetts Ave., Cambridge, MA 02139, USA.

Also add information on how to contact you by electronic and paper mail.

If the program is interactive, make it output a short notice like this when it starts in an interactive mode:

```
Gnomovision version 69, Copyright © 19yy name of author
Gnomovision comes with ABSOLUTELY NO WARRANTY; for details type "show w". This is
free software, and you are welcome to redistribute it under certain conditions; type
"show c" for details.
```

The hypothetical commands "show w" and "show c" should show the appropriate parts of the General Public License. Of course, the commands you use may be called something other than "show w" and "show c"; they could even be mouse-clicks or menu items—whatever suits your program.

You should also get your employer (if you work as a programmer) or your school, if any, to sign a "copyright disclaimer" for the program, if necessary. Here is a sample; alter the names:

Yoyodyne, Inc., hereby disclaims all copyright interest in the program "Gnomovision" (which makes passes at compilers) written by James Hacker.
<signature of Ty Coon>, 1 April 1989
Ty Coon, President of Vice

This General Public License does not permit incorporating your program into proprietary programs. If your program is a subroutine library, you may consider it more useful to permit linking proprietary applications with the library. If this is what you want to do, use the GNU Library General Public License instead of this License.

DOS AND UNIX
EQUIVALENCIES

f you take a close look at Unix and DOS commands, you'll find there are many parallels. This is true because DOS took much of its design from Unix, so if you have learned to use DOS, then you already know quite a bit about Unix.

After each set of parallel commands, an example is given showing actual usage in both DOS and Linux. In most cases, the commands don't do exactly the same thing, but are roughly equivalent. See the chapters in this book or use the **man** command to learn more about these Unix commands under Linux. Under DOS, use the **help** command.

DOS	UNIX	DESCRIPTION
attrib **attrib +r file.txt**	chmod **chmod +r,-w file.txt**	Change read/write permissions of a file.
backup **backup setup_file**	tar **tar -cvf backup.tar**	Create a backup or archive.
cd **cd \mydir**	cd **cd /mydir**	Change directory.
date **date 07/04/1999**	date **date -s 07/04/1999**	Set system date.
deltree **deltree \temp**	rm -r **rm -r /home/temp**	Remove entire directory tree (delete files and subdirectories).
dir **dir**	du **du -ab**	Report on disk use.
fc **fc pgm1.c pgm2.c**	diff **diff pgm1.c pgm2.c**	Compare two files.
copy **copy sample.htm c:\website**	cp **cp sample.htm /home/bob/www**	Copy files.
time **time 13:28**	date **date -s 1328**	Set system clock.
dir **dir \windows**	ls **ls /root**	List a directory.
dir **dir /s c:\windows*.ini**	find **find /etc -name "*.rc" -print**	Find a file.

DOS	UNIX	DESCRIPTION
del **del panda.zip**	rm **rm panda.zip**	Remove a file.
edit **edit panda.txt**	pico **pico panda.txt**	Edit a text file.
fdisk **fdisk**	fdisk **fdisk /dev/hda**	Define disk partitions.
format **format c:**	mke2fs **mke2fs /dev/hda2**	Format a file system or disk.
find **find /I "wigdet" *.txt**	grep **grep -i "widget" *.txt**	Search for text within files.
help **help find**	man **man grep**	Display help for commands.
md **md \newdir**	mkdir **mkdir /newdir**	Make a new directory.
mode/ctty **mode CON LINES=43**	stty **stty rows=43**	Set modes on console or serial and/or printer port.
more **more outlist.txt**	more **more outlist.txt**	Display output screen by screen.
print **print autoexec.bat**	lpr **lpr .profile**	Print a file.
rename **rename big.txt large.txt**	mv **mv big.txt large.txt**	Move or rename a file.
rmdir **rmdir \temp**	rmdir **rmdir /home/temp**	Remove a directory.
scandisk **scandisk c: /AUTOFIX**	e2fsck **e2fsck -p /dev/hda2**	Check file system and fix errors.
sort **sort /+6 < number.fil**	sort **sort -k 6,7 number.fil**	Sort a file.
type **type ascii.txt**	cat **cat ascii.txt**	Display a file on the screen.
xcopy **xcopy /s *.ps c:\tmp**	cp -r **cp -r *.ps c:**	Copy files and directories recursively.

GLOSSARY

This glossary will help as you explore Linux. You'll no doubt encounter many of these terms in your travels about Unix and the Internet, so bone up now on your geekspeak, and you'll be prepared when the acronyms start flying.

Anonymous FTP A public archive of files that anyone can access without a user ID or password.

Archie Internet-based software used to search for files at anonymous FTP sites.

Article A message posted to a Usenet newsgroup; see *post*.

ASCII (American Standard Code for Information Interchange) A set of 128 standard characters guaranteed to be displayed the same way on any computer. The ASCII character set consists of numbers, letters, and other special characters that you can find on a standard U.S. keyboard. Examples of non-ASCII characters are ü, é, â, and £.

Attachment A file attached to an email message. Attachments are often graphics, compressed documents, or programs.

Bash Acronym for Bourne Again Shell, the default Linux shell.

Background A task that runs behind the scenes, allowing no user interaction. See also *Foreground*.

Bandwidth A measure of the amount of data a network can send or receive at one time. Think of bandwidth as the size of the pipe through which data flows from one computer to another.

BBS (bulletin board system) A computer you can dial to access files and participate in electronic discussions. Unlike the Internet, BBSs are not always networked and often require that you have a password or membership before you can access them.

Binary file A file containing items other than plain text (ASCII characters), such as a program or graphics.

Bit The basic unit of data a computer processes. A bit can have a value of 1 or 0.

Bounce An email message that could not be delivered and is returned is said to have *bounced*.

Browser As in World Wide Web browser; a piece of software like Netscape, Mosaic, or Lynx that displays World Wide Web documents.

Client Also called client software. Software that connects your computer to another (server) computer.

Compression The compacting of files to save storage space and reduce transfer time. Common compression tools for Unix are gzip and zip. You will often find software packages distributed as compressed files on the Internet.

Copyleft The idea that anyone who redistributes a piece of software, with or without changes, must pass along the freedom to further copy and change it.

Cross-posting Posting the same message to several Usenet newsgroups.

Current directory The directory in which you are currently working. You display its value with the pwd command.

Cyberspace A term coined by William Gibson in the science-fiction novel *Neuromancer.* Though commonly used to refer to the Internet, it describes the virtual space one occupies when participating on any computer network.

Daemon A background process that takes a predefined action when a certain event occurs. An example is the printer daemon, which manages the print queue. (Pronounced like *demon*.)

Directory A place where related files are grouped. Directories may contain files or subdirectories (directories below the first level), resulting in a tree-like organization of files.

Domain name The name assigned to a computer on the Internet (for example, *http://www.snarch.com*). The suffix on the domain name tells you the type of organization that operates the system (for example, com = business, edu = university, gov = government, mil = military, org = organization). Sometimes the organization type is followed by a two-character country code (au = Australia, for example, as in outback.edu.au).

Download What you do when you transfer a file from another computer to your own. Common usage implies moving a file from a public library to one's personal space.

Email (electronic mail)   Electronic messages sent or received over the Internet, other online services, or computer networks.

Encryption Scrambling a file so that it can't be read without special decoding software and a password. PGP is the most commonly used encryption software.

Enlightenment A window manager for GNOME that lets you control the look and feel of the desktop.

FAQ (frequently asked questions)   A document that provides answers to frequently asked questions on a specific topic. (It is pronounced like *fact* without the final consonant.)

File permissions A set of permissions associated with a file or directory that tells who can read, write, or execute the file or directory.

File system A chunk of hard disk formatted so that Linux can use it, with a hierarchical (tree-like) structure for storing files. This might be a hard disk drive or a partition on a disk drive.

Filter A program in a pipeline that reads a stream of data, performs some operation on each line, and sends out the modified lines.

Finger A program that displays information about another user on the network.

Flame Expression of a strong opinion or criticism, usually in an email message or Usenet posting.

Foreground A program running in the foreground is one you can interact with. See also *Background*.

Free software Software that is covered under the GNU Public License (see Appendix B). Free, in this context, refers to freedom and not cost. Not to be confused with *Freeware* or *Shareware*.

Freeware Software that is free of charge. Not to be confused with *Free software* or *Shareware*.

FTP (File Transfer Protocol or File Transfer Program)   A means of transferring files between computers on the Internet.

Geek Someone who enjoys being with computers as much as or more than being with people.

GIF (Graphic Interchange Format)   A graphics file format used on the World Wide Web. See also *JPEG*.

GNOME The GNU Network Object Model Environment, a contrived acronym for a nifty graphical user interface for Linux.

GNU An acronym for GNU's Not Unix. The GNU project's goal is to provide a complete set of free Unix software.

Gopher A menu-based interface to collections of information on the Internet.

Header The lines in an email message that precede the message body. These lines identify the sender, the recipient, and the path traveled by the message.

Home page A World Wide Web document that is the online home of a person, business, or organization; the first in a series of Web documents.

Host A computer on a network that provides access to files or information. See also *Server*.

HTML (Hypertext Markup Language)   The language used to create and format documents for display by a World Wide Web browser.

HTTP (Hypertext Transfer Protocol)   The way the computers on the World Wide Web communicate. When you type **http://** into a URL, you're telling your browser that the file you want resides on a Web server (as opposed to a gopher or FTP server).

Hypertext A way to link documents so they can be explored by selecting highlighted words or phrases (hypertext links) in Web documents. These links, in turn, are linked to other documents, which are displayed as you select each link.

Internet The set of networks that connects over a million computers and an estimated 40 million people worldwide.

IP (Internet protocol)   The rules that govern the way computers communicate on the Internet. Internet protocol allows large chunks of data to travel in small packets across computer networks before they're reassembled at their destination.

IRC (Internet Relay Chat)   A multiuser system that allows people to chat live with other Internet users.

ISP (Internet service provider)   A company that provides Internet access and services.

JPEG (Joint Photographic Experts Group)   An acronym for a file format that compresses graphics files to reduce their size. JPEG files are commonly found on the World Wide Web. See also *GIF*.

Kbps (kilobits per second)   A measure of the speed at which data moves across a network or modem. A kilobit is equal to 1024 bits, or 128 bytes. The higher the number, the faster the transfer.

KDE   The K Desktop Environment is the desktop manager for X Windows. KDE can be used instead of GNOME.

LILO   An acronym for Linux Loader. LILO is a boot manager that allows you to select which operating system to load at startup.

Listserv   Software that distributes email to groups of mailing list subscribers. Majordomo and Listproc are similar programs.

Mailing list   An email discussion group. Mailing list subscribers automatically receive members' postings. Mailing lists are usually managed by automated software like Listserv or Majordomo.

Man page   A page from an online Unix manual.

MIME (Multipurpose Internet Mail Extension)   A format for encoding and attaching binary files to email messages. You must have special MIME-decoding software (or a mail reader that supports MIME) to decode a MIME-encoded attachment.

Modem   Hardware your computer uses to communicate with another computer over a telephone line. Modems convert analog telephone signals to digital signals (a form your computer can process) and vice versa. Modem speeds are measured in bits per second (bps). The higher the bps value, the faster the modem can send or receive data.

Mount   Making another file system available. One can mount a floppy disk, a CD-ROM, a partition on a hard drive, or a directory on a remote machine.

Name server   A networked computer that tracks the relationships between Internet domain names and their actual addresses. For example, a name server will know that the domain name xyz.com has the address 193.252.47.19.

Nerd A socially inept person, slavishly devoted to intellectual or academic pursuits—pocket protectors, taped glasses, and plaid shirts are optional.

Netiquette Internet etiquette; a set of generally agreed upon rules for proper behavior on the Internet.

Newsgroup A Usenet discussion group.

Newsreader Software that reads and posts Usenet messages. Tin is commonly used on Unix for this purpose.

NNTP (Network News Transport Protocol)   The communication method used to distribute Usenet postings.

Packet A small chunk of data sent over a network. Packets include the message, the sender's and receiver's identities, and some error-control information.

Pager A tool on the Gnome Panel to help you manage the applications currently active on your desktop.

Perl A popular interpreted programming language widely used for writing shell scripts.

Pipeline A sequence of programs through which a stream of data passes. Each stage or filter performs some operation on the data.

POP (Post Office Protocol)   A communication method used by SLIP/PPP software to send and receive email. POP also stands for Point of Presence—a computer system that accepts local dial-ins for a large regional network.

Post What you do when you send a message or article to a network newsgroup.

Postmaster The person who administers the email system on a network and responds to users' questions and complaints.

PPP (Point-to-Point Protocol)   A communication method that allows a personal computer to connect directly to the Internet using a standard telephone line. PPP is gradually replacing the older SLIP technology.

Protocol A prescribed method of communication allowing different types of computers to exchange information over a network.

Recursion See *Recursion*.

Redirection Piping the output of a command to a file or another program, instead of having it displayed on the screen.

Regular expression A text string that includes special characters for pattern matching.

RFC (Request for Comments)   The standards that define the Internet and how it works. RFC also refers to the way these documents are discussed and approved by the Internet community.

Root directory The directory located at the top of the Linux file system, represented by the forward slash character.

RPM (Red Hat Package Management)   A utility that helps you install and uninstall software packages on a Linux system.

Server A computer that responds to requests from a client computer. See also *Host*.

Shareware Software you can try for free before buying it. See also *Freeware* and *Free software*.

Shar file A shell archive file; a bunch of program source code files bundled together so they can be easily transmitted by email.

Shell A program that acts an intermediary between the user and the operating system. Commands entered by the user are passed from the shell to the operating system for execution.

Shell account A type of Internet account where you dial in to a service provider's system and use Unix commands there to access email and Internet resources.

Shell prompt A character at the start of the command line that indicates that the shell is ready to receive your commands. In the Bash shell, the prompt is a percent sign for normal users and a pound sign for superusers.

Shell script A short program written in an interpreted language to automate routine command-line tasks.

Signature A brief, personal message or tag line at the end of an email or Usenet message. A signature should generally not exceed five lines.

SLIP (Serial Line Internet Protocol)   A communication method that allows a personal computer to connect directly to the Internet using a standard telephone line. See also *PPP*.

Standard input The source of input for a program. This is assumed to be the keyboard unless input is redirected from a file or another program.

Standard output The destination for output from a program. This is assumed to be the screen unless output is redirected to a file or another program.

Talk A program for online chats between two users.

Tar file A file created by the tar (tape archive) command, which bundles a bunch of files together and creates an archive (commonly called a tar file) on a tape, hard disk, or floppy disk. The most common use is to package multiple files or directories into a single file for easy transfer or archiving.

TCP/IP (Transmission Control Protocol/Internet Protocol)   A set of rules that enables different types of computers to communicate over a network; the basis for all Internet communications.

Telnet Software that allows Internet users to log into another computer remotely.

UNIX An operating system developed by AT&T's Bell Labs, later sold to Novell, and now owned by SCO. UNIX is a trademarked name, whereas Unix is a generic term.

Unix A generic term for any UNIX-like operating system. Linux is an implementation of Unix.

Upload What you do when you transfer a file from your computer to another.

URL (universal resource locator)   The assortment of colons, slashes, and other funny characters that make up the address of a Web document—for example, http://www.xyz.com/welcome.html.

Usenet An electronic conferencing system that enables millions of Internet users to wallow in dung. Also a place where you can post messages or read the messages posted on various topics by other users.

UUencoding A means of converting binary files to ASCII format so they can be emailed to other Internet users. The uuencode program converts the binary file to ASCII format, and the uudecode program returns the file to its original form. See also *MIME*.

VT100 A standard terminal type supported by many computer systems. Telnet programs emulate this type of terminal in order to connect to many Internet sites.

Web A common abbreviation for the World Wide Web.

World Wide Web Originally designed as a means for researchers to share documents, the World Wide Web (commonly referred to as the Web or WWW) has become the Internet's primary tool for storing, presenting, and researching information. The Web is a collection of electronic documents linking together documents, images, and sound files located on the Internet.

WWW A common abbreviation for the World Wide Web.

INDEX

Italic page numbers indicate illustrations and are listed separately from references to text.

SYMBOLS

A

F

G

partitioning
    with Disk Druid, *16*
    a hard drive, 8–10
partition mount points, 16, *18*
partitions
    creating DOS, 8–10, 17
    creating Linux, 14–18
    linking files to different, 156
    size and types of Linux, 16
passwd command, 97, 139–40
Passwd package, 260
passwords, changing, 139–140, 282, *286*
patches, 321
Paths, Linux vs. DOS, 118
PATH variable, 109, 110, 206, 265
pattern matching, 192, 195, 196, 198–199
    in Perl, 224
PCMCIA device supplemental diskette, 12, 13
PCMCIA support
    RAM needed for, 15
    selecting, 13
pdksh shell, 99, 204, 370
percent sign (%), files beginning with, 149
peripherals. *See* hardware
Perl
    about, 215
    comparison operators, 219
    defined, 399
    help using, 224
    packages, 349
    pattern matching, 224
    print command, 216
    statement end symbols, 216
Perl Institute, 224
Perl scripts
    creating, 215–216
    conditional statements in, 219–221
    iteration in, 221–223
    variables used in, 216–218, 223
PGP (Pretty Good Privacy) program, 256–257
PhotoShop for Linux, *56*, 337
Pico text editor
    about, *171–172*
    cutting and pasting text with, *174*–175
    exiting, 173–174
    extra features of, 175
    help using, 175

inserting a file into a file with, 174
menu of commands, 173–175
moving through a document with, 172–173
PID, 107
Pine Composer. *See* Pico text editor
Pine Information Center, 175, 241
Pine mail system
    about, 234
    commands, 108, 237, 238–239
    FOLDER INDEX screen, *236*, 237, 238
    help using, 241
    INBOX folder, 235–236
    managing mail with, 236–237
    MESSAGE TEXT screen, *236*, 237, 238
    package, 335
    power uses of, 238–241
    starting, 235
ping, 78–79
pipes or pipelines
    creating, 199–200
    defined, 106, 399
    piping input/output through, 95, 106–107, 239
    for uuencoded email, 255
PKZIP and PKUNZIP (DOS/Windows), 251, 252
.pl extensions, 215
plug-and-play modems, 67
plus sign (+)
    in gnoRPM, 310
    in Pine, 235
    in shell scripts, 213
POP (Post Office Protocol), 399
ports
    defining a printer port, *23*
    selecting a mouse port, *21*
    setting up a modem port, 64–67
post, 399
postmaster, 399
postscript printing, 149
pound sign (#), prompts beginning with, 100
PPID, 107
pppo device listing in ifconfig, 72
PPP-HOWTO file, 73
PPP packages for Linux, 335, 364
PPP (Point-to-Point Protocol)
    about, 68, 399
    configuring and defining, *70*, 282, *283*,
        284, 323

Q

R

WordPerfect, 59
World Wide Web, 402
write access, 133
    for directories, 134
WWW, 402

X

X-Chat, 85, *86*
    package, 336
xclock command, 142
Xconfigurator, 26, 37
    package, 373
    rerunning, 30, *280*
xdos command, 268
XFree86, 26, 36, 372–375
X Games package, 19
Xgammon, *56*, 329
X hardware support packages for Linux, 372–374
Xpaint, *57*
    package, 338

X Server, 37
X Windows
    architecture and components, 37
    configuring, 26–31, *280*
    Internet tools, 83–86
    Linux packages for, 374–375
    omitting at installation, 9
    running DOSemu under, 268
    running Windows on, 271, *272*
    starting your system in, 31
    text editors, 175–182
    using virtual consoles under, 97–98

Z

zcat command, 251
.Z files, 247, 250
zip command, 251–252, 255
Zip package, 331
zless command, 251
zmore command, 251

redhat®

www.redhat.com

Copyright 1999 Red Hat, Inc.

PLAYING LINUX GAMES

by AL KOSKELIN

The first complete guide to gaming for Linux users, *Playing Linux Games* covers Linux basics as well as game-specific hardware and software issues. Linux can be a great gaming platform and this book has everything you'll need to get games up and running fast, including dozens of games, drivers, and information files on the bundled CD-ROM. You'll learn:

- How to find, install, run, and troubleshoot games on Linux

- How to get the software or drivers you need to play games under Linux

- How to set up a LAN to play games over a network

- How to install and play the games currently available for Linux (including games for other operating systems that can be emulated on Linux)

- Game-specific tips, techniques, and strategy

AL KOSKELIN studies computer science and writing at the University of Wisconsin-Stevens Point. He is the co-founder of the popular Linux Games Web site (http://www.linuxgames.com).

350 pp., paperback, $34.95 w/CD-ROM
ISBN 1-886411-33-6

LINUX MIDI & SOUND

by DAVE PHILLIPS

Linux MIDI & Sound offers in-depth instruction on recording, storing, playing, and editing music and sound under Linux. The author, a programmer and performing musician, discusses the basics of sound and digital audio, and covers specific software and hardware issues specific to Linux, including:

- A clear introduction to the fundamental concepts of digital sound

- Linux-specific issues including available toolkits, GUI libraries, and driver support

- Reviews of available software with recommendations

- Recommended components for building a complete system including a digital audio player/recorder, soundfile editor, MIDI recorder/player/editor, and software mixer

- Coverage of hard disk recording, advanced MIDI support, network audio, and MP3

- A complete bibliography and an extensive list of Internet resources

- A CD-ROM with dozens of software packages

A performing musician for over 30 years, DAVE PHILLIPS became interested in computers as a means for playing, editing, and recording music. He is an expert in MIDI, Csound, and Linux. He currently maintains several educational Web sites on these topics.

300 pp., paperback, $39.95 w/CD-ROM
ISBN 1-886411-34-4

APPLE CONFIDENTIAL:
THE REAL STORY OF APPLE COMPUTER, INC.

by OWEN W. LINZMAYER

"The Apple story . . . in all its drama." — The New York Times Book Review

"Written with humor, respect, and care, it absolutely is a must-read for every Apple fan." — InfoWorld

"An irreverent work that captures the essence of that which is Apple."
— Gil Amelio, former Apple CEO

In *Apple Confidential*, journalist and Mac guru Owen Linzmayer traces the history of Apple Computer from its legendary founding to its recent return to profitability. Backed by exhaustive research, the book debunks many of the myths and half-truths surrounding Apple, the Macintosh, and its creators. With facts, photos, timelines, and quotes, every page brings a new discovery about this fascinating company, including:

- The forgotten founder who walked away from hundreds of millions of dollars

- The trials and tribulations of taking the original Macintosh from research project to finished product

- Apple's disastrous oversight that allowed Microsoft to dominate the personal computing industry

- The careers of CEOs Sculley, Spindler, Amelio, and Jobs

- Complete timelines of the development of the Apple II, Apple III, Lisa, Macintosh, Newton, NeXT, and Windows

- The triumphant return of Steve Jobs to Apple

OWEN W. LINZMAYER is a San Francisco-based freelance writer who has been covering Apple for industry magazines since 1980. He writes a monthly column for *MacAddict* magazine and is the author of four other Macintosh books, including *The Mac Bathroom Reader.*

268 pp., paperback, $17.95
ISBN 1-886411-28-X

STEAL THIS COMPUTER BOOK: WHAT THEY WON'T TELL YOU ABOUT THE INTERNET

by WALLACE WANG

"A delightfully irresponsible primer." — Chicago Tribune

"If this book had a soundtrack, it'd be Lou Reed's 'Walk on the Wild Side.'" — InfoWorld

"An unabashed look at the dark side of the Net — the stuff many other books gloss over." — Amazon.com

Steal This Computer Book explores the dark corners of the Internet and reveals little-known techniques that hackers use to subvert authority. Unfortunately, some of these techniques, when used by malicious hackers, can destroy data and compromise the security of corporate and government networks. To keep your computer safe from viruses, and yourself from electronic con games and security crackers, Wallace Wang explains the secrets hackers and scammers use to prey on their victims. Discover:

- How hackers write and spread computer viruses
- How criminals get free service and harass legitimate customers on online services like America Online
- How online con artists trick people out of thousands of dollars
- Where hackers find the tools to crack into computers or steal software
- How to find and use government-quality encryption to protect your data
- How hackers steal passwords from other computers

WALLACE WANG is the author of several computer books, including *Microsoft Office 97 for Windows for Dummies* and *Visual Basic for Dummies*. A regular contributor to *Boardwatch* magazine (the "Internet Underground" columnist), he's also a successful stand-up comedian. He lives in San Diego, California.

340 pp., paperback, $19.95
ISBN 1-886411-21-2

Distributed to the book trade by Publishers Group West

If you can't find No Starch Press titles in your local bookstore, here's how to order directly from us (we accept MasterCard, Visa, and checks or money orders—sorry, no CODs):

PHONE:
1 (800) 420 7240 OR
(415) 863-9900
MONDAY THROUGH FRIDAY,
9 A.M. TO 5 P.M. (PST)

FAX:
(415) 863-9950
24 HOURS A DAY,
7 DAYS A WEEK

E-MAIL:
SALES@NOSTARCH.COM

WEB:
HTTP://WWW.NOSTARCH.COM

MAIL:
NO STARCH PRESS
555 DE HARO STREET, SUITE 250
SAN FRANCISCO, CA 94107
USA

UPDATES

This book was carefully reviewed for technical accuracy, but it's inevitable that some things will change after the book goes to press. Visit the Web site for this book at http://www.nostarch.com/ rhl_updates.htm for updates, errata, and information about downloading packages that are not included on the CD.

SOFTWARE LICENSE AGREEMENT

This book includes a copy of the Publisher's Edition of Red Hat Linux from Red Hat Software, Inc., which you may use in accordance with the GNU General Public License. The Official Red Hat Linux, which you may purchase from Red Hat Software, includes the complete Official Red Hat Linux distribution, Red Hat Software's documentation, and 90 days of free e-mail technical support regarding installation of Official Red Hat Linux. You also may purchase technical support from Red Hat Software on issues other than installation. You may purchase Official Red Hat Linux and technical support from Red Hat Software through the company's web site (www.redhat.com) or its toll-free number 1.888.REDHAT1.

No Starch Press License Agreement

THIS IS A LEGAL AGREEMENT BETWEEN YOU, THE END USER, AND NO STARCH PRESS. BY OPENING THIS SEALED DISK PACKAGE, YOU ARE AGREEING TO BE BOUND BY THE TERMS OF THIS AGREEMENT. IF YOU DO NOT AGREE TO THE TERMS OF THIS AGREEMENT, PROMPTLY RETURN THE UNOPENED DISK PACKAGE AND THE ACCOMPANYING ITEMS (INCLUDING WRITTEN MATERIALS AND BINDERS OR OTHER CONTAINERS) TO THE PLACE YOU OBTAINED THEM FOR A FULL REFUND.

LIMITED WARRANTY

CUSTOMER REMEDIES. No Starch Press' entire liability and your exclusive remedy shall be, at No Starch Press' option either (a) return of the price paid for this book or (b) replacement of the SOFTWARE.

NO LIABILITIES FOR CONSEQUENTIAL DAMAGES. In no event shall No Starch Press or its suppliers be liable for any damages whatsoever (including, without limitation, damages for loss of business profits, business interruption, loss of business information, or other pecuniary loss) arising out of the use of or inability to use the SOFTWARE, even if No Starch Press has been advised of the possibility of such damages. Because some states do not allow the exclusion or limitation of liability for consequential or incidental damages, the above limitation may not apply to you.

This agreement is governed by the laws of the State of California.

Should you have any questions concerning this agreement, or if you wish to contact No Starch Press for any reason, please write No Starch Press, 555 De Haro St., Suite 250, San Francisco, CA 94107, or email info@nostarch.com.